British Rule and Rural Protest
in Southern Ghana

Society and Politics in Africa

Yakubu Saaka
General Editor

Vol. 11

PETER LANG
New York • Washington, D.C./Baltimore • Bern
Frankfurt am Main • Berlin • Brussels • Vienna • Oxford

Li Anshan

British Rule and Rural Protest in Southern Ghana

PETER LANG
New York • Washington, D.C./Baltimore • Bern
Frankfurt am Main • Berlin • Brussels • Vienna • Oxford

Library of Congress Cataloging-in-Publication Data

Li, Anshan.
British rule and rural protest in southern Ghana / Li Anshan.
p. cm. — (Society and politics in Africa; vol. 11)
Includes bibliographical references.
1. Protest movements—Ghana—History—Case studies. 2. Ghana—Rural conditions.
3. Ghana—Politics and government—To 1957. I. Title. II. Series.
HN832.A8 A57   303.48′4′09667—dc21   00-048748
ISBN 0-8204-5188-6
ISSN 1083-3323

Die Deutsche Bibliothek-CIP-Einheitsaufnahme

Li, Anshan:
British rule and rural protest in southern Ghana / Li Anshan.
–New York; Washington, D.C./Baltimore; Bern;
Frankfurt am Main; Berlin; Brussels; Vienna; Oxford: Lang.
(Society and politics in Africa; Vol. 11)
ISBN 0-8204-5188-6

For my parents, my wife Kaifang
and my kids Suzanne and Martin
who share my happiness

TABLE OF CONTENTS

LIST OF TABLES

PREFACE

The scientific study of African history is relatively recent in western universities. Its development was parallel to and stimulated by the African nationalist movements that achieved independence in the 1950s and 1960s was an attack on assumptions about the African past made by Africa's colonial rulers. One of the most persistent of these assumptions was the notion that resistance to colonial conquest was a futile effort of archaic societies to resist the forces of history. This notion was first attacked by the Nigerian scholar, Kenneth Onwuka Dike, who argued that the forces that most effectively resisted British penetration of the Niger Delta in the 19th century were modern African merchants who participated actively in international trade and were fighting to keep control of their markets. A broader challenge to colonial orthodoxy was launched by Terence Ranger and his colleagues at Dar es Salaam, who argued that resistance was rational, that it was effective in shaping colonial rule and that there was a continuity between early resisters and modern mass nationalists. These early works spawned a series of studies by both African and foreign scholars of those movements that resisted conquest and of the ways in which African peoples continued to resist after the revolts were suppressed.

Much of this writing was linked to the nationalist and nation-building imperatives of the independent period. New nations were interested in defining themselves and in rooting their nationalist movements in earlier history. Increasingly, however, as groups within the independence coalitions began to articulate their separate interests and oppose each other, scholars both within and outside Africa became aware that resistance was not always simply resistance to colonial rule. Gerald Caplan argued that there was in southern Africa a "scramble to protection" as threatened elites allied themselves with various colonial powers to protect themselves against enemies both within their own societies and outside. Increasingly, scholars recognized that African societies, like other human societies, have their internal tensions, which peoples are divided by ideology and by interest. In a major article, Allen and Barbara Isaacman argued that these tensions and oppositions shaped the way African peoples responded to the colonial intrusion, that elites were often more concerned to protect themselves against the challenge of other elites or of the young or poor than they were with what seemed like a minor external threat. Resistance to colonial rule, the Isaacmans argued, was often linked to conflicts within the resisting societies. Increasingly too, studies of resistance focused not only on the great early revolts, but also on movements concerned to limit colonial arbitrariness and ameliorate the conditions under which African workers, peasants and women worked. Thus, in different contexts, Africans demonstrated, went out on strike, withheld their crops from markets, and even in some cases, attacked colonial representatives or burned their headquarters.

Li Anshan's book is written within the Isaacman problematic. When Anshan first applied to the University of Toronto, we were delighted to be able to contribute to a dialogue between China and Africa. More than half of the students in our African history program have come from Africa. We have always been interested not only in training scholars, but also in the exchange of ideas and in the understanding that comes from learning about the traditions and historical experience of other societies. Anshan did not disappoint us. He was from the first a meticulous scholar, who participated openly in the exchange of ideas with Canadian and African fellow students. When it came time to choose a research subject, he chose peasant protest. Coming from China, with its rich peasant traditions, and particularly its history of peasant revolts the subject seemed to be one where he could bring his understanding of Chinese peasant history to bear on the experience of African peasants. The Chinese experience seemed particularly relevant for Ghana, where a broad-based peasant class had developed.

Anshan soon found that the issues for many of those who protested were not peasant issues. Ghanaians protested for many different reasons. They defended their cultures and religions. They resisted the chiefs, who were instruments of colonial rule. They struggled to define the boundaries of local authority. They opposed modern agricultural science when it was arbitrarily imposed on them. The title of his thesis was soon changed from "peasant protest" to "rural protest," though even this term ignores the fact that some protest movements involved town dwellers. The richness of this study is that it captures that broad range of issues that moved people to action and that it gives a picture of the issues that concerned Ghanaians. Anshan makes clear that Ghanaian social movements were not simply concerned to end or ameliorate colonial exploitation, but to defend local culture and religion, and in particular, as he puts it so well, to defend the small against the big. It also underlines that just as independence has not involved a total break from the colonial past, so too, colonial rule did not involve a total break from the pre-colonial past. The young men's groups that play such an important part in this study were an important institution in pre-colonial Ghana and they have continued to play a role in independent Ghana. Li Anshan's study also underlines the importance of historians confronting the particular historical experience of whatever community they are studying and not impose a pre-conceived schema on it. An analytic framework is important, but it must be tested against the facts of the past. Anshan does this very well. I am proud to have supervised this work as a thesis and am delighted that those interested in Africa will be able to read it.

Martin A. Klein
University of Toronto

ACKNOWLEDGMENTS

This work is based on my Ph.D. dissertation that I finished in the summer of 1993. Intellectual work cannot be done alone, in particular in my case. For aid in this study, I have many to thank. My debt goes far beyond those listed in the bibliography. My supervisor, Professor Martin Klein, deserves special mention. He has taken care of me since my first day in Canada; he guided me to choose the subject, arranged my trip to London and Accra, gave excellent suggestions and raised important questions about my arguments, and showed no mercy to my writing errors. My appreciation also goes to Professors Jonathan Barker and Gwendolyn Mikell, who offered sharp and expert comments, and to Professors Milton Israel and C. Thomas McIntire, who worked hard at my draft.

I would like to thank those who commented critically on one or more chapters: Professor Jack Gerson, University of Toronto; Dr. Addo-Fening, University of Ghana; Dr. Gareth Austin, London School of Economics; Dr. Nana Brukum and Dr. Ako Okoro, University of Toronto. Dr. R. J. S. Southall, University of Birmingham, sent me his research materials on Cadbury Company in care of Martin Klein. Dr. Jarle Simensen, University of Trondheim, and Mr. Paul Jenkins, Basel Mission Archive, provided me with invaluable information. My friends and academic colleagues Professors P. Zachernuck, Nykanike Mosissi, I. Abdullah and S. Rockel, Dr. J. Palsetia, Dr. Mei Jianghai and her husband Mr. Xu Junshen, and Professor Zhang Xiangmin helped me in one way or another. I would like to show my sincere thanks to all of them.

During my stay in Ghana, so many Ghanaian friends helped me in one way or another: Mr. Badoe who met me when I landed at Kotoka Airport, and his wonderful wife; Mr. Joseph Mensah and his friends who accompanied me in my first days in Accra; Mrs. Brukum who worried so much about my appetite; Brother Jimmy who took me to Nsawan, one of the first cocoa towns; Ms. Olivia Kpodoe, Ms. Thelma Ewusie, Ms. Gartrude Botchway, Ms. Judith Botchway, Mr. Frank Abloth of the Ghana National Archives, and the staff of the Library of the Institute of African Studies and Balme Library, the University of Ghana, who gave me valuable assistance in my research; and so many friendly gestures and smiling faces which have been embedded in my memory. I would like to thank Professor John Fynn, Professor Kwame Arhin and Dr. Kofi Baku for their advice in finding source materials. The assistance of the staff of the Department of History and the Institute of African Studies, University of Ghana, made my research in Ghana a great enjoyment.

I am deeply indebted to the Alumni Association and the Department of History, University of Toronto, for grants that enabled me to make trips to Great Britain and Ghana collecting materials for this thesis, and to the staff of the Public Record Office of London, Great Britain, for their generous assistance. Two anonymous reviewers and the Series Editor Professor Yakubu Saaka offered me excellent suggestions and the Production Coordinator Bernadette Alfaro of Peter Lang Publishing Inc. constantly gave me some professional help in the revision, I would like to thank all of them. I am grateful to Miss Jean Vale for her painstaking efforts in proof reading my draft. In spite of these, all mistakes remain mine.

For permission to include in the book portions of my previously published articles in *Journal of Religious History* (20:1, 1996) and *The International Journal of African Historical Studies* (28:2,1995), I am indebted to the copyright holders. Finally, I want to thank my parents in China, who raised me in intellectual surroundings and sparked my interest in history, and my in-laws, who helped take care of Suzanne and Martin, my two lovely kids, while I was away in Ghana doing my research. I owe too much to my wife Tian Kaifang, who accompanied me to London while expecting our first child, and who has shown extraordinary patience during my work. Without her help and encouragement, I could never have finished this book.

INTRODUCTION

Generally speaking, three factors changed Ghana (the Gold Coast)[1]: colonialism, Christianity and cocoa.[2] The three factors caused great tension as well as protest in rural areas. This work is a study of social protest in southern Ghana, mainly but not exclusively in rural areas.

As an empirical study based mainly on government documents, this study explores social protest through a series of case studies: a struggle to maintain their local culture, contentions between different social groups or sections, conflicts between tradition and modernity, and encounters between politics and science, which reflect the change and continuity in southern Ghana under colonial rule. These cases were not necessarily "away in the location" geographically, as Beinart and Bundy have suggested in their intellectually stimulating work.[3] On the contrary, some of them were right in the center, but for a long time "away in the location" for researchers.

In historical research, a balanced study of a society should try to test some theories and models through evidence, rather than voluntarily to provide new cases to help prove those theories. This study intends to examine some general theories and offers a few examples towards the formulation of some suggestive conclusions.

A Critique: The Theory of Rural Protest

Since the 1960s, scholars have become increasingly interested in the theme of rural protest or rural resistance. However, the nation-building priorities of the newly independent countries have more or less shaped academic research, and the first historical works on rural protest were concerned mainly with the linkage between primary resistance and modern nationalism. At the International Congress of African Historians in 1965, A. B. Davidson first pointed out that it was impossible to understand the African past without the re-establishment of the truth about resistance and rebellion.[4] T. O. Ranger tried to link rural resistance with later nationalist movement.[5] This "continuist" approach, as Ranger termed it himself, although pioneering in nature, was limited to protest against whites, thus failed to picture the more complicated conflicts within rural communities. What is more, this school treated resistance as the only response towards colonialism. This approach was adjusted by other Africanists, such as Allen Isaacman, who indicates resistance was not the only form of the response towards colonial rule. Collaboration and neutrality were other forms.[6]

In the 1970s, the underdevelopment theory was applied to the study of African history. Samir Amin and Walter Rodney tried to establish a direct correlation between the development of Europe and the underdevelopment of Africa.[7] This theory has its own limitation. Using Frederick Cooper's words, it "leaves the struggle of cultivators, peasants and workers against capital as little more than transitory and futile gestures in the face of the inevitable course of the world economy."[8] At the same time, social scientists began to apply the mode of production theory and class analysis in their works. These works provided a new method for the study of peasants but did not touch the issue of protest. As Allen Isaacman points out, "much of the literature has focused on class analysis without class struggle."[9] Another problem with these works is that they presented theoretical generalizations without detailed case studies.[10]

The 1980s began with a collection of critical essays on African peasants, which called for a wider range of themes and a deeper study into the ways and types of peasant protest, the appearance of "distinct peasant consciousness" and religious resistance.[11] Scholars began to question the narrow paradigms of the previous schools of thought. As a result, rural class struggle and peasants' protests moved to the center of their research. At the same time, "protest" gradually became a catchall word used to express all kinds of conflicts. Although it is possible to analyze conflicts in the colonial period in terms of protest, and as a social phenomenon rural protest should have its place in nationalist movement, yet there is a clear tendency to glorify the term.

The study of the strategy of protest is an example. The strategy is so important that sometimes it alone could decide the result of the protest. As a consequence of glorification, ineffective protest strategy has been less studied or omitted altogether. For example, most social scientists have exalted "exit" as one of the "most frequent and effective responses to oppression." [12] Explaining the "exit" strategy extensively in his study of Tanzania, Goran Hyden concludes that the small is powerful. The African peasants, being the only class not captured by other classes, could protest against the government by "exit", meaning to withdraw from the cash crop and return to subsistence production.[13] But in the Gold Coast, the "exit" strategy was not so frequently used. The simple fact is that cocoa needs more than five years of intensive care to bear fruit; once on track, it would be next to impossible to "exit." However, when world prices, taxation, living standards and local factors combined and the situation became really hard, some cocoa farmers did exit, such as in the periods of 1964-65, 1977-78 and 1979-81.

It is also important, however, to analyze each incident as a particular case rather than to generalize. In the writing of African colonial history, the experience of colonialism has often led to moral judgments, which sometimes prevents a better understanding of history. As a result, there has been little critical analysis of the protests that occurred during the colonial period. For example, in the protest against cutting-out of diseased cocoa trees in the Gold Coast and Nigeria, or in the opposition to an anti-erosion scheme in Malawi, or in the anti-dipping movement in Eastern Griqualand, the protest as a political phenomenon was significant. Yet the rationale behind a protest is one thing, to make a careful and objective study of the protest is another.

There has been a dichotomous structure in the historiography of rural social protest from the very beginning, either nationalist/colonialist, or poor/rich, or weak/strong. Several weaknesses emerged from this dichotomous structure. First, although the usual case would involve the poor or the weak against the rich or the strong, yet the weak could turn out to be strong when they were organized, as in the cocoa hold-up of 1937-38 in the Gold Coast.[14] The approach also overemphasizes the struggle, neglecting dissent within the group. The history of rural protest in southern Ghana reveals that conflicts between different social groups or even within the same group were far too complicated to capture in dichotomous variables. Furthermore, stratification existed among the so-called "poor" or "rich" groups. The best example is *Asafo*, a commoners' organization in the Gold Coast. "Within the ranks were to be found christians and non-christians, educated and illiterate, rich and poor."[15] In some cases, commoners could be richer than chiefs.

Another weakness in the writing of colonial African history is to ignore different responses of various ruling groups towards the "native policy." The study of rural protest has been concentrated on the opposition of peasants to the super-ordinate power or classes, such as the government, European firms and merchants. Very little research has been done on the divisions within the ruling class. Two points need to be elaborated here. First, different social groups had different attitudes towards colonial rule based on their perceived self-interest. Some protested, some remained neutral, some allied and collaborated. Secondly, there were various or even opposite responses within the traditional ruling class itself. Their attitude towards colonialism depended upon their respective position in the new system:

whether they were co-opted to or had some share in the system.

The study of religious protest affords us a good example. Previous research has concentrated on two subjects: the leader's charismatic qualities and followers' initiative. Obviously, it is essential to study the religious leaders in order to reach an impartial conclusion. Certain leaders are embedded in people's memory and beliefs: Andre Matswa of the *Kimbanguist* movement, Isaac Shembe, the founder of South African Zionism, or Alice Lenshina, the prophet of the Lenshina movement of Zambia, to name only a few. As a mobilizer, the religious leader was instrumental in the protest. But there has been a tendency to stress his or her personal character rather than to analyze the leaders as a social group.

Indigenous priests often took an active part in protest, such as in *Abirewa* of the Gold Coast, in *Majimaji* of Tanganyika, in the Watchtower Movement of colonial Central Africa, or in the separatist church movement. The colonial government usually used the "conspiracy" theory to explain this phenomenon. For example, in the *Majimaji* rebellion, the German government found rebels had obtained the *maji* (magic water) from a priest and concluded priests were "reactionary, ultra-conservative" elements, who had imposed a pattern of irrational behavior on people and tried to restore their declining power. John Iliffe expresses succinctly this point of view: "This 'conspiracy' theory saw the rising as a savage response to progress introduced by European rule, and implicitly denied that rational explanation was possible. It became the semi-official explanation and something of a dogma to colonial enthusiasts." Refuting this explanation, he argues that the real cause of the rebellion was not priests but the German policy.[16] In other words, "No matter how attractive the leader is, the social-structural conditions must be propitious for a movement to originate," as Audrey Whipper points out in her book on Kenyan religious protest.[17]

This study of masses explains how colonial policy affected people and how they responded to the change of the conditions. However, it does not answer why the priests were so vigorously involved in the protest, why they always became leaders in the protest and what were their motivations and aims. To answer these questions, we have to look at a related issue: the change of priests' status as a social group under colonialism. Although the change of their position during the colonial period cannot define the nature of protests, since protests usually involved more social strata than priests alone, yet this change fundamentally affected their attitude towards colonialism and was closely linked to their role in the protests. This aspect of the question has been ignored for a long time.[18]

Another relevant issue is the scale of the protest. Previous studies usually equated "peasant protest" to "rural protest." However, the peasants or peasantry are not an equivalent to rural community, although they are the overwhelming majority of it. Besides the peasants or peasantry, there were other social strata in the rural community, such as chiefs, priests, petty traders, educated and semi-educated, who may or may not be peasants. Therefore, rural protest, or "rural social protest" as Allen Isaacman terms it, is a wider concept than peasant protest. In this work, I found it difficult to confine the topic even to rural community, since it is equally difficult to distinguish between rural and urban areas under colonial rule.

This difficulty results from two facts. First, in colonial Ghana, there was no rigid division between urban and rural areas. The definition of "town" in the Ghanaian sense is quite different from the western notion. Thomas Hodgkin points out that in Africa the cause of a town's existence and the basis of its economic life is not industry, but commerce.[19] In accordance with general colonial usage, "town" usually denoted the seat of a divisional chief, thus the divisional capital. With a number of villages under its authority, such a place certainly possessed a central function as the headquarters of traditional government.[20]. Consequently, it is not easy to differentiate between rural dwellers and urban residents, especially when they were both involved in cash-crop cultivation or trading activities.

Secondly, "rural protest" usually involved "urban" participation. The 1924 Accra incident is an example. Although the attempted deposition of the Ga *Mantse* by commoners was termed "urban response" and "urban protest" by some scholar,[21] destoolment[22] was such a popular movement that it happened in many districts during the colonial period. It becomes clear that without studying destoolment in rural areas, we can hardly understand the Accra incident. The cocoa hold-up in 1937-38 was another example, with farmers, chiefs, drivers, traders and lawyers involved. The same as the boycott launched by an Accra chief Nii Kwabena Bonne III in February 1948 and the following protest in Accra. Although this incident occurred in the capital, many cocoa farmers joined the protest either in Accra or in their own towns. Again, the protest against the cutting-out of diseased cocoa trees became a national movement; local newspapers carried articles written by teachers, lawyers or ex-servicemen, linking various issues such as unemployment and inflation with the policy of cutting-out.

Although this study is mainly of rural areas, it also tries to link rural protest with urban areas whenever applicable and put southern Ghana in the context of the colony, or West Africa, in order to make a balanced conclusion. This approach is decided by the colonial experience. It treats protest in such a way as to make African history part of the general process of world history. In other words, the history of protest is meaningful and inspiring only if we put it in a wider context.[23]

The Context: The Colonial Episode

Historians generally agree that British colonial policy in the nineteenth century could be divided into three periods: the period up to the 1820s, the 1820s to 1870s and the 1870s to 1900. All acknowledge that there was a change during the 1870s, be it policy or means.[24]

The year 1874 witnessed a gradual change in British policy towards the Gold Coast. In February 1874, the British army defeated the Asante. The Gold Coast Colony was formed and confirmed by a Royal Charter of July 24, 1874.[25] In the same year, the British reoccupied Anlo that had been abandoned in 1859, and included it in the Protectorate. This manoeuvre seems to have three purposes: to check smuggling, to alter the Germany's attempt to invade the area and to pursue the fiscal and territorial policy that was carried out west of the Volta. In early 1877 there were eleven coastal district stations in the Protectorate. The Native Jurisdiction Ordinance (1883) purported to define and govern the political relationship between the government and protected Kings. Akuapem, Yilo Krobo and Manya Krobo were first proclaimed under the Ordinance.[26] By 1893 there were twelve administrative stations, Akuse, Keta, Ada, Prampram, Winneba, Saltpond, Cape Coast, Shama, Dixcove, Axim and Tarkwa. In 1895, Governor Griffith proposed the division of the Gold Coast into western and eastern provinces, "for the greater convenience of administration."[27]

Griffith's proposal, however, was not realized until March 1900 when an Order in Council grouped fourteen districts into two judicial provinces, West and East. A scheme for reorganizing the district administration was planned in 1901. It divided the Colony into Western, Central and Eastern Districts, each under a District Commissioner. [28] This scheme was put into operation in 1902. On December 8, 1903, it was ordered that from January 1, 1904, three districts should be changed to provinces. Thus the three provinces formally came into being in 1904.[29] The 1924 Ordinance provided that southern Togoland become part of the Eastern Province. In 1946, the Colony was reorganized into two provinces. The Central Province was divided up between the Western Province and the Eastern Province.[30] Finally in 1952-53, the Gold Coast changed from provincial administration to regional administration.

The change of administrative areas during the colonial period shows that the making of those areas to a large extent resulted from *real politik*.[31] This pragmatism had several consequences. First, the division was not consistent.

The Volta River District is a good example. By the end of the 1800s, the District underwent several changes. In 1888 the only interior station permanently occupied was Akuse, the headquarters of the Volta River District. At the end of 1888 the Volta River district was redefined to include Eastern Krobo and Western Krobo, Akuapem, Shai, Eastern Akyem, Kwahu, Akwamu, Krepi(Peki) and all territory "to the North of the said countries which may at any time be comprised in the Protected Territories." In March 1896 a District Commissioner was appointed to the newly created Trans-Volta District comprising the territories of Krepi and Kwahu with the headquarters station at Anum.[32]

Secondly, administrative units were defined more by political situation than by geographical position. Thirdly, the naming of districts or divisions reflected the arbitrary nature of colonial administration. Many local names were changed or abandoned for the convenience of European pronunciation. For example, Keta means "head of the sands", a name of the leader of the first migrants there.[33] But Europeans called it Kwittah, Kwitta or Quittah, and spellings differed from writer to writer.[34]

Ethnicities and Migrations

Southern Ghana, or southern part of the Gold Coast, was characterized by its ethnic diversity, economic importance and political significance. The population included the major ethnic groups: the Akan, the Ewe, the Ga-Adangbe and the Guan.[35] Although each group had its own characteristics, the long-time intermingling made some special marks on the development of the area.[36]

Migration was a distinct feature of the people of southern Ghana. In general, there were three phases of migration: the early migration to settle in their present homeland, later migration caused by wars between different states, and the latest migration caused by the spread of cocoa.

In the early period, almost all ethnic groups were migrants. Some scholars suggested that Ghana were largely unoccupied before the arrival of Europeans, and most Ghanaian people entered the country especially the forest areas after the Europeans.[37] A. Adu Boahen refuted this opinion and pointed out Ghanaians did migrate to the present Ghana, but much earlier than European. He argues that before the fourteenth century there was "multiplication and movements of populations within Ghana", the Akan as "an integral part of the negroes of West Africa" "originated somewhere in the Benue-Chad region" and moved to the region of Asante.[38]

The origin of the Akan is still a subject of debate, yet one fact is certain: the Akan were not indigenous but moved to the present home from other place.[39] Recent archaeological research, however, clearly indicates that there is an "Akan cradle", which straddled the geographical area between Brong, Adanse and Assin. Anquandah suggests that there was a multilineal development of proto-Akan social units in a number of areas such as the northern Brong savanna, the Adanse forestlands, the Etsi coastlands and Assin. These social groups were probably the descendants of "Neolithic" farmers who spread out to inhabit the forest land between the river Comoe and the river Volta between 500 B.C. and A.D. 1000. [40]

As to the origin of the Ga-Adangbe, some suggest that they were originally from the Niger or Kwara River area. Under the pressure of the Fulani, they first migrated to the banks of the lower Volta and then occupied the coastal region. Later the Ga moved to the Accra Plains and got their name Ga to distinguish them from the Adangbe.[41] Adu Boahen suggests that the origin of the Ga people should be traced to Tagulogo near Lolovo Hill in Ghana because of the language similarity between Ga and the Adangbe and Krobo, who claim their ancestors originated in this region. [42] Recent archaeological evidence indicates that during the Early and Middle Iron Age, there was an expansion of village settlements, which suggests an indigenous culture.[43] The Ewe claim that they came from the east, they do not trace the origin farther than Nuatja (Nushie) in the Republic of Togo.[44] The Guan's origin and distribution is regarded as "extremely complex and highly speculative."[45]

From the slave trade to the early nineteenth century, the contact with Europeans created many conflicts between different groups, such as the Asante-Denkyera war (1699-1701), the Akyem-Akwamu war (1729-30), and the wars between coastal Fante and Asante during the eighteenth and nineteenth centuries. The flow of refugees was the direct consequence of the wars. Akwamu immigrants came to Akuapem after the fall of Akwamu kingdom. Krobo hills accepted a lot of war refugees. The resettlement of the Dwabens was another example of migration caused by war.

The most important and last migration was by cocoa farmers. The introduction of cocoa in the late 1800s had stimulated a new migration and people began to purchase fertile land nearby or far away, to try their fortune with cocoa. Migrant farmers were mainly Akuapems, Ewes, Krobos and Gas. For example, by 1948 those described as Akuapems numbered 89,373. Among them about 50,000 migrants living in other districts, particularly in the cocoa growing areas of Akyem Abuakwa.[46]

Intermingling and Interactions

Another characteristic of the peoples of southern Ghana is their intermingling, which caused both exchange and conflict. This interaction may be studied from three aspects: cultural-linguistic, socio-economic and political-military. The Akan, or the Twi-speaking people, seem to have contributed a great deal to this process.

The Akuapem Guan-speaking people accepted many Twi words into their vocabulary. Having studied this phenomenon, Wilks concludes that Twi-speaking settlers in the early 1600s brought about the linguistic unity of the earlier population in Akuapem.[47] Thanks to their unique geographic position, the Ga-Adangbe absorbed as much as possible the characteristics of other people. The Ga *Mants's* (Ga chief) stool was copied from the Akan. There is "absorption of a considerable group of Guan speakers into the Adangme-speaking population."[48] The Krobos learned the stool rites, royal drums, shrines and rites of war-gods from the Akan.[49] The Anlo Ewe used Akan terms to describe various titles. They refer a ward chief not *tofia*, an indigenous term, but *Asafohenega*, an Akan derived term.[50]

From socio-economic aspect, trading activities had been going on among the southern peoples for a long time. There was a traffic network between Kumasi and the coast region, which Wilks described as "the four southern great-roads."[51] The southern Ghanaians carried their daily trading activities along these roads. Take the southern-eastern part for example. The Adangbe people participated in a substantial trade with those in the Akuapem hills. They supplied the Akuapems with clay pots for carrying palm oil and obtained food stuffs from them. Akyem Abuakwa had many markets in the state, which were linked to Accra by different paths.

The coastal peoples benefited most from their favorable geographic location. The Ga exchanged salt and fish for products of the Akuapem hills. Accra had once controlled the market at Late of Akuapem where they collected duties from traders passing through the interior to Accra. The control of this market fell into the Akwamu between 1646 and 1681.[52] This geographical advantage also allowed Keta to become an important market center. A demand for fish by the hinterland Ewe led to the trading network between them and the coastal people. The coastal waters, lagoons and rivers provided good fishing. Trading between the coastal peoples in the east and west brought about a series of port markets. The slave trade engaged coast chiefs and merchants as middlemen, who exchanged slaves with Europeans for sundry goods.[53]

The interactions also involved political and military aspects. Akan political culture was very influential. Priests used to rule the early Guan communities in Akuapem. The separation of functions between priests and occupants of stools was the result of the introduction of Akan system of chieftaincy.[54] The Akan custom of destoolment was introduced into many states since it was no longer possible under the British administration to kill an unpopular chief as they had done previously. Among the Ga, the first destoolment occurred in 1918, which was described as "a turning point in Ga political history since it was unprecedented."[55] In 1929, Anlo state also decided to "import" the custom of destoolment "as a check on any recalcitrant Holder of any Stool of the Anlo (Awuna) State."[56] As late as 1930, the states of Manya Krobo, Yilo Krobo, Shai and Osudoku passed a resolution relative to the variation of custom in which they "wish to adopt the practice of deposition as obtaining in the Akan-speaking States."[57]

The Akan military organization was divided into four columns. They were *Adonten*, the central column, consisting of scouts, advance guard, main body, the Commander-in-Chief; *Kyidom*, the rear column; *Benkum*, the left wing; *Nifa*, the right wing.[58] This organization also spread around south Ghana. The Ewe obviously copied this Akan system, though the Ewe army was divided into three columns instead of four.[59] Another sign of Akan influence was the introduction of the *Asafo* system. The Krobo people adopted this system, and in Accra the *Asafo* songs were mainly in Twi. Commissioner Crowther suggested in 1907 that the *Asafo* in Accra was an imitation of the Akan *Asafo*.[60]

Cocoa and Hold-ups

In southern Ghana, cocoa and politics are synonymous.[61] Cocoa was supposedly brought into the Gold Coast by Tetteh Quaishie, an African farmer from Akuapem who returned with a few cocoa plants and pods from Fernando Po in 1878 (or 1879). Governor Sir William Brandford Griffith introduced better methods in cocoa cultivation from Sao Tome in 1886.[62] By 1900, cocoa production was spreading very rapidly in southern Ghana.

The political economy of cocoa has been studies rather extensively. What is important here is the politics of cocoa hold-up. Cocoa hold-up was the term used to refer to cocoa farmers' main form of economic protest against fixing of the cocoa price by foreign companies: organized refusals to sell cocoa beans to

European firms, sometimes accompanied by a partial boycott of European merchandise.[63] The earliest hold-up was in 1908, when farmers declined to sell their cocoa in protest against low price and the control of the market by a cartel of big commercial firms. The most widespread were the hold-ups of 1930-31 and 1937-38.[64] J. B. Danquah suggested what the farmers were really fighting for was the principle of a free labor market relieved of cartels, pools, and combines.[65] Other scholars believe that price and pool were what the farmers protested against.[66]

As a collective protest, the cocoa hold-up had several features. First, although the hold-up was not solely for the cocoa price, the fall in price was always the trigger of the hold-up. This fall in price, largely influenced by the world cocoa market, hurt almost everybody in the Gold Coast society, and was commonly seen as a conspiracy of European firms against local cocoa farmers. The hold-up also provided an opportunity for the articulation of other discontents of farmers, who had many grievances against the marketing system or the increase of price of imported goods that resulted in the rise of living standard.

Secondly, since it was collective, organization was needed. This usually involved some chief farmers at the beginning doing organizational work and with chiefs as the leader. Some traditional measures were used to enforce solidarity: oaths were taken according to local customs and chiefs issued a proclamation by gong-gong[67] forbidding farmers to sell cocoa or buy foreign goods. In a few cases, some small farmers or laborers were fined or severely punished by local tribunals for selling cocoa to European firms. Since this kind of action was carried out according to the Paramount Chief's order, the government sometimes had to step in to warn the Paramount Chief of the illegal restraint upon trade.

Thirdly, organization required unity, especially because the opposition was a combination of powerful buyers who frequently acted in concert. There had been conflicts between laborers and farmers, small farmers and big farmers, farmers and chiefs, especially between farmers and brokers. Evidence shows foreign firms wanted to take advantage of this friction. In the hold-up of 1937, the firms claimed the pool, or the buying agreement, was directed against brokers rather than farmers, but protesters assumed European firms and the government should take the full responsibility. For the common interest, the chiefs, farmers, brokers and truck drivers united at the start of the hold-up. This is a good example of unity. But in other hold-ups, the unity seldom lasted long.

Fourthly, the result was almost the same. All the hold-ups failed, except for the 1937-38 one that achieved partial success in the appointment of the Nowell Commission by the British Government to investigate the cocoa marketing system. The failure of "local capitalism" was due to the stronger economic position of European firms, their greater influence with the British government, the incomplete solidarity within the hold-up and the absence of hold-ups in other producing countries.

We cannot, however, neglect another common feature in almost all the hold-ups: the farmers' boycott of European goods. For example, in the 1930-31 hold-up, gong-gong was beaten in towns and villages "threatening one year's imprisonment to anyone who buys European goods or sells cacao."[68] In the 1937-38 hold-up, the market women were urged to boycott the British cotton goods, which had an impressive impact upon the trade.[69] Obviously, the protest was more than the matter of cocoa. The farmers' consciousness of the linkage between the price of cocoa and the imported goods shows their recognition of the basic nature of the capitalist system. Therefore their protest, if not directly, was indirectly against the foreign control, be it the European firms or colonial government.

Another important issue was the division in the hold-up movement. When the hold-up started, it usually involved almost every member of the community, since the oath forbade any action otherwise. As the hold-up continued, different elements began to show different attitudes under the pressure of foreign firms, the Government, or simply the difficult conditions. The hold-up of 1930-31 failed because of the split of the leadership when there existed a substantial opposition from small brokers and small farmers.[70] The poor farmers complained that the hold-up was a plot to facilitate the acquisition of large stocks of cocoa for shipment rather than a genuine attempt to better the conditions of all producers. They felt bitter about the oath sworn upon them not to sell cocoa since this was the only source of their income.[71] There was also a strong disagreement in the 1937-38 hold-up movement. The poor farmers sold cocoa to Europeans and some of migrant laborers even "stole" their one-third share of cocoa beans in order to sell for cash.[72] All this division predicted the final breakdown of the hold-up. As Sam Rhodie points out, "Once the Government had attacked the authority of the chiefs and encouraged social and economic conflicts, the hold-up was doomed."[73]

The Content: Case Studies

This study concentrates mainly, but not exclusively, on rural areas, and deals with four types of protest: the people against the colonial Government, the commoners against the chief, the religious leaders against the secular authority, and lesser chiefs against Paramount Chiefs.

Colonial rule was an encroachment on the daily life of Africans. The common people most cared about issues directly relating to daily life. One such concern was over land. For a long time, land had been a difficult issue for the Gold Coast government. In the Gold Coast, and in most part of Africa for that matter, land traditionally belonged to the whole community and no one could own it. The chief was in charge of the land as a guardian. From 1875, the colonial Government tried every means to control the concession of land by claiming the ownership by the Queen of the "waste land" of the Colony. This claim met strong resistance from Africans, especially in the protest against the Lands Bill of 1897. In 1910, the Forest Bill was passed in an effort by the government to set up Forest Reserves. Although this measure was designed to curb the wave of concessions to foreign companies, the Ghanaians regarded it as an intrusion on their traditional land tenure and strongly protested against it.

Another daily life issue concerned cocoa. In 1936, a cocoa disease called swollen shoot was found in the Eastern Province, which became so rampant that it devastated cocoa trees in most producing area of southern Ghana from the late 1930s till the 1950s. In order to control the disease, the government introduced a method of cutting-out of cocoa trees, which met resistance from farmers. This work has studied the protest against the cutting-out at different stages, as well as the consequences of the protest. It tries to examine how the nationalists used the protests as a tool and therefore, how the protest against the cutting-out fit into the broader framework of the independence movement.

The second type of protest is that of commoners against chiefs. The study of the political history of colonial Ghana has generally focused on two indigenous political forces: the chiefs' involvement in the struggle against or collaboration with the government, and the role of the western-educated elite in the emergence of nationalist movement.[74] Martin Wight argued that there were two indigenous political forces in the colony: the native rulers and the educated class.[75] David Kimble mentioned the commoners' role in local politics in his excellent work on colonial Ghana. However, he held almost the same view as Martin Wight when he analyzed the conflict between educated Africans and chiefs.[76] Even Ghanaian scholars hold the same view. In his

Danquah Lecture, Robert K. A. Gardiner used such title for one section: "Reactions to British rule: the chiefs and intelligentsia."[77]

However, neither chiefs nor educated class can explain a widespread political phenomenon: commoners or young men deposed many chiefs. The complementary side of the picture is that another important challenge came from young men, who though holding no political position, had the right in traditional system to check the excessive power of chiefs. The change in the political situation was so fast, the nature of the chief's authority so modern, the "apparatus of government" so new that the young men's role in traditional power structure was totally disregarded and their participation in state affairs became less and less possible. The young men organized as *Asafo* companies to protect their own interests. During the colonial period, the *Asafo* played a crucial role in local political affairs. One theme of my work is to study this third force in local politics.

The third subject of this book is the conflict between religious leaders and secular authority. Although the causes of imperialist partition of Africa are debatable, the very first problem the colonial government had to tackle was its relationship with the indigenous political system. It is a truism that British colonial rule disrupted traditional political system, but by what means or in what way is by no means self-evident. A close linkage between religion and politics did exist in traditional system in the Gold Coast. This tie seemed to have been weakened in the modern period, but European rule speeded up the separation between religious and secular power.

The colonial government regarded the priests, a very important group in the traditional Gold Coast, as religious servants rather than a source of authority. As a result, the priests' power decreased dramatically.[78] They came under the authority of the chief, the only political force recognized by the colonial government.[79] This downgrading caused discontent among priests, which they took every opportunity to voice. One chapter studies a religious movement called *Abirewa* that occurred in the southern Ghana in 1906-08 and tries to trace its cultural origin and political implication.

The fourth type of protest was that of the lesser chiefs against their Paramount Chiefs. By imposing an authority structure upon the Gold Coast, the British neglected the checks and balances in the indigenous system. They took the chief as a tyrannical monarch whose power had no limitation. As a result, they disregarded other strata in the traditional ruling class. At the first stage, the Europeans made no attempt to distinguish between different levels of local authority, thus encouraging the tendency of localities to separate. Later, when they noticed the difference between the lesser chiefs and the Paramount Chiefs, they supported the Paramount Chiefs' authority at the expense of the lesser chiefs. Two chapters deal with the conflict between a chief and Paramount Chiefs (*Omanhene, pl. Amanhene*). In the Asamankese affair, locally the case was against the Paramount Chief and colonial officers, but it involved the propaganda of the West African Youth League, lasted more than fifteen years and caused a debate in British Parliament and policy change in the colony. The Jumapo affair was of a more economic nature, but it also disclosed the essence of British colonial policy regarding the concept of justice.

The final chapter tries to draw some suggestive conclusions from the case studies. Dealing with legitimacy, forms and significance of the rural protest in southern Ghana in 1904-1952, it argues that colonialism was after all a situation of paradox; protest played an important role in local politics and in most cases caused changes in colonial policy. In challenging the colonial establishments, rural social protest converted African commoners into political actors and made a great contribution to the formation of independence movement.

NOTES

[1] The Gold Coast, or colonial Ghana, includes four parts: the Gold Coast Colony, Asante, Northern Territories, and the British mandated Togoland.

[2] For a history of the spread of Christianity, see C. J. Williamson, *Akan Religion and the Christian Faith* (Accra: Ghana University Press, 1965); H. Debrunner, *A History of Christianity in Ghana* (Accra, 1967); F. L. Bartels, *The Rise of Ghana Methodism* (London: Cambridge University Press, 1965). For cocoa, see R. Szereszewski, *Structural Changes in the Economy of Ghana   1891-1911* (London: Weidenfeld & Nicholson, 1965); Polly Hill, *The Migrant Cocoa-farmers of Southern Ghana* (London: Cambridge University Press, 1963); Christer Gunnarsson, *The Gold Coast Cocoa Industry 1900-1939, Production, prices and structural change* (Lund,1978).

[3] W. Beinart & C. Bundy, *Hidden Struggle in Rural South Africa: Politics and popular movements in the Transkei and Eastern Cape 1890-1930* (London: James Currey, 1987), p.1.

[4] A. B. Davidson, "African resistance and rebellion against the imposition of colonial rule," in T. O. Ranger, ed., *Emerging Themes of African History* (Nairobi: East African Publishing House, 1968), pp.177-188.

[5] T. O. Ranger, *Revolt in Southern Rhodesia 1896-7: A study in African resistance* (London: Heinmann, 1967); "Connection between 'primary resistance' movements and modern mass nationalism in East and Central Africa," *Journal of African History*, 9:3(1968), pp.437-54; "Resistance in Africa: from nationalist revolt to agrarian protest," in Gary Okihiro, ed., *In Resistance: Studies on African,*

Caribbean, and Afro-American history (Amherst: University of Massachusetts Press, 1986), pp.32-52.

6 Allen Isaacman, *The Tradition of Resistance in Mozambique: Anti-colonial activity in the Zambesi Valley 1850-1921*(Berkeley: University of California Press, 1976); Allen Isaacman and Barbara Isaacman, "Resistance and collaboration in Southern and Central Africa. ca. 1850-1920," *International Journal of African Historical Studies*, 10:1(1977), pp.31-62.

7 Samir Amin, *Neo-Colonialism in West Africa* (Penguin, 1973); Walter Rodney, *How Europe Underdeveloped Africa* (Dar es Salaam: Tanzania Publishing House, 1972).

8 Frederick Cooper, "Peasants, capitalists and historians: a review article," *Journal of Southern African Studies*, 7:2(1981), p.288.

9 Allen Isaacman, "Peasants and rural social protest in Africa," *African Studies Review*, 33:2(1990), p.10. An exception is C. Meillassoux's *Maidens, Meal and Money: Capitalism and domestic community* (London: Cambridge University Press, 1981).

10 A typical example is Barry Hindness and Paul Q. Hirst's *Pre-Capitalist Modes of Production* (London: Routledge & Kegan Paul, 1975). For criticism, see Robin Law, "In search of a Marxist perspective on pre-colonial tropical Africa," *Journal of African History*, 19:3(1978), p.443; Martin A. Klein, *Peasants in Africa: Historical and contemporary perspectives* (London: Sage, 1980), pp.14-18.

11 Klein, *Peasants in Africa*, p.32.

12 James Scott, *Weapons of the Weak: Everyday forms of peasant resistance* (New Haven: Yale University Press, 1985), p.245. Using a Malaysian village as a case, this work analyzes the struggle between rich and poor not only in material life, but also in cultural aspects.

13 Goran Hyden, *Beyond Ujamma: Underdevelopment and an uncaptured peasantry* (London: Heinmann, 1980).

14 The cocoa hold-up showed that "organized resistance to foreign monopoly could be powerful, even in a colonial context.." Gareth Austin, "Capitalists and Chiefs in the cocoa hold-ups in South Asante, 1927-1938," *The International Journal of African Historical Studies*, 21:1(1988), p.95.

15 R. Addo-Fening, "Akyem Abuakwa c.1874-1943: A study of the impact of missionary activities and colonial rule on a traditional society" (Unpublished PhD. Thesis, University of Ghana, 1980), p.449.

16 John Iliffe, *Tanganyika under German Rule 1905-1912* (London: Cambridge University Press, 1969), pp.21-26.

17 Audrey Wipper, *Rural Rebels: A study of two protest movements in Kenya* (Nairobi: Oxford

University Press, 1977), p.11.

[18]For a more recent study, see Anshan Li, *"Abirewa*: A religious movement in the Gold Coast, 1906-8," *The Journal of Religious History*, 20:1(1996), pp.32-52.

[19]Thomas L. Hodgkin, *Nationalism in Colonial Africa* (New York: New York University Press, 1956), p.64.

[20]David Grove & L. Huszar, *The Town of Ghana: The role of service centres in regional planning* (Accra: Ghana Universities Press, 1964), p.1; Kofi N. Awoonor, *Ghana A Political History* (Accra: Sedco & Woeli, 1990), p.11.

[21]Dominic Fortescue, "The Accra crowd, the *Asafo*, and the opposition to the Municipal Corporations Ordinance,1924-5," *Canadian Journal of African Studies*, 24:3 (1990), pp.348-375.

[22]In southern Ghana, the *stool* represents the soul of a community. Stools are carved wooden seats, and regarded as sacred objects. Every state has a stool. In abstract sense, the stool usually means the symbol of authority of a chief. Hence "enstoolment" (enstool) means the installation of a chief, and "destoolment"(destool), the deposition of a chief. See P. Sarpong, *The Sacred Stool of the Akan* (Accra: Ghana Publishing Corp., 1971).

[23]For a more detailed historiographical survey of rural protest, see Li Anshan, "Rural protest and historical study," *Hong Kong Journal of Social Sciences*, 12 (Autumn, 1998), pp.155-174.

[24]See J. Gallagher and R. Robinson, "The imperialism of free trade," *Economic History Review*, 2nd series, 6(1953), pp.1-15; R. Robinson, J. Gallagher and A. Denny, *Africa and the Victorians, The official mind of imperialism* (London: Macmillan, 1970); D. C. M. Platt, "The imperialism of free trade: some reservations," *Economic History Review*, 2nd series, 21(1968), pp.296-306; "Further objections to an 'imperialism of free trade' 1830-60," *Economic History Review*, 2nd series, 26(1973), pp.77-91; D. K. Fieldhouse, *Economics and Empire 1830-1914* (London: Weidenfeld & Nicolson, 1973).

[25]C. W. Newbury, *British Policy Towards West Africa: Selected documents, 1786-1874* (Oxford: Clarendon Press, 1965), pp.534-536; R. B. Bening, "Administrative areas of the Gold Coast Colony, 1874-1899," *Universitas*, 3:3(1974), pp.59-78.

[26]"State", or *oman*, is a geographical area, linguistic homogeneity and a complexity of religious institutions that subsumes the political and social order. It covers boundaries that may be large or include peoples other than the original lineage group. Kofi N. Awoonor, *Ghana: A Political History*, pp.11-12. The term is used in this study according to the context.

[27]*CO96/255*. G.C. Conf. 27 March 1895.

[28]V. C. Climo, *Precis of Information Concerning the Colony of the Gold Coast and Ashanti* (London: War Office, 1904), p.5. Appendix IV, pp.190-192; *CO96/382*. G.C.Conf. Nathan to Chamberlain, 3 September, 1901.

[29] *ADM6/29. Government Gazette*, 1903. pp.995-6. See Appendix II; *CO96/417*. Despatch. Gold Coast. No.209. Rodgster to Lyttelton, 29 April, 1904, "Journal on tour of inspection through the Eastern Province." See also *The Gold Coast Colonial Civil List, 1904*. Francis Agbodeka suggests "there was a change from the nineteenth century political divisions of Eastern and Western Districts to Eastern, Central and Western Provinces which came into use around 1914." F. Agbodeka, *Ghana in the Twentieth Century* (Accra: Ghana Universities Press, 1972), xiii. This statement is incorrect.

[30] *The Provinces and Districts (Colony) Order. No.40 of 1946.*

[31] See for example David Brown, "Anglo-German rivalry and Krepi politics 1886-1894," *Transactions of the Historical Society of Ghana*, 15:2(1974), pp.201-216.

[32] *CO96/235*. Encl. 5 in G.C. Conf. 17 August, 1893. *CO96/274*. G.C. No.219 of 1 June 1896; *CO96/159*. C.O. Minute No.18641 on G.C. No.449.

[33] *Keta Study*, Occasional paper No.15 (Kumasi: University of Science and Technology, Faculty of Architecture, no date), p.15.

[34] Mary Gaunt, *Alone in West Africa* (London: T. W. Laurie, 1912), p.284; J. B. Yegbe, "Research material at the Ghana National Archives on the history of Anlo 1850-90" (Legon: Institute of African Studies, 1966), p.10.

[35] Akan (Twi and Guan), Ga, Adangbe and Ewe are genetically related and belong to the Kwa sub-family of the Niger-Congo family. See J. H. Greenberg, *The Languages of Africa* (Bloomington: Indiana University, 1966), p.8.

[36] The study of ethnic groups is not the subject of this work. Some detailed studies have been done. For example, M. Manoukian, *The Akan and Ga-Adangme Peoples of the Gold Coast* (London: Oxford University Press, 1950); M. J. Field, *The Social Organization of the Ga People* (London: The Crown Agents, 1940); L. E. Wilson, *Krobo People of Ghana to 1892: A political and social history* (Athens: Ohio University International Studies, 1992); Hugo Huber, *The Krobo, Traditional Social and Religious Life of A West African People* (St. Augustin: The Anthropos Institute, 1963); Kwamena Poh, *Government and Politics in the Akuapem State 1730-1850* (London: Longman, 1973); Otutu Bagyire VI, Abiriwhene, "The Guans: A preliminary note," *Ghana Notes and Queries*, 7(1965), pp.21-24; Ansa K. Asamoa, *The Ewe of South-Eastern Ghana and Togo on the Eve of Colonialism* (Tema: Ghana Publishing Co., 1986).

[37] W. E. F. Ward, *A History of Ghana*, pp.58-63; F. M. Bourret, *Ghana: the Road to independence*(Stanford: Stanford University Press, 1960), pp.9-10.

[38] Adu Boahen, "The origins of the Akan," *Ghana Notes and Queries*, 9(1966), pp.3-10; A. Bohen, "Ghana before the coming of Europeans," p.96; A. Bohen, "Ghana before the coming of

Europeans," *Ghana Social Science Journal*, 4:2(1977), pp.93-106.

[39]E. L. A. Meyerowitz, J. B. Danquah and others suggested that the Akan came from Ethiopea, ancient Ghana, north Africa, or the valley of Tigris and Euphrates. E. Meyerowitz, *Akan Traditions of Origins* (London: Faber & Faber, 1952), pp.124-129. J. B. Danquah, "The Akan claim to origin from Ghana," *West African Review*, 26(Nov. and Dec. 1955). D. Tait, G. W. Irvin and R. A. Mauny disagreed with this view but failed to provide any alternative hypothesis. D. Tait, "Akan traditions of origins," *Man*, 53(January, 1953), no.10, pp.11-12; G. Irwin, "The origins of the Akan," *Universita*, 4:5 (1961), pp.138-41; R. A. Mauny, "The question of Ghana," *Africa*, 24(1954), pp.200-212; J. R. Goody, "Ethno-history and the Akan of Ghana," *Africa*, 29(1959), pp.67-80.

[40]James Anquandah, *Rediscovering Ghana's Past* (Accra: Sedco, 1982), pp.85-112.

[41]Several authors have suggested that the Ga and the Adangbe belonged to "one big nation" at the beginning. See T. H. Odonkor, *The Rise of the Krobos* (Tema: Ghana Publishing Co., 1971), pp.1-2; I. Quaye, "The Ga and their neighbours 1600-1742" (Unpublished PhD. Thesis, University of Ghana, 1972), p.13.

[42]A. Adu Boahen, "Ghana before the coming of Europeans," p.96; K. B. Dickson, *A Historical Geography of Ghana* (London: Cambridge University Press, 1969), p.27. See also L. E. Wilson, *Krobo People of Ghana to 1892*, pp.12-32.

[43]James Anquandah, *Rediscovering Ghana's Past*, p.115.

[44]A. Boahen, *Topics in African History* (London: Longmans, 1966), p.64; "Ghana before the coming of Europeans," p.96; Ansa K. Asamoa, *The Ewe of South-Eastern Ghana*, pp.2-5.

[45]Kwamena Poh, *Government and Politics*, pp.13-18.

[46]Ivor Wilks, "The growth of the Akwapim State: A study in the control of evidence," in J. Vansina, R. Mauny & L. V. Thomas, ed., *The Historian in Tropical Africa*(London: Oxford University Press, 1964), pp.390-411. For the migration of cocoa farmers, see Polly Hill, "The history of the migration of Ghana cocoa farmers," *Transactions of the Historical Society of Ghana*, 4:1 (1959), pp.14-28; Hill, Polly, *The Migrant Cocoa-farmers of Southern Ghana A study on rural capitalism* (London: Cambridge University Press, 1963), pp.219-238.

[47]Wilks, "The growth of the Akwapim State," p.391. Two reasons contributed to linguistic change in Akuapem. The *Akwamuhene* forced the Guan to learn Twi during his rule over Akuapem and there was a large influx of Akwamu (Twi-speaking) immigrants after the destruction of the Akwamu empire. Kwamena-Poh, *Government and Politics*, p.132.

[48]M. E. Kropp Dakubu, "Bowdich's 'Adampe' word list," *Research Review* (Legon: Institute of African Studies, 1969), pp.47-48.

[49]Wilson, *Krobo People of Ghana to 1892*, pp.24-32; Hugo Huber, *The Krobo*, p.292.

[50]C. K. Nukunya, *Kinship and Marriage among the Anlo Ewe* (London: the Anlone Press, 1969), pp.11-13, 21.

[51]Wilks, *Asante in the Nineteenth Century: The Structure and Evolution of a Political Order* (London: Cambridge University Press, 1975), pp.1-42.

[52]Ivor Wilks, "The rise of Akwamu empire, 1640-1710," *Transactions of the Historical Society of Ghana*, 3:2(1957), p.101.

[53]King Ladzekpo of Anexo, a notorious slaver, went to Liverpool in 1800 by a slave ship to sell his own slaves. Asamoa, *The Ewe*, p.20. no.31.

[54]Kwamena-Poh, *Government and Politics*, p.133.

[55]Samuel S. Quarcoopome, "Political activities in Accra 1924-45" (Unpublished M.A.Thesis. University of Ghana, 1980), p.5.

[56]*ADM11/1/1393*. Case No.88/1913. Destoolment. Anlo State Resolution dated at Keta this 31st day of May, 1929.

[57]*ADM11/1/1393*. Case No.88/1913. Destoolment. Acting Commissioner of Eastern Province to Acting Secretary for Native Affairs, 13 August 1930.

[58]R. S. Rattray, *Ashanti Law and Constitution* (London: Oxford University Press, 1929), pp.121-122.

[59]There were left, right and center columns, but the rear guard had no recognized status.

[60]I. Quaye, "The Ga and their Neighbours," pp.267.

[61]Bjorn Beckman, *Organising the Farmers: Cocoa, politics and national development in Ghana* (Uppsala: The Scandinavian Institute of African Studies, 1976); Gwendolyn Mikell, *Cocoa and Chaos in Ghana* (New York: Paragon House, 1989).

[62]K. B. Dickson, "Origin of Ghana's cocoa industry," *Ghana Notes and Queries*, 5(1963), pp.4-9. Who introduced cocoa to Ghana is a debatable issue among scholars, but not among the Ghanaians. Tetteh Quashie is a national hero and there is a Tetteh Quashie Circle in Accra. For various views on the issue, see Polly Hill, *The Migrant Cocoa-farmers of Southern Ghana*, pp.170-176.

[63]G. Austin, "Capitalists and chiefs," p.66. The contemporary literature includes J. B. Danquah, *Liberty of the Subject A Monograph on the Gold Coast Hold-up and Boycott of Foreign Goods (1937-38)*(Kibbi, 1938) and *Cmd5845. Report on the Marketing of West African Cocoa.* A general study is John Miles's "Rural protests in the Gold Coast: the Cocoa Hold-ups, 1908-1938," in C. Dewey and A. Hopkins, ed., *Imperial Impact Economic development in Africa and India under colonial rule* (London: Athlone, 1978), pp.152-170.

[64]S. Rhodie, "The Gold Coast hold-up of 1930-31," *Transactions of Historical Society of Ghana*, 9(1968), pp.105-18; Josephine Milburn, "The 1938 Gold Coast cocoa crisis: British business and the Colonial Office," *African Historical Studies*, 3(1970), pp.57-74.

[65]Danquah, *Liberty of the Subject*, p.19.

[66]John Miles, "Rural protest in the Gold Coast," pp.152-79; Austin, "Capitalists and chiefs," pp.63-95.

[67]Gong-gong is a traditional instrument used only by the chief in emergency to make a announcement or to gather people.

[68]*ADM87/5.* October 9, 30; November 18, 28; December 2, 1930. Quoted from Sam Rhodie, "The Gold Coast Cocoa hold-up of 1930-31," p.105.

[69]According to a report, Lancashire was having a bad time with cotton goods for West African trade, because of "the West African native is boycotting British goods, particularly Lancashire cotton goods." Quoted from R. Howard, *Colonialism and Underdevelopment*, (London: Croom Helm, 1978), pp.215-216.

[70]See E. Y. Twumasi, "Aspects of politics in Ghana, 1923-39: A study of the relationship between discontent and development of nationalism"(D.Phil. Dissertation, Oxford University, 1971), pp.233-240.

[71]Twumasi thinks that small brokers and small farmers opposed the hold-up since they "were less dependent on market forces." This argument is not convincing. See his dissertation, p.238. Here I argue the opposed: they were against the hold-up simply because they were bound to the market and cocoa was their only means to survive.

[72]*ADM23/1/798.* See R. Howard, *Colonialism and Underdevelopment*, pp.216-218.

[73]Rhodie, "The Gold Coast hold-up of 1930-31," p.118.

[74]For exceptions, see T. Johnson, "Protest tradition and change: An analysis of southern Gold Coast riots 1890-1920," *Economy and Society*, 1:2 (1972), pp.164-93; R. Stone, "Protest tradition and change: a critique" and T. Johnson's reply, *Economy and Society*, 3:1(1974), pp.84-105; J. Simensen, "Rural mass action in the context of anti-colonial protest: the *Asafo* movement of Akim Abuakwa, Ghana," *Canadian Journal of African Studies*, 8:1 (1974), pp.25-44; "The *Asafo* of Kwahu, Ghana: a mass movement for local reform under colonial rule," *The International Journal of African Historical Studies*, 8:3 (1975), pp.383-406; R. Addo-Fening, *et al, Akyem Abuakwa and the Politics of the Inter-war Period in Ghana* (Basel: Basler Afrika Bibliographien, 1975); Anshan Li, "*Asafo* and destoolment in colonial southern Ghana, 1900-1953," *The International Journal of African Historical Studies*, 28:2 (1995), pp.327-357. This "elite history" in African historiography has been criticized elsewhere.

[75]Martin Wight, *The Gold Coast Legislative Council* (London: Faber & Faber, 1946), p.181.

[76]D. Kimble, *A Political History of Ghana The rise of the Gold Coast nationalism 1850-1928* (Oxford: Clarendon Press, 1963), p.458.

[77]Robert K. A. Gardiner, *The Role of Educated Persons in Ghana Society* (Accra, 1970), p.20. F. Agbodeka's *African Politics and British Policy in the Gold Coast 1868-1900 A study in the forms and force of protest* (London: Longman, 1971) This study on protest concentrates on primary and early resistance led by chiefs.

[78]A colonial officer noticed the priests' power was diminishing. He once wrote in a report: "It is not difficult to foresee, however, that they will make every effort to retain ascendancy over the people." *ADM/11/1/10*. C.S.O. No.05094. Conf.M.P.No.688/07. Dispatch, 21 November 1907.

[79]*ADM36/1/8*. Fetish 1920-46. Regulations regarding the practice of native doctor issued in various states.

CHAPTER I

Abirewa: The Religious against the Secular

From 1906 to August 1908, a religious movement spread first throughout Asante, then to the Gold Coast Colony. At first, the colonial government regarded it as helpful for law and order, and did not pay much attention to it. Later, the movement gained such popularity that many chiefs began to complain about its subversion of their power. Having realized the political implication of the movement, the government finally put an end to it in 1908.

Origin and Principles

In 1906 a new "fetish"[1] by the name of *Abirewa* appeared in Asante. The place of its origin is still a mystery. Some suggested that it had come from the Northern Territories. Others believed that it had been brought from the Ivory Coast, or Gyaman country.[2] All information indicates that it came from the hinterland to the north, but the government believed that it had been introduced from the French colony.[3] There are several versions regarding the origin of *Abirewa*. According to one legend, an old woman in the interior fell sick and died. Upon entering the "world of spirits," a great man standing at the door said to her "your time to die has not yet come, witchcraft has killed you, return to the earth!" Offering her a charm to protect her against any kind of evil magic or witchcraft, he sent her back to life, telling her "you will die a natural death in old age." The news spread very quickly and the religion became famous throughout the hinterland and was called "*Abirewa*" (old woman). Other versions had the same features. First, *Abirewa* was sent by God, implying the power of the religion. Secondly, it came to serve the people "by destroying the evil." Thirdly, it appeared particularly as anti-witchcraft.[4]

Abirewa was made of some black substance wrapped in string and laid on the top of a small mound. *Abirewa* was accompanied by a male god *Manguro* made of fibers and cowry shells bound together. Together they were called "*Borgya*." The medicine that the worshippers of *Abirewa* had to drink was made of the root of a certain tree, ground into powder and diluted with water. Its preparation was a great secret known to only the priests. *Abirewa* had its own temple, or shrine, which had been prepared before the high priest's introduction of it. *Manguro* had a long horn, giving forth a terrifying sound, which was said to collect all the evil spirits or witches. When someone died, the priests would decide whether the person was killed by *Abirewa*. If so, the property of the dead would be confiscated and usually divided between the priest and the chief.[5]

Unlike some other religious movements, *Abirewa* lacked institutional leadership and systematic organization. The high priest was said to be in Bunduku, and there were three kinds of people involved in the introduction of *Abirewa*. Some were strangers, who benefited from selling the medicine said to be able to kill witchcraft. Some converted to it and became priests. Most were already priests, or were elected by villagers.[6] Membership in *Abirewa* was open to both men and women without having to serve any probation. After a ceremony, the applicant was admitted or rejected according to the priest's judgment. Members were initiated by taking an oath to observe certain rules. The rules seemed so beneficial to the people that even a colonial officer admitted "it is difficult to find fault with the principles of this new religion for it inculcates speaking the truth and living a good life as essential."[7] According to a missionary, the principles of *Abirewa* included twenty commandments:

1. You shall not covet your neighbor's property or else you will die.
2. Don't envy rich men and wealthy persons, or else you will soon stiffen in death!
3. If you plan evil against your neighbor, you are a child of death!
4. Never walk past a neighbor's farm without weeding a little or doing any necessary repairs to the fence, or death will soon catch you.
5. If during a meal you become angry and leave the food, you must wipe the mouth with a cola nut and then ask *Abirewa* for pardon—otherwise *Abirewa* will kill you!
6. Disobedience against chiefs means death!
7. Selling of stolen things: Death!
8. Slandering your neighbor: Death!
9. Using magic against your neighbor: Death!
10. Adultery with your neighbor's wife: Death!
11. Refusing a request for help: Death!
12. Bringing others into debt by litigation: Death!
13. Having community with the witches: Death!

14.   Cursing your neighbor: Death!
15.   Carrying firewood in bundles into town: Death!
16.   You must clean away the remainders of food after eating at once, or else you will die!
17.   Neglecting to further the interests of *Abirewa* brings death!
18.   Coming to the shrine in an unclean state: Death!
19.   Forgetting about *Abirewa* when traveling: Death!
20.   If you neglect to pay your debts: Death! [8]

Akan society was generally organized in groupings of kin or small states where face-to-face relations were of paramount importance. A close look at the code reveals that the principles really stress those relations in three aspects: to obey and respect authorities whether that of the elders, the chief, the government, the souls of ancestors, or the new religion; to be kind and cooperative with others, especially neighbors; and to behave properly according to social norms. All these laws seemed to be very constructive and even the colonial officials believed that *Abirewa* would "work for law and order."[9]

H. Debrunner suggests that the intention of all these laws with their terrible threats was obvious: "to reknit society by the imposition of new moral and legal sanctions. In this way, they hoped to overcome the various stresses and frictions in society which were brought about by the culture contact."[10] This observation is true in the sense that the cultural contact and economic expansion brought about rapid social changes, and the people wanted to hold the dissolving society together by adjusting themselves to the new situation. But the "imposition of new moral and legal sanctions" was not necessarily guaranteed. To achieve this the priests had to hold on to their power if it still remained in their hands, or to regain the power if it had been lost. Since the latter was the case in the southern part of the Gold Coast,[11] *Abirewa* offered an excellent opportunity for the priests to recover their power. As a result, all the rules ordered respect for *Abirewa*. Besides numbers 17, 18 and 19 in the above-mentioned code, there were other versions of the principles. "You must obey your Fetish and Chief." Here the authority of the religious leader obviously came before the chief's. "To respect the departed souls of your Ancestors and family Fetishes." "To bewail no person whom the fetish kills." All precepts stressed the indisputable authority of the religion in terms of its legitimacy and judgment.

Reactions and Suppression

Since *Abirewa* became a challenge to chief's authority and a threat to Christianity, the reaction from missionaries and chiefs was not at all favorable. Missionaries complained about the "barbarous" character of local religions. Their criticism was due to both their attitude of cultural superiority and their devotion to the mission of converting "pagans" to Christianity. This deep-rooted prejudice prevented them from seeing the real value of traditional religion and those practices "which to the unscientific mind seem barbarous, but which, when critically examined, cover a mine of truth and inspiration."[12]

When *Abirewa* was spreading in the south, the Basel missionaries urged the Government to suppress it. They called *Abirewa* a "dangerous religion" and laid several charges against it. First, it was a practice of human sacrifices and threatened people with terror. "It is a messenger of death and has done more harm than all the witches and sorcerers together." Secondly, the property of the person killed by *Abirewa* all went to the priest, which withdrew wealth from the region and made people poor. Thirdly, the ill treatment of the body of the person killed by *Abirewa* was harmful for public sanitation. The missionaries also warned the people were becoming completely spell-bound, "It is binding the whole nation into a league as strong as that of any Dervish Band, a league of men and women convinced that no shot can harm them, no sickness can attack them, no untimely death can come upon them, nothing can touch them as long as they obey implicitly and unquestioningly every law and demand of the priest." [13]

Unlike missionaries who stressed "uncivilized" and "inhuman" aspects of *Abirewa*, chiefs generally worried about its effect in reducing their power and privileges to the priests' advantage. Chiefs either opposed it because of its political implications or supported it if they could benefit from it. On August 3, 1907, F. C. Fuller, the Chief Commissioner of Asante, held an enquiry concerning the spread of *Abirewa*. Participants were chiefs and priests. Among the twenty-one participants, ten supported, ten opposed and one made no comment. Supporters either were informed of its introduction or got one third of the property of the dead. Their power was acknowledged and legitimized by their villagers. In contrast, chiefs opposed *Abirewa* not because of its principles or practice, but because of its introduction without their knowledge. Typical of the opposing group, a chief named Frimpon accused the *Abirewa* of body-mutilating and sending away the property of the dead, but his real concern was: "My people did not inform me before introducing the fetish into my village so that proves that the Fetish is held higher than myself... The

Fetish should be introduced with the knowledge of the chiefs." The majority of chiefs complained their people were being taken away by the new religion. One chief found that "those of my people who have accepted the fetish no longer visit or salute me."[14] From this testimony, it is evident that what caused the chiefs' discontent was not *Abirewa* itself, but the appropriation of their power by priests.

Common people, by contrast, seemed to have welcomed the new religion. Once it was brought to Asante, it spread "with astonishing rapidity" and attracted a lot of people. A priest named Yaw Wua, who had served the government for thirty-seven years, was initiated into *Abirewa*. Soon he had six thousand followers, some were other chiefs' subjects. *Abirewa* was also found in the Central Province, especially in the Aguna District. It involved so many people that almost all the chiefs were frightened. According to a missionary's report, "People believe in it, love it and become devoted to it more and more by [*sic*] every day." The gathering of the ceremony became so big that "Every time the dance stops, the people indulge in feasting and drinking; the noise of these orgies can be heard far away." In the Eastern Province, the more the chiefs tried to prohibit it, the more people converted to it. In less than a year, worshippers of *Abirewa* were found in all towns in New Dwaben and Kwahu, in almost every town in Eastern Akyem and also in Akuapem.[15]

The government's reaction was different. When *Abirewa* appeared in Asante, the colonial officials reported it immediately. Western District Commissioner T. E. Fell held a meeting with the chiefs and people of Sunyani, together with Sei Kwahu, who had introduced *Abirewa* to the region. After the meeting, he concluded that "Personally I don't object to its existence in Sunyani where the Chief and people honestly appear to think it a safe-guard against quarrels, bad Fetish and bad medicines." Five days later he suggested that government should not forbid *Abirewa* because "it is of no political importance whatever, that it tends rather to settle than unsettle the people." [16] As Chief Commissioner of Asante, F. C. Fuller followed the same course of action. After he received various complaints about the new religion, he called a meeting with chiefs and priests. After the meeting, he decided that the worship of *Abirewa* would be allowed with the approval of head chiefs. Chiefs and priests should be responsible for breach of the law occasioned by the worship. No part of a deceased man's property should be sent out of the country. *Abirewa* should not show hostility to Christians or missions.[17]

Without a general policy, the government left it to the chiefs to decide, who could either support *Abirewa* or leave it alone. In either case they helped its spread. Even if the chiefs wanted to suppress it, they could do nothing without the government's backing. As a result, *Abirewa* spread so rapidly that it caused still more complaints from chiefs and also alarmed district commissioners. On June 6, 1908, Commissioner C. N. Curling of the Eastern Province received a letter from the *Omanhene* of Eastern Akyem, complaining that "certain fetishism called '*Abirewa*' had been brought to Akim from Ashanti and that most of my people had received and were worshipping same," and requesting that "steps may be promptly taken with a view to the entire abolition of this fetishism in my country."[18]

Chiefs in the Central Province had the same fear. According to Provincial Commissioner Eliot, chiefs regarded *Abirewa* with fear, and "those Chiefs who have not already come under the influence of the priests would view with satisfaction any action on the part of the government to suppress this heathen worship." He also enclosed in his letter a report by a Basel missionary in the Winneba District, who claimed that the "*Abirewa* is creating a 'reign of terror'."[19] Here Eliot expressed his opposition and began to talk about the possibility of suppression. A month later Curling again reported that *Abirewa* had spread to Akuapem, New Dwaben, Eastern Akyem and Kwahu. The chiefs of these districts were all afraid of the subversion of their authority by the new religion. Since they could not stop it without assistance, Curling took action, "suppressing the fetish from New Juabin upwards." He hoped that the Governor would support his action.[20]

From all these steps, we can sense a kind of emergency in Central and Eastern Provinces. However, the final decision was made after the Acting Colonial Secretary submitted a report on *Abirewa* on June 29, 1908. He pointed out the possible political significance of this new religious movement. On July 17, the Executive Council decided to abolish *Abirewa*. Since "it appears to the Government that the celebration of the rite, ceremony and worship of the fetish known as *ABIREWA* tends towards the commission of crime," the Order was issued to have it suppressed and "whosoever continues this order shall be liable to a fine not exceeding twenty-five pounds."[21]

The most interesting point is Asante Chief Commissioner Fuller's attitude. At first, he was quite optimistic about the new movement, saying "I am inclined to believe that the '*Abirewa*' worship will work for law and order." He criticized the Basel missionaries who "have assumed such an extremely hostile attitude towards it" and suggested Abirewa was "in fashion" and "the Christian Missionaries find that they are unable to attract congregation when on 'preaching tour' so they have only too readily... accepted and utilized a vague rumor of mutilation of dead bodies, to counteract the proselytizing success of the *Abirewa* propaganda."[22]

After a meeting with some chiefs and priests, Fuller decided that *Abirewa* should be allowed if chiefs approved of it. Ten months later, C. H. Armitage, Acting Chief Commissioner of Asante, expressed the same view and explained the attitude of missionaries. "The Missionaries naturally object to '*Abirewa*', as the dancing and singing associated with it attract the people and militate against their efforts to proselytize the Ashantis." But the Acting Colonial Secretary at Accra took the matter more seriously. He pointed out that the political importance that the movement might have been neglected by the Ashanti authorities."[23]

This opinion, together with the news that the colony had taken action to suppress *Abirewa*, seemed to have changed Fuller's mind. Since "the Detractors failed hopelessly to establish, or prove, a case against '*Abirewa*' as an institution likely to promote crime," Fuller decided to "fight the new worship by ridicule." In a circular addressed to all the Paramount Chiefs of Asante, he enclosed a letter from Commissioner Fell on this subject. Fell said that the priets of *Abirewa* lived in the neighborhood of Bontuku were becoming "inordinately rich" and large presents of money they received were from Ashanti. "Over these payments the natives of the French side are laughing in their sleeve and... that they clap their hands and say 'By these tricks of Fetishes we are getting back from Ashanti all the moneys and tributes they took from us in the old days.'"[24]

But after fifteen days, Fuller decided that he had found enough excuses for the suppression and resolved to strike a "crushing blow" to this worship "owing to a sudden eruption of *Abirewa* fanaticism." This was an astonishing turnaround. The charges he laid against *Abirewa* included ill treatment of corpses, subversion of chiefly power and wholesale collections for the benefit of the high priests living in French colony. He quickly convened a meeting of all the chiefs of the Central Province in Asante "together with all their *Abirewa* Priests (whom I inveigled into Coomassie by guaranteeing them their personal safety)."[25] Four to five thousand people attended the meeting. The Chief Commissioner made a thoughtful speech: "I have waited to see the working of this Religion for a whole year and I tell you the net result is that crime is encouraged by it; that the land is being impoverished by it; and that the land has become unsettled by it."

He attacked *Abirewa* severely despite the fact that only half a month earlier he had said he could not "discover any political or criminal danger in the cult." In order to justify his action, the Chief Commissioner piled up a series of charges. He ridiculed the Asante as cowards, and scolded them for being credulous, thus permitting them to be laughed at by their neighbors for sending back "part of the wealth that the Ashanti had taken from them in former times." He accused the priests of cheating the rich and undermining the chiefly power. He also blamed the chiefs for supporting the worship.[26]

Debrunner argues that the main reason for the suppression was the priests' direct involvement in witch-hunting.[27] Fuller expressed the same view in his book.[28] But a study of the evidence reveals a quite different picture. It was the missionaries who first called the attention of the government to the political implications of this new religious movement. This new religion threatened to become "a greater danger" to Christianity, trade, peace and prosperity of the country "than any other superstition yet known"; "Let us not forget that this *Abirewa* has spread from Dweso and it is in this district the last insurrection originated. This is rather significant!"

The Acting Colonial Secretary noticed "its organization and constitution emanate from a mind of a caliber out of the common." He suggested the fact that "the injunction of obedience to the government and the power and material prosperity of the priesthood are secured" must be "an attempt to avert official disfavor." Provincial Commissioners Curling and Eliot strongly supported the suppression especially because of the subversion of chiefly power by the priests. Curling also worried about the underlying doctrine of *Abirewa* that "those who have drunk the medicine need fear nothing, need obey no one, for no one can harm them. They are immune from danger of all kind [sic] whether from man or beast and spiritual as well as temporal."[29] A doctrine defying everything could not be allowed.

By August 1908 most colonial officials and chiefs realized *Abirewa* was a threat to their authority and *Abirewa* was suppressed. John P. Rodger, the Governor, showed his concern about the danger of *Abirewa* and was greatly relieved when it was suppressed.[30] Although the charges against it focused on criminal acts, the real reasons for its suppression were more political than humanitarian; namely to prevent the weakening of chiefly power and to kill the potential for disturbances. However, two questions remain to be answered. Why did so many people believe in *Abirewa*? Why did the priests try so hard to spread *Abirewa*?

Causes: A Tentative Explanation

The colonial government was obviously more concerned about the effect of *Abirewa*, it never analyzed the causes of this religious movement. A missionary explained why people welcomed *Abirewa*, "because it fosters and encourages just these things which they delight in, drumming, obscene dances, feasting and drinking etc. Then the doing away of people, who are not wanted and that seems to satisfy the old love for manslaughter and cruelties, which seem to be a part of their very nature." [31] Full of cultural bias, this explanation shows no intention even to try to understand the movement. The missionaries cared much more about the actions of the followers than anything else. However, the most important factor seems not to be the nature of *Abirewa* itself, but its social significance.

There are two more thoughtful interpretations regarding the *Abirewa* movement in the Asante area. Malcolm McLeod suggests that the breakdown of political control and the suppression of older anti-witchcraft cults gave young men the chance to import and profit from *Abirewa*, and some chiefs seemed "to have ineffectually tried to combat the movement which further reduced their power."[32] T. C. MaCaskie refutes this explanation and argues that this was the case only in some areas, while in other areas chiefs were able to make use of *Abirewa* to strengthen their own decreasing power.[33] But neither has mentioned the possibility that a change in the status of the priest may have resulted in the rise of the movement. In order to understand fully *Abirewa* as a protest, we have to study its historical origin and the favorable situation for its spread. The previous status and authority of priests shaped its non-institutional leadership, and the grievances of the people played an important role in the advance of the movement.

Cultural Heritage

G. Parrinder suggests that in West Africa, religious belief resembles a triangular structure. At the apex is God, the supreme and creator spirit. The two sides of the triangle are the lesser deities and ancestors, and the base is composed of those beliefs and practices called magic. P. Sarpon agrees that this summary would "apply to Ghanaian religious thought."[34] In Akan religion, *Nyame* (or *Nyankopong*) is God, the Creator and the Supreme Being, who keeps a loving but watchful eye on people. The world is full of spirits, the minor gods or lesser deities (*abosom*), who are worshipped by people. They believe that ancestors keep a close contact with the living members of the lineage and try their best to protect them.[35] This structure shows while the priest acted as representative of the deities, the chief as secular leader also played the sacred role as intermediary with the ancestors.

People in the Gold Coast also believed in witches (*abayifo*, sing. *obayifo*) and witchcraft. The belief acted as a sanction against antisocial behavior: witches were wicked people and their ill feeling, hatred or envy caused harm. Besides supporting the moral order of the community, the belief also explained why a particular person at a particular time and place suffered particular misfortunes. People believed all the tragedy and misfortune were due to such evil works as witchcraft, curses, or bad medicines. But the distinguishing feature of witchcraft was that the killing or harming was wrought by the silent, invisible projection of influence from witches. Their attack on the individual took various forms, such as sickness, barrenness, sorrow or death.[36] It was believed that the misfortunes caused by witches could be protected or cured by medicine or traditional religion.

There has been a long tradition of use of medicine for special purposes. Among the Akan, the word "medicine" has a much more comprehensive meaning than the term usually indicates. It is common to use it to describe magic, religious object and the related ritual. The Akan believe that there is some medicine for every kind of illness or misfortune. M. Field once stated that no activity in life can not be assisted by medicine. A hunter can "medicine his gun and his bullets to make them unerring;" a blacksmith can "medicine his tools;" a fisherman or a lorry-driver can medicine their canoe or lorry. Even a suitor could "medicine himself to make his charms irresistible."[37]

Generally speaking, there are three kinds of medicine: common remedies used by everybody without ritual, family secrets handed down through generations and medicines known only to the professional priests.[38] Medicine is so closely linked with religion that it is suggested that the Akan or the Ga made no or little distinction between medicine and religion, or "fetish". [39]

For the Akan, *asuman* means certain particular articles, for example, charms and amulets. They are supposed to be inhabited by *abosom*, or the lesser deities, and are all supplied by priests. There are also natural phenomena, such as rivers, hills and forest, which are abodes of *abosom*. Different people have different classifications of these minor gods. People consider it good to have a minor god living among them. Early Europeans mentioned articles worn by people or hung in the house or a tree at the entrance of a village.[40] They were put there for a protective purpose.[41] In fact, *Abirewa* was so closely linked with *Sakrabudi*, an old religious object, that one priest was carrying *Sakrabudi* on his back and

Abirewa in front. The practice of *Abirewa* was "also in close resemblance to the *Katawere* and other fetishes."[42]

The belief in God or minor gods and related rituals, the fear of witchcraft and the use of medicine were essential elements of the traditional religion in the Gold Coast. These factors were all conditions favorable to the spread of *Abirewa*. This cultural heritage explains the people's willingness to convert to the new religion. But why should the movement spread at this particular time? To answer this question, we have to understand the dramatic change that occurred at the beginning of this century and its impact upon the people.

Situation of Crisis

At the end of the nineteenth century, the spread of Christianity, the introduction of cash crops and the establishment of colonial rule significantly altered Gold Coast society. As a result of the penetration of Christianity, traditional religion began to lose its believers. For example, at Late, a "fetish town," priests were reported in 1880 as having withdrawn from the vicinity of a new chapel. The mission hoped "may they soon creep into the holes of moles and bats." According to a report, "the belief in fetishes had weakened, especially among the younger generation who no longer believe in them."[43]

A colonial officer also noticed the difference in attitude between the old and the young. In 1886, he attended a religious ceremony, where he noted the old people, "particularly the old women, appeared most impressed by what they saw; and they apparently had the most implicit faith in the genuineness of the whole proceeding;" while the younger people appeared skeptical and some "openly laughed."[44]

A rapid change of daily life caused wealth, anger and jealousy, but most important the crisis in faith. Epidemics brought about a high rate of child-death or barrenness. More and more people got into debt as a result of being involved in litigation over land rights. A chief expressed his sorrow and despair when he talked about the dramatic change after 1900: "If our tribe is degenerating, our fame declining and the former splendor of our kingdom vanishing, whence does it come, if not from the wrath of the tutelar spirits and the anger of the ancestors!" Then he named all the changes: "the thunder of the big guns," "the noise of the church bells," "the wires of the telephone," all these made their spirit unhappy.[45]

This disastrous impact on the Gold Coast society created a sense of insecurity and fear.[46] Human relations became tenser than ever, and more and more witches were suspected or accused. In spiritual or temporal crisis, people resorted to old ways, relying on the vitality of traditional belief and the strength of the priests, who were believed to be able to remove stress, as well as to seek out and cure social disturbances. As a result, the fear of witchcraft became widespread, and powerful religion was sought for protection; thus arose various kinds of anti-witchcraft cults.

There are two interpretations regarding anti-witchcraft phenomenon among the Akan. One school argues that anti-witchcraft cults are the creation of the twentieth century and have arisen to meet the challenge and strain brought about by the colonial situation.[47] Jack Goody rejects this view and suggests that anti-witchcraft cults first appear far back in the pre-colonial period.[48] These two views both hold some truth, but neither is convincing enough. A synthesis is needed in order to make sense of this historical phenomenon.

On the one hand, although very few early sources mentioned this matter, no doubt the anti-witchcraft did exist in the Gold Coast before colonial rule. Joseph Dupuis described the struggle for the throne between the Asante King and a usurper during 1818-1819, an event that had much resemblance to the way witchcraft and anti-witchcraft are understood today.[49] Some early Europeans also recorded the methods of witch finding that they came across in the Gold Coast.[50] It seems that chewing or drinking a decoction of certain poisonous bark and corpse-carrying, two major methods used in early witch-finding, were both adopted in the *Abirewa* ceremony.

On the other hand, the frequency of this phenomenon indicates colonial rule did bring about such a severe change that there was a marked increase in uncertainty and strain among people. Goody argued that the British occupation in many ways brought about "an increased rather than a decreased personal security."[51] He is certainly right if by "personal security" he only meant life security. But economic anxieties caused by more opportunities, political oppression caused by colonial rule and chiefs' abuse of power, and social disorientation caused by the declining of traditional institutions, all resulted in increased **insecurity** and **uncertainty**. Fear, envy, accusations and confessions provided a favorable climate for increasing witchcrafts and anti-witchcrafts.

Change of Status: the Priests

In order to understand the significance of *Abirewa* as a new religious movement, we also have to analyze the change of the social status of the priests after the arrival of Europeans, especially after the establishment of colonial rule.

According to Casely Hayford, in the Akan traditional system, the King (or chief) was the spiritual head, but the actual working of the system was in the hands of priests.[52] Danquah suggested that the priest was the first and highest person in the Ga-Adangbe state, while in the Akan institutions a priest was "the maker of a country, but not the governor of it."[53] The Guans were ruled by priests. The system was later introduced into the Akan by Guan Priest Okomfo Anokye, a man of Awukugua in Akuapem who helped Osei Tutu win the fight against Denkyira and form the Asante Kingdom.[54] The Ga form of government was an "absolute fetishocracy," where "foretelling fetish-priests" controlled the supreme power.[55] No matter how the priests were described, it is no doubt that they had played a crucial role in the traditional state system.

Priests generally performed three functions: ritual performance, daily protection and war preparation. During the annual festival, the priests offered sacrifices to God or ancestors, purification of the nation for the past year and prayer for direction and protection for the coming year.[56] They performed sacrifices to *abosom* and also acted as their mouthpiece. This oracular function of the *abosom* was very important because people had to consult them about their fate. In daily life, priests were supposed to protect people by foretelling and curing. In case of illness or misfortune, people always went to them to seek advice or cures. Priests were good healers and doctors. Their knowledge of herbs and plants greatly contributed to the mystery of their calling. [57] During wartime, the King and elders would consult oracles from their own religion, or even the shrine in other places.[58] The priests were supposed to help prepare for the battle and be able to prophesy the result of the war. "Eat fetish" or "drink fetish" was also a way of swearing the oath of allegiance by which a whole army was bound together.[59]

In the traditional system, priests had also enjoyed economic benefits. T. J. Hutchinson, a colonial officer, once described his impression of priests in the interior country at Akyem: "The fetish house is ornamented with swords and axes having golden handles; the drums are ornamented with gold also. The fetish man or high priest is always rich."[60] The priests' fortunes generally came from three sources: service charges, punishment and duties. They served deities by holding various ritual ceremonies. They had the right to make a prophecy or judgment on grand occasions, such as royal succession and funeral, or in cases of crisis. They received handsome presents and payment for service.[61] In the nineteenth century, they earned a good living and received handsome payment for service. They afforded protection for runaway slaves and received presents from "influential and rich people who washed themselves with holy water or made vows in sickness". The denial of protection to slaves was also a way to make money. In Asante, priests would deliver fugitive slaves to their master on receiving two ounces of gold and four sheep.[62]

Secondly, priests could inflict a punishment by confiscating the property of the dead. According to Hutchinson, a priest was so powerful that if a person died without having conciliated him, he had the power of ordering the corpse to be placed in an upright position inside the house. "Should the body retain its perpendicularity all the property it possessed when living is claimed by the family; if it fall, which the fetish man has knowledge enough of the peculiarity of gravity in a dead body always to secure, the effects of the defunct must of course be at once handed over to the Moloch of superstition."[63]

The third way to obtain wealth was through the imposition of a customs tariff. Some priests imposed "heavy dues" on traders and secured law and order in return. In Krachi, the priest dominated the King and "gets hold of the custom money which is on all articles transported to the interior especially on salt." In Accra, the priests of *Nai* (sea) could claim a duty of 16 dollars and rum from every captain anchoring in the roads at Accra, besides annual presents from the merchants. In addition, they had other source of income. The ferrying of Sakumo was a large source of revenue to traditional rulers. The rate of ferrying was 25 strings. "The amount collected on Monday and Tuesday belongs to the priests."[64]

In the eighteenth century, European traders fully recognized the great influence of local priests and sought their help on several occasions. When the French tried to establish themselves on the Fante coast in the early 1750s, both the British and the French tried to win support from the priests of *Nananom Pow* by offering goods worth twenty ounces and sixty ounces of gold respectively. Later in 1765, when the war broke out between the Asante and the Fante, both Dutch and British traders sent messengers with gifts to the Fante priests asking them to urge on chiefs to settle the dispute with the Asante. [65]

All these practices began to change after the arrival of Christian missionaries. In 1835 the Wesleyan Methodists began their work at Cape Coast and the Basel Mission moved to the Akuapem ridge.[66] Since the missionaries' success directly depended upon their undermining traditional religion, it became their primary task to destroy it and its related structures. "Fetishism" became the immediate target of this general assault.

In 1851, the Mankessim Case put the local religion on trial. In order to retaliate against the Christians who insulted the worshippers of the local religion, a group of priests and priestesses attempted to murder four prominent African Christians by poison. The plot was discovered and they were charged with conspiracy. Nineteen were convicted. The priests were sentenced to be publicly flogged and to be imprisoned with hard labor for five years, and the priestesses were given two years imprisonment. The trial shocked the community and some people were crying: "What can we now do in sickness or distress? Whither can we fly for succor? Our gods have been proved to be no gods. Our priests have deceived us."[67] Christianity gradually gained the upper hand in the Gold Coast. Missionaries produced the New Testament in local languages, which became a convenient help in converting Africans. Some priests "renounced their paganism," while more and more people abandoned local religion and converted to Christianity.[68]

But the fatal attack on traditional religion came from the colonial government. Early Europeans described African religion as "fetish", or "fetishism", and painted an uncivilized picture of priests. The same attitude prevented colonial officers from understanding local religion, much less the status and function of priests. For them, the traditional ruler simply meant a single chief, or Monarch; and the important thing was the position of traditional rulers under the colonial administrative and judicial set-up.[69] Although the government tried to make use of the local authority, it failed to see the role of priests in the traditional power structure. The fate of the *Dente Bosomfo* is a typical example.

The Krachi people were Guans. *Dente* was a powerful local god who had been worshipped not only by the Krachi, but also by the neighboring people, including the Asante. During the nineteenth century, it seems the *Dente Bosomfo* (the priest) was superior to the *Krachiwura* (the King) not only in religious matters, but also in political, economic and military authority. But the fact was ignored by the German and British colonial governments. The *Dente Bosomfo* was executed in 1894, followed by the decline of religious power.[70] Reindorf wrote in 1895 the power of the priest over lands and revenue was gradually falling into the hands of the Kings.[71] The same thing happened in Ga towns, where Europeans only recognized the power of the secular ruler, the *Mantse*, therefore causing the change of the power structure and disturbances among the Ga people.[72]

Although Christianity weakened the local religions, it by no means replaced them. In crises of life such as birth, marriage, misfortune, illness or death, traditional religion had a greater role than Christianity. Since priests had lost their political influence, economic benefits and social privileges, and could hardly contest their rivals politically, the best way for them to regain their lost power was to revive traditional religion. As noted by a contemporary, this aim was achieved more or less by the new religion. The chiefs who had allowed *Aberewa*'s service in their villages at last repented of so doing, because their subjects no longer came for cases as before, "they have to decide all their cases before the priest of *aberewa* in the villages, even the oath matters; the chiefs consequently see that they have put themselves in a strait."[73]

However, the analysis by no means suggests that the deterioration of priests' status was the only element involved in the *Abirewa* movement. Besides the priests' attempts to regain their lost power, another important factor was people's grievances towards their chiefs.

Voice of Grievances: the People

Since the chiefs were generally appointed or approved by the government, their authority was not well accepted nor did it go unchallenged. It is interesting to compare what happened in Asante before and after 1901. Before the Asante uprising, the government did not have any title to rule Asante by conquest. Governor Maxwell once told Captain D. Stewart, Resident of Kumasi: "You should interfere as little as possible in the ordinary administration carried on by the Kings and Chiefs of a tribe. They should be encouraged to manage their own affairs, and they are entitled to hold their own courts of justice." [74] Therefore Kings and chiefs generally retained their power.

At the same time, there existed two legal systems: English Courts and Native Courts, but very few local cases went to the former. There were complaints about this "unsatisfactory" situation, especially inland, where local courts dealt with all other cases, except those of murder and the most important land disputes. Although Kwahu was part of a district under the Supreme Court Ordinance, it was reported "there has not been for the last six months a single case brought from there either to the District Commissioner's Court or to the Divisional Court; there having been no Resident District Commissioner, the native courts have dealt with all the cases that have arisen."[75] It is quite clear that people still trusted their own rulers in matters of justice.

Things changed dramatically after 1901. The traditional leaders who had been involved in the uprising were severely punished. About sixty Asante chiefs were sent down either to the coast or to join their Paramount Chief Prempeh in exile in the Seychelles. Governor M. Nathan suggested all the vacant stools be filled "with men duly elected and recommended to me by Resident in Coomassie."[76] New chiefs were picked up not because they were entitled to offices according to local law or custom, but based on their loyalty to the government during the uprising. As a result, the people's reaction towards these new chiefs was non-cooperative. In 1906, the Chief Commissioner reported on the new conditions in the Southern District. The people there began "to recognize that government is the chief guardian of their interests, judging by the way they have sought advice on every matter, however small, that concerned them, and they have displayed a trusting and friendly spirit towards the Commissioner of their district that is most pleasing to record."[77]

This indicated the decreasing power of the chief over his people not only because of the change of his status to a "subordinate authority", as Busia has suggested,[78] but also because of his lack of both legitimacy and accountability. People began to turn to the government, the real boss, for protection. This contemptuous attitude partly explained the conversion to *Abirewa* and religious leaders.

The problem of legitimacy became more serious owing to the improper behavior of those newly elected chiefs, who now enjoyed the government support and neglected checks and balances in the traditional law and showed very little concern for the interests of the people. There were various complaints about the abuse of chiefly power.[79] As a result, a movement developed at the beginning of twentieth century to destool the appointed chiefs, an interesting phenomenon which will be discussed with later.

In 1905, the people at Agona refused to serve their chief, Kwame Boakye. The government interfered but the rebellion burst out again in September 1906. The government supported the chief and the rebellious leaders were punished. Rebellions against chiefs appointed by the government occurred in the same year at Ejisu, Akropong, Ahinkuro and Nsuatre. In some areas, even the Queen-mother and elders were punished for their opposition to their chiefs.[80] Disturbances also occurred in the Eastern Province. According to official reports, between 1906 and 1908, two chiefs were murdered and three chiefs deposed. Other religious movements emerged in the region at the same time. In 1906, a religious practice called *"Yi Abeyi"* or "witch-finding" caused a serious riot at Abetifi. The origin of *Yi Abeyi* is not quite clear, but a group of young men were involved. *Yi Abeyi* was also responsible for an attempt made by the people of Wenchi to destool their chief, Kobina Akyere, one of the principal chiefs of Akyem Abuakwa. He was, however, reinstated by the government.[81] The suppressed religious movement *Katawere* was revived in Akyem Abuakwa, Otutu and Ati also caught the government's attention and were suppressed.[82] There were other sabotages. In Asante, a great deal of unrest occurred among the young men.[83] In Adda District, a series of cases of alleged poisoning gave rise to intervention by the Provincial Commissioner. The ensuing trial disclosed that secret poisoning societies existed in the District.[84] All these show tension did exist between the chiefs and their subjects.

Conclusion

The traditional power structure in the Gold Coast had its own characteristics, the function of priests was one of them. The establishment of colonial rule began with its encroachment on the traditional power structure. Poor understanding of African society and cultural imperialism based on technological superiority made it impossible for the colonial government to make optimum use of traditional power. The intervention by European authorities and the abuse of power by the chiefs created tensions that inevitably resulted in protests from those who were hurt by the newly established system. *Abirewa* provided an example of this kind of protest.

As a religious movement, *Abirewa* was surely a success. It not only attracted many people in a short time, becoming a great threat to both the secular authority and the missionaries; it was also revived time and again despite the government's suppression.[85] But as a political protest, *Abirewa* movement was a failure. Lacking institutional leadership, a unique doctrine and a sound organization, it could cause disturbances within the system, but it could not overthrow or even change the system. Moreover, it met a joint counter-attack from the government, chiefs and missionaries. With strong opposition, failure was inevitable. Later, in the 1930s and 1940s, religious movements with the same content but different names occurred in Asante and the Gold Coast. Among them, *Tigare*, which bore the resemblance of *Abirewa*, was the best known and most widespread.[86]

However, the change of social status of the priest only affected a small group of people: the religious leaders whose political power and economic benefits were weakened. There were other more detrimental changes attempted by the government that caused greater alarm among the people of the Gold Coast, the Forest Bill of 1911 was one of them.

NOTES

1. From the Portuguese, *feitico* meaning "charm, amulet," the word was first used by early Europeans to describe everything related to African local religion. *Abirewa* was referred to as "religion" or "fetish" by contemporaries, Africans and Europeans. Owing to its derogatory denotation, it will not be used in this work except in quotes.

2. *CO96/471*. Extract from the Annual Report on Ashanti for 1907. Encl.(5)in (Confidential) Sir John P. Rodger to Crewe, 17 August 1908; F. C. Fuller, "Meeting held on the 6th August 1908 outside the fort at Coomassie." Encl.(2) in (Confidential), Rodger to Crewe, 25 August 1908. See also A. Ffoulkes, "*Borgya* and *Abinwa*, or, the § latest fetish on the Gold Coast," *Journal of the African Society*, 13(1908-1909), p.388; T. C. McCaskie, "Anti-witchcraft cults in Asante: an essay in the social history of an African people," *History in Africa*, 8(1981), p.138.

3. *CO98/17*. Report on the Native Affairs Department for the year 1908. It is believed in Asante that "Northern societies are almost totally free from witchcraft." See M. McLeod, "On the spread of anti-witchcraft cults in modern Asante," in J. Goody, ed., *Changing Social Structure in Ghana: Essays in the comparative sociology of a new state and an old tradition* (London: International African Institute, 1975), p.112.

4. *CO96/471*. *Abirewa* a new dangerous religion; C. N. Curling (Commissioner of East Province) to the Secretary for Native Affairs, 1 July 1908. Sub-encl. to Encl.(7)(8) in (Confidential) Rodger to Crewe, 17 August 1908.

5. In some places, one third of the property of the dead went to his or her family. The most detailed description is found in Ffoulkes, "*Borgya* and *Abinwa*," pp.387-397. But the meaning of *Borgya* in his article is different from this version.

6. *CO96/471*. "Palaver held on the 3rd Aug. 1907 in connection with certain allegations brought about against the '*Abirewa* Fetish' worship," Encl.(1) in (Confidential) Rodger to Crewe, 17 August 1908.

7. *CO96/471*. Curling to the Secretary for Native Affairs, 1 July 1908.

8. H. Debrunner, *Witchcraft in Ghana* (Accra: Presbyterian Book Depot Ltd, 1961), pp. 112-113. This is the most detailed account of those principles. For other versions, see *CO96/471*. *Abirewa* a new dangerous religion; Palaver held on the 3rd Aug. 1907.

9. *CO96/471*. Fuller to the Colonial Secretary at Accra, 8 August 1907. Encl.(1) in (Confidential) Rodger to Crewe, 17 August 1908.

10. Debrunner, *Witchcraft in Ghana*, p.113.

11. C. C. Reindorf, *The History of the Gold Coast and Asante* (Accra: Ghana University Press, 1966[1895]), p.109. M. J. Field, *The Social Organization of the Ga People*, pp.74-81. D. J. E. Maier, *Priests and Power The*

case of the Dente Shrine in nineteenth-century Ghana (Bloomington: Indiana University Press, 1983), pp.37-60,120-33.

[12]Casely Hayford, *Gold Coast Native Institutions* (London: Sweet & Maxwell, 1903), p.101.

[13]*CO96/471. Abirewa* a new dangerous religion.

[14]*CO96/471.* Palaver held on the 3rd Aug, 1907.

[15]*CO96/471. Abirewa* a dangerous religion.; *CO96/471.* Curling to the Secretary for Native Affairs, 1 July 1908.

[16]*CO96/471.* T. E. Fell (Western District Commissioner) to Fuller, 26 May and 1 June 1907, Sub-encl.(1) and (2) to Encl.(1) in Rodger to Crewe, 17 August 1908.

[17]*CO96/471.* Palaver held on the 3rd Aug, 1907.

[18]*CO96/471.* Amoaku Atta to the Commissioner of Eastern Province, 6 June 1908. Sub-encl. to Sub-encl to Encl.(8) in Rodger to Crewe, 17 August 1908.

[19]*CO96/471.* E. C. Eliot (Commissioner of Central Province) to the Secretary for Native Affairs, 8 June 1908. Sub-encl. to Encl. (7) in Rodger to Crewe, 17 August 1908.

[20]*CO96/471.* Curling to the Secretary for Native Affairs, 1 July 1908.

[21]*CO96/471.* Account of the *'Abirewa'* Fetish by the Acting Colonial Secretary. Encl.(6) and Encl.(9) in Rodger to Crewe, 17 August 1908.

[22]*CO96/471.* Fuller to the Colonial Secretary at Accra, 8 August 1907. Encl.(1) in Rodger to Crewe, 17 August 1908.

[23]*CO96/471.* C. H. Armitage (Acting Chief Commissioner of Asante) to Acting Colonial Secretary, 1 June 1908. Encl.(5) in Rodger to Crewe, 17 August 1908. *CO96/471.* Account of the *'Abirewa'* Fetish by the Acting Colonial Secretary.

[24]*CO96/471.* Fuller to Acting Colonial Secretary, 22 July 1908; Fell to Fuller, 5 July, 1908. Encl to Sub-encl.(1) to Encl.(10) in Rodger to Crewe, 17 August 1908.

[25]*CO96/471.* Fuller to the Acting Colonial Secretary, 15 August 1908. Fuller swallowed his words by detaining two of the priests as hostages after the meeting.

[26]*CO96/471.* Fuller to the Acting Colonial Secretary, 22 July 1908; Meeting held on the 6th August 1908.

[27]Debrunner, *Witchcraft in Ghana*, p.123.

[28]Sir Francis Fuller, *A Vanished Dynasty Ashanti* (London: John Murray, 1921), pp. 221-222.

[29]*CO96/471. Abirewa* a new dangerous religion; *CO96/471.* Account of the *'Abirewa'* Fetish by the Acting Colonial Secretary.; *CO96/471.* Curling to the Secretary for Native Affairs, 1 July 1908.

[30] *CO96/471.* (Confidential) Rodger to Crewe, 17, 25 and 29 August 1908.

[31] *CO96/471. Abirewa* a new dangerous religion.

[32] M. McLeod, "On the spread of anti-witchcraft cults in modern Asante," pp. 107-117.

[33] T. C. MacCaskie, "Anti-witchcraft cults in Asante," pp.138-141.

[34] G. Parrinder, *West African Religion* (London: Epworth Press, 1969), p.12. P. Sarpong, *Ghana in Retrospect* (Tema, 1974), p.44.

[35] J. B. Danquah, *The Akan Doctrine of God* (London: Frank Cass, 1968[1944]). For a special case, see J. K. Fynn, "The *Nananom Pow* of the Fante: myth and reality," *Sankofa The Legon Journal of Archaeological and Historical Studies*, 2(1976), pp.54-59. For an early illustration, see A. B. Ellis, *The Tshi-speaking Peoples of the Gold Coast of West Africa* (Chicago: Benin Press, 1964[1887]), pp.22-109.

[36] Debrunner's book is the most comprehensive research on this subject. See also M. Manoukian, *Akan and Ga-Adangme Peoples*, pp.55, 60-61, 103-104. For a general study of African witches and witchcraft, see a special issue of *Africa*, 8:4(1935) and M. Gluckman, *Custom and Conflict in Africa* (Oxford: Basil Blackwell, 1970), pp.81-108.

[37] Field, *Search for Security* (London: Faber & Faber, 1960), p.40.

[38] Kofi Appiah-Kubi, *Man Cures, God Heals Religion and medical practice among the Akans of Ghana* (New Jersey: Allanheld, Osmun & Co., 1981), p.37.

[39] Appiah-Kubi, *Man Cures, God Heals*, p.2; M. Field, *Religion and Medicine of the Ga* (London: Oxford University Press, 1937), pp.110-134. Even the stool was referred to as "fetish" or medicine, see Field, *The Social Organization of the Ga People*, p.73.

[40] Pieter de Marees, *Description and Historical Account of the Gold Kingdom of Guinea (1602)*(London: Oxford University Press, 1987), translated by Albert van Dantzig & Adam Jones, pp.82-83, p.85, p.104. A. B. Ellis, *The Land of Fetish* (London: Chapman and Hall, 1883), the title caused great confusion which the author regretted in his *The Tshing-speaking Peoples*, p.176. Lady Hodgson, *The Siege of Kumassi* (London: C. Arthur Pearson, 1901), pp.59-69.

[41] As late as 1953, during a research in Late a man gave the names of nearly forty fetishes in one quarter alone. See, J. K. Ansah, *The Centenary History of the Larteh Presbyterian Church 1853-1953* (Larteh, Larteh Presbyterian Church, 1955), xiii.

[42] *CO96/471.* Fell to Fuller, 26 May 1907. Encl. (1) in Rodger to Crewe, 17 August 1908; *CO98/17.* Report on the Native Affairs Department for the Year 1908.

[43] D. Brokensha, *Social Change at Larteh*, pp.10-15. See also Ansah, *The Centenary History of the Larteh Presbyterian Church 1853-1953.*

[44]Ellis, *The Tshi-speaking Peoples*, pp.136-137.

[45]Quoted from Debrunner, *Witchcraft in Ghana*, p.66.

[46]M. Field's *Search for Security* is a detailed study of the psychotherapy practiced by the priests at various shrines in rural Ghana. Although the time is different, the study shows how people became increasingly preoccupied with a sense of insecurity and troubled by desire, depression and fear.

[47]B. Ward, "Some observations on religious cults in Ashanti," *Africa*, 26(1956), pp.47-61.

[48]J. Goody, "Anomie in Ashanti?," *Africa*, 27(1957), pp.356-363. See also his essay in J. Goody, ed., *Changing Social Structure in Ghana*, pp.91-106.

[49]J. Dupuis, *Journal of a Residence in Ashantee* (London: Frank Cass, 1966 [1824]), pp.114-117; McCaskie, "Anti-witchcraft cults," pp.128-129.

[50]W. Bosman, *A New and Accurate Description of the Coast of Guinea*(London: Frank Cass, 1967 [1705])p.124. T. E. Bowdich, *Mission from Cape Coast Castle to Ashantee* (London: Frank Cass, 1966 [1819]), p.163. W. Hutton, *A Voyage to Africa* (Frank Cass, 1971 [1821]), p.88. T. J. Huchinson, *Impressions of Western Africa* (London: Longman, 1858), p.70.

[51]Goody, "Anomie," p.362.

[52]Casely Hayford, *Gold Coast Native Institutions*, p.101. But his view is challenged by Ghanaian historian J. K. Fynn. Fynn acknowledges the important function of the priests in the religious life of the Akan people, but argues that in all Akan states, "priests and priestesses were subservient to the political establishment." See his article, "The *Nananom Pow* of the Fante: myth and reality," pp.54-59.

[53]J. B. Danquah, *Gold Coast   Akim laws and customs and the Akim Abuakwa Constitution* (London: George Routeledge, 1928), p.23. He did not agree with Casely Hayford's view that fetishism was a national institution, but admitted that the fetish system no doubt existed among all the people in Akanland. See, J. B. Danquah, *The Akim Abuakwa Handbook*, pp.83-84.

[54]Otutu Bagyire IV, "The Guans: A preliminary note," *Ghana Notes and Querries*, 7(1965), p.23. Kwamena-Poh, *Government and Politics*, p.19.

[55]B. Cruickshank, *Eighteen Years on the Gold Coast of Africa* (London: Frank Cass, 1966[1853]), Vol.II, pp.124-190.

[56]Bowdich, *Mission from Cape Coast Castle to Ashantee*, pp.274-280. R. S. Rattray, *Religion and Art in Ashanti* (London: Oxford, 1927), pp.121-143.

[57]Kofi Appiah-Kubi, *Man Cures, God Heals*, pp.35-80; H. Fink, *Religion, Disease and Healing in Ghana* (Trickster Wissenschaft, 1990), trans. by Volker Englich. For an early example, see J. Beecham, *Ashantee and the Gold Coast* (London: Dawsons of Pall Mall, 1968 [1841]), p.192.

[58]Maier, *Priest and Power*, pp.38-40.

59 Cruickshank, *Eighteen Years on the Gold Coast*, pp.172-76; Beecham, *Ashantee and the Gold Coast*, pp.193-222.

60 T. J. Hutchinson, *Impressions of Western Africa*, p.70.

61 In Krachi, gifts and payments were also sent to *Dente* for permission to establish branch shrines, a King gave no less than £100 to the *Dente Bosomfo* for a consecrated stone for establishing a branch. *CO879/30*. African (West) No.384. Sunter to Colonial Office, Burnham, Somerset 25 October 1890. Quoted from Maier, *Priests and Power*, p.59. See also Beecham *Ashantee and the Gold Coast*, pp.189-190.

62 Reindorf, *The History of the Gold Coast*, pp.107-108.

63 Hutchinson, *Impression of West Africa*, p.70.

64 Muller to Basel, 28 March 1884. Quoted from Maier, *Priests and Power*, p.55; Reindorf, *The History of the Gold Coast*, p.108.

65 J. K. Fynn, *Asante and its Neighbours 1700-1807* (London: Longmans, 1971), p.103. *Nananom Pow* was an important shrine situated at the outskirts of Mankessim. According to J. K. Fynn, it was made the abode of gods deliberately by the Borbor Fante for political consideration. See his article "*Nananom Pow* of the Fante," pp.54-59.

66 Williamson, *Akan Religion and the Christian Faith*, pp.4-5.

67 Cruikshank, *Eighteen Years on the Gold Coast*, Vol.II, Ch. XI; Reindorf, *The History of the Gold Coast and Asante*, p. 234.

68 D. Kemp, *Nine Years at the Gold Coast* (London: Macmillan, 1898), pp.182-184. The New Testament in Fanti was produced in 1895, and by 1900 it was translated into all the major languages of southern Ghana. Ga was the fifth and Twi the seventh African language, into which the entire Bible was translated. C. P. Groves, *The Planting of Christianity in Africa 1914-54* (London, 1958), Vol.IV, pp.358-59.

69 "The Native Jurisdiction Ordinance" in G. E. Metcalfe, ed., *Great Britain and Ghana Documents of Ghana history, 1807-1957*(Accra: University of Ghana, 1964), pp.390-393.

70 Maier, *Power and Priests*, pp.37-60.

71 Reindorf, *The History of the Gold Coast and Asante*, p.109.

72 Field, *The Social Organization of the Ga People*, p.77.

73 Quoted from McCaskie, "Anti-witchcraft in Asante," p.140.

74 C. W. Newbury, *British Policy towards West Africa Selected documents 1875-1914* (Oxford: Clarendon Press, 1971), p.296.

[75] *CO96/342*. W. Brandford Griffith, Memorandum: Jurisdiction in Ashanti. 9 August 1899.

[76] *CO879/67*. No.649. William Low (Colonial Secretary) to Joseph Chamberlain, 8 March 1901. Quoted from Newbury, *British Policy Towards West Africa*, p.333.

[77] *Colonial Reports: Ashanti, 1906*. Quoted from K. A. Busia, *The Position of the Chief in the Modern Political System of Ashanti*, p.110.

[78] Busia, *Position of the Chief*, p.110.

[79] *CO98/11*. The Governor's Address to the Legislative Council. 26 September 1904. Minutes of the Legislative Council, 1904.

[80] Busia, *The Position of the Chief*, pp.105-106.

[81] *CO98/16*. Report on Native Affairs Department, 1906-1907. See also J. Simensen, "Commoners, Chiefs and Colonial Government, British policy and local politics in Akim Abuakwa, Ghana, under colonial rule," pp.68-70a.

[82] *CO98/16*. Report on Native Affairs Department 1906-1907. *CO99/20*. Native Affairs Department Annual Report for 1907. *CO98/17*. Report on Native Affairs Department for the year 1908.

[83] *CO96/471*. Fuller to the Acting Colonial Secretary, 22 July 1908. Encl. in Rodger to Crewe, 17 August 1908.

[84] *CO98/16*. Report on Native Affairs Department 1906-1907.

[85] *CO96/543*. Encl. in (Confidential A), Clifford to Harcourt, 24 March 1914. *The Gold Coast Nation*, 26 March, 2 April, 7 May, 26 November 1914. The latest evidence of *Abirewa* was in 1921. See *ADM36/1/8*. Acting Commissioner of Central Province to District Commissioner of Nsuaem, 5 September, 26 September 1921.

[86] *ADM11/1/1679*. Native custom and fetish (1 August 1908 to 2 November, 1948); *ADM36/1/8*. Fetish 1920-46. Acting Commissioner of Central Province to District Commissioner of Nsuaem, 5 September, 26 September, 1921. Appiah-Kubi, *Man Cures, God Heals*, pp.41-58. See also Debrunner, *Witchcraft in Ghana*, pp.128-130.

CHAPTER II

Forest Bill: The People against the Government

Like the rest of West Africa, there was no land without owners in the Gold Coast. This simple fact was not recognized by the British at first. After 1874, the British colonial government attempted to establish the Crown ownership of "waste lands" in the Gold Coast, which met constant resistance from the people. The resistance reached its climax when the Forest Bill was passed in 1911. This chapter will study how the colonial government tried to control land by means of the Forest Bill and how the people of the Gold Coast struggled to defend their indigenous land system. In addition, it will examine the role played by the Eastern Province, an aspect neglected by historical scholarship for a long time.[1]

The Problem of Land

In West Africa, the problem of land caused a lot of tension, especially during the first two decades of colonial rule.[2] Traditionally, land in the Gold Coast was considered in three respects: the earth itself; the usufruct or right of occupation; and the crop, trees, and houses that were separate from the earth itself. The earth was not conceived of as being a commodity that could be personally owned, bought and sold.[3]

There was no land without owners and land tenure varied in the Gold Coast. Usually there were stool land, family land and individual land.[4] The King or the chief did not own all the land of the state. He had rights over three types of land: land which was his ancestral property, land attached to the stool which he could deal with only with the consent of the councilors, and the general land of the state over which he exercised paramountcy.[5] Secondly, there was family land. The uniqueness of this type was that the land was not regarded simply as the property of the living members of the family; it also belonged to ancestors and future generations.[6] Until the establishment of the cocoa industry, most land was family land, owned by a lineage and worked on a system of shift cultivation. The third type was individual land, a type of ownership "which is **not** foreign to the indigenous law."[7] According to an official report published at the end of the nineteenth century, the family land could be traced to the individual land ownership.[8]

But individual land was not common until the nineteenth century. The reason was that upon the death of an owner, his land would become the property of the family. What is more, most of the land could originally be acquired only through the joint labor of groups of people in clearing land of the dense jungle.[9] However, it seems that both family land and individual land were out of the control of the chief. Among the Akyems, "All rents accruing from lands let to strangers for normal uses (i.e. agriculture and building) belong wholly to the landowner, and are not shared by the *omanhene*."[10] Rattray once described the importance of land to the community in Asante, "this communal and family interest in land protected it from forfeiture, even when a clansman had committed some capital offence, and that the king, despotic as he was in many ways, did not dare to seize the offender's land, because he would have had opposition from the whole clan."[11]

In Asante, it was customary to inform the chief when family land was leased. But this was purely an act of courtesy. Konor Mate Kole, the Paramount Chief of Manya Krobo in the Eastern Province, stated the situation in his area in 1912. In the case of private ownership that was possible in some instances, the land was "quite out of the control of the chief." The sale of such land was subject to the consent of the owner's family. "Most of the plantations (palm-oil trees, cocoa and rubber) are the individual property of the owners and can be sold without reference to anyone but members of the owner's family." It was the same with the Ga and the Adangbe communities, where self-acquired land could be sold without the consent of the senior member of his group while family land could be sold only with the family's assent.[12] Since the property was a source of revenue to the stool-holder, absolute alienation of stool land was rare, and only under exceptional circumstances. There had to be a valid reason for sale, such as raising funds to provide monies for important purposes, like the payment of debts, or to provide for education or expenses for illness.

Land as a commodity was a rather new concept in the Gold Coast.[13] At the very start, the European contact with the Gold Coast was commercial. Gold and slaves were at the top of the trading list.[14] Legitimate trade initiated the production of cash crops, such as palm oil and rubber, and the principle of private property was gradually introduced into the Gold Coast. Four factors stimulated the commercialization of land. First, European traders paid rent to the local chiefs for the sites of their trading stations, and such land became known as valuable or potentially valuable among the coastal people.[15] The exploitation of minerals, especially the gold rush in the 1880s, also made it clear that land had achieved exchange value. The second was the introduction of cash crops. In the case of cocoa, the need for farmers to be assured of their returns over a longer period was an impetus for land ownership. Thirdly, as a result of cocoa farming, in the 1900s, land in southern areas became less available, thus far more valuable. The shortage of land even stimulated the "macro-movements of farmers" into central Asante and the eastern areas.[16] Fourthly, there were more specific European influences, such as English legal ideas, the concepts of freehold and mortgage, and a monetary system.

As a result, land became a valuable commodity in the Gold Coast. Divisional Chiefs and others became actively involved in selling and leasing lands, as well as in legal cases involving land disputes. It was reported in 1900 in Wassaw district that the rise in the value of lands had been a cause of many strife and litigation among chiefs themselves. Many of them neglected the administration of the affairs of their country because of the involvement in land litigation.[17]

Generally, there were three kinds of land deals: land leased to those migrants who came to the south-eastern part to try their fortune in cocoa, land concessions to European mining companies and palm oil concessions. About 1896-7, migrants from several Akuapem towns started to buy forest land for cocoa-growing in Akyem Abuakwa. Some of the purchases were very large, running into square miles. Soon after 1900 the desire to participate in the migration produced a scramble for land in Akyem districts. People of the patrilineal Akwapim area as well as Krobo, Shai, Ga and other farmers from south-eastern Ghana began to buy land through companies that were modeled on the older *huza* system of the Krobo people. "These companies, which were basically groups of friends (not relatives) from one home town, were land-purchasing clubs which enabled rich and poor alike to buy land for cocoa-growing."[18]

There was a sharp increase in cocoa production at the end of the nineteenth century.[19] The Colonial Office gave a very optimistic prediction about the situation in the coming years. "Cocoa is the sole article of export which shows any increase for 1901, and that was considerable, being 994,777 *Ibs.* in weight, and amounting to £15,537 in value. A further increase is expected for the current year, and there is every reason to hope that this satisfactory state of things will continue year by year."[20]

There were other forms of land deals as well: grants, loans, leases, gifts, or pawning.[21] But the commonest was the land concession to European companies. From 1900 to 1910, the total area granted under the Concessions Ordinance was 970 square miles.[22]

Although the Forest Bill seems to have originated from alienation of land, or the concern with deforestation, the essence of the Bill was primarily an issue of ownership, an issue that caused protest from the last decade of the nineteenth century. Without studying the resistance against the Crown Lands Bill in 1894 and the Lands Bill in 1897, it would be impossible to understand the protest against the Forest Bill.

The Government's Measures

In 1874, the Gold Coast Colony administratively separated from Sierra Leone. The Public Lands Ordinance was issued in 1876 to establish title to land for public buildings.[23] In 1894, a Crown Lands Bill was introduced to gain control of "reckless land concessions." The Ordinance's intent was to vest "all waste land and forest land in the Gold Coast in the Queen for the use of the Government of the Colony," causing an unanimous protest from the Kings, chiefs and people.

They were strongly opposed to the notion of "waste land," since all the land in the Gold Coast was owned by somebody. This right had been recognized by the Ordinance of 1876, and the government had to pay money for lands purchased for whatever purposes. The Crown Lands Bill would transfer African property to the colonial government, in which "no native of the Gold Coast has a voice and over whose policy and conduct the people of this country have no control whatever."[24] In 1895 the Bill was dropped, and the government issued in the Gazette of October 1895 a notification that the government would recognize no documents transferring land, unless they bore the signature of the Governor or his deputy.[25]

In 1897 the Lands Bill was introduced. It stated that all public land in the Colony may be "administered" by the government of the Colony. The government wanted to "facilitate the acquisition of public land by private persons," subject to the control of a Concessions Court, and "to preserve waste and forest land and minerals being improvidently dealt with." The Bill dealt with the old contentious matter: the acquisition of the public lands should be administered by the government "for the general advantage."[26] The Ghanaian people strongly objected to this principle. Demonstrations and protest meetings were held.[27] Petitions were first presented to the Governor, then to the Secretary of State, and finally to the Queen. In 1897 the educated and chiefs founded the Gold Coast Aborigines' Rights Protection Society.[28]

In 1898 a deputation from the Gold Coast went to London and were received by the Secretary of State Joseph Chamberlain. They had three main objections to the Lands Bill. First, the so-called "unoccupied land" did not exist; it belonged either to a family, a chief or a King. Secondly, the Lands Bill proposed that the Governor was to appoint some Commissioners in charge of every concession. The petitioners asked that the handle of concessions should be judicial and not administrative.

Thirdly, they also opposed the proposal that "everyone who obtains land by land certificate should take it to English law, instead of subject to native law."[29] After a long discussion with the deputation, Joseph Chamberlain acknowledged in substance the validity of the objections.

Consequently, only Part III of the Lands Bill that dealt with concessions was amended and passed as Concessions Ordinance of 1900. The main principles of the Ordinance can be summarized as the following: 1) the land of the Colony was acknowledged to be the property of the indigenous people; 2) no grant of rights in or over land shall be valid unless its validity has been certified by the Supreme Court; 3) a concession can not be for more than 99 years, or be of larger area than 5 square miles for mining or 20 square miles for other purposes.[30]

The passage of the Concessions Ordinance marked a major failure of the British attempt to establish government control of land. Since land was not only an economic issue, but also involved political sovereignty, social structure and religious belief, this was a great victory for the Africans in their struggle against colonial encroachment of their traditional system. Moreover, it provided a basis for the argument in their later protest against the Forest Bill.[31]

The origin of the Forest Bill lay in land alienation and deforestation. In May 1905, Dr. Fisch in Aburi Botanic Garden wrote that deforestation had been responsible for the decreased rainfall in the Akuapem hills. In that year, the Acting Secretary for Native Affairs, the Commissioner of the Eastern Province and the Director of Agriculture attributed the problem of deforestation to careless clearing, bush fire, timber felling and tapping of rubber trees.[32] When the Chief Justice was passing through the Akuapem area, he was shocked to see how rapidly the country was being deforested. He immediately wrote to the Governor and suggested an ordinance be passed providing that the Governor in Council could declare any parts of the Colony to be forest reserves and that in any forest reserve it should be unlawful to make any new farm.[33]

In 1907 an ordinance was passed to prevent the cutting of immature timber. Then the Gold Coast government invited Mr. H. N. Thompson, the Conservator of Forests in southern Nigeria, to examine the forest resources of the Colony and Asante. In 1908 Thompson presented his report that revealed a very serious situation. He argued that it was necessary to provide for forest conservation.[34] In 1909, the Department of Forestry was established and began the task of framing protective legislation. It seems that the Forest Bill was written to prevent deforestation.[35]

Some sources indicate, however, that land alienation remained a great concern of the British government for several reasons. Since the introduction of the

Concessions Ordinance, there was a great increase in cocoa production. In eleven years, the production had increased more than seventy-four times![36] Besides the expansion of cocoa, there came a second "gold boom" in 1901-1902.[37] Both stimulated concessions. All these were accompanied by increasing land deals and land disputes. For example, after gold was found in Pankesi and a concession was signed in 1901, a land dispute immediately occurred between the chief of Pankesi under the King of Western Akyem and the chiefs of Obo and Obomeng under the King of Kwahu. The chief of Pankesi was removed and detained by the government because he refused to accept the Governor's ruling. But his people continued to block the work of the Gold Coast Proprietary Mines Limited and threatened to attack the managing director and his men.[38]

There were boundary disputes as well. Take the Eastern Province for example. Boundary disputes were frequent between the Dwaben, Akyem and Krobo ever since the Dwaben took refuge in Akyem Abuakwa in 1875.[39] Riots and disturbances occurred frequently in Accra, Ada, Keta and other districts.[40] There was a complaint that there were too few policemen to maintain order. In March 1902, a Department for Native Affairs was formed with the intention to deal with "Riots and disturbances, tribal lands disputes" among other issues.

Since the Concessions Ordinance admitted the indigenous right over land, more and more people were involved in legal cases because of land disputes. In his tour of the Eastern Province in 1904, the Governor heard many complaints that people were "ruined by their fondness for litigation and by the exorbitant legal fees."[41] Again in 1909 when he made another tour in the Province, the chiefs "complained bitterly of the expense and delay involved in settling native land dispute in the Supreme Court."[42] All these caused a serious problem for the government that did not have control of land and could hardly interfere with the issue legally. Most importantly, the British government was still thinking of Crown ownership as a way of getting revenue from the mining companies. Even after meeting with the deputation, Joseph Chamberlain wrote to the Governor of the Gold Coast about the possibility of getting income from the land concession: "I consider it absolutely necessary for the Colonial Government to supervise grants of land," so as to "obtain for the Government a reasonable income from profitable operations."[43]

Frequently the "whole question of the property in land in this Colony" was discussed between the Governor and the Secretary of State in London. In 1910, the Governor wrote again to the Secretary of State, "I fear that it will be found that a very large proportion of the land in this colony has already been alienated under 'The Concessions Ordinance, 1900'."[44] In July 1911, the new Governor Thorburn suggested "a special officer be appointed to take action when necessary to see that its requirements are promptly complied with by concessionaires."[45] All these seemed to be private conversations, with no intention to consult the Africans.

Another example illustrates this point. In reply to Mr. Thompson's address on Forestry to the African section of the Liverpool Chamber of Commerce, an article by Hazzledine, a spokesman for the Chamber, appeared in the *West African Mail* of October 14, 1904 with this heading:

West African Forests.
Are they to belong to the Government Official or
the Enterprising Merchants?
Are they to be Preserved or Used?
A Vital Question for the Trade

Here again the colonial mentality is reflected: the African forests did not belong to Africans! It was only a matter to be decided by Europeans, government officials or enterprising merchants. So the essence of the issue was the question of ownership. After the first wave of protest, the Forest Bill was amended. Since the government stressed that ownership would not be changed, the Bill was passed in the Legislative Council in November 1911, and a new wave of protest followed.

Protest against Forest Bill

As the Forest Bill resembled the Crown Lands Bill and the Lands Bill, the protest was a continuation of those in 1894 and 1897. The striking feature of the protest against the Forest Bill was that it did not develop over either the issue of deforestation or the problem of alienation. Like the previous protests, it concentrated on the central issue: ownership. The protest was against both the principle and the details. It was made clear that "the principles involved in the Forest Bill are the same as those of the Lands Bill."[46]

Since the Gold Coast became a protectorate by the 1844 Bond, the people still believed in their independence. J. Sarbah made this point quite clear in his work. The Gold Coast was British territory, but "not so by conquest or cession." Even the Colonial Office stated on March 11, 1887, as published in a Parliamentary Blue Book of that year, "it is inaccurate to state that after the successful Ashanti Expedition of 1874 the Protectorate was annexed by Great Britain and became a colony, 'inasmuch as the greater portion of the Gold Coast Colony still remains a Protectorate, the soil being in the hands of the natives and under the jurisdiction of the native chiefs.'" [47]

The protest against the Forest Bill was argued along the same line. The deputation from the Gold Coast asserted the fact that "the Crown had never laid claim to acquisition of the lands of the country either by conquest, cession, or purchase."[48] This principle was also acknowledged by some colonial officials. For example, Cruickshank, once Acting Governor, wrote in 1853, "Indeed we had no legal jurisdiction in the country whatever. It had never been conquered or purchased by us or ceded to us." [49] Even as late as 1911, the Attorney-General of the Gold Coast still agreed that "no land in the Colony other than the forts and their immediate surroundings, and such land as has from time to time been acquired by the Government for specific public purposes, can be considered to be Crown Land." He also agreed "all land in the Colony is owned by someone."[50]

Secondly, the Forest Bill vested a great power in colonial officials. The Governor in Council could declare certain land subject to forest reservation and prohibit anyone from taking timber, collecting rubber, etc. Since the power to constitute a forest reserve was located in the Governor's office, local forest was to be managed by the government.[51] This arbitrary power aroused strong protest, although the government stressed that ownership would not be altered by this Ordinance. For Africans, the Concessions Ordinance "has worked well so far, and contains ample provisions for safeguarding all interests."[52] Under the Forest Bill certain lands were to be declared as forest lands, and the government had the power to grant them in the form of leases to whomsoever the government might think proper.[53] After the petition of September 1911, the amended Bill came up for its second reading. Though the Governor thought there was a major change, the petitioners thought the Bill passed "without tangible alteration in the principles." They argued that although no change would occur when the forest reserves were established, yet the power to take up leasehold grants would be the same as the official acquisition of lands.[54]

For the chiefs, their principle objection to the Bill was that "the Government proposes to take over our lands and look after them." Chief Kumah made it clear that "I did not approve of the way in which the Government were proposing to take over the forests, and that I did not like the Bill at all." The representative of Chief Mensah of Elmina said, "My principal objection to the measure is the power taken by the Government to lease our lands." The government ought not to place itself on the same level as ordinary concessionaires. [55]

Thirdly, the Forest Bill defined unoccupied land as land not used for permanent habitation and has not been cultivated for ten years.[56] It was true that some land was left "unoccupied" because of shifting cultivation, a common practice in West Africa. If the Bill passed, such areas would come under the definition and be compulsorily reserved. The chief's authority relied on land, the land was inherited from the ancestor. As Casely Hayford emphasized, "The existence of a tribe is entirely bound up in its land, and without it the community would break up." To take away the control and management of the lands by the Kings and chiefs was to destroy the whole fabric of traditional institutions.

This issue was dealt with seriously in their protest. Dr. Papafio, a member of the deputation to London representing the Eastern Province, stated before the Secretary of State the importance of the relation between land and stool. If the power of management and control of the land were transferred from the chief to the government, it would result in the breaking up of the traditional system. It was on this account that "they really object to this Ordinance." They would not allow the government to interfere in matters connected with their land. "It was managed by our ancestors, and we have to look after it and pass it on intact to our posterity without interference from anybody." The Bill would eventually "uproot the cherished institutions of the people, divest the stools of all inherent rights and interests in the soil, and ruthlessly tear asunder the social and political systems of the Gold Coast."[57] In other words, any change in the indigenous land tenure meant a direct attack on the African political structure and social system.

For the people in the Gold Coast, forest conservancy was not unknown. The Chief Justice mentioned that the Ga *Mantse* (*pl. Mantsemei*, chief) in Accra made a law for forest protection in 1824, and stated "we should be only following the native practice in declaring such forest reserves." In many places, shrines and graveyards were reserved. Besides, there were forest areas reserved for cultivation purposes. Although the Chief Justice admitted that he was not acquainted with the mining districts, he made a rather absurd conclusion that the deforesting was the result of farms, either cocoa or *amankani* or yam; and cutting of forest trees for timber or firewood in the mining districts had no effect on the forest. "Consequently to put an end to farms is in many parts of the Colony to put an end to deforesting."[58]

From an African perspective, the cause of deforestation was different. People complained about mining companies that cut timber indiscriminately, "those who are really deforestating the country are the mining companies, who indiscriminately cut timber for timbering their mines on every part of the area granted.[59] Preferring to manage forests themselves, all the chiefs interviewed agreed to adopt some measures to prevent deforestation. They were willing to have some experts give instructions or conduct training courses; this suggestion was brushed aside. H. C.

Belfield, the Special Commissioner, accused this as "not a practical proposal worth serious consideration."[60]

Owing to the strong protest against the Forest Bill, the Secretary of State appointed H. C. Belfield to study the land problem in the Gold Coast. This Commissioner was asked to direct his attention to certain specific questions relating to the land and concession.[61] After investigating for three months, Belfield drew several important conclusions. The Crown had acquired rights over three kinds of land: fortified stations on the coast; such land in the immediate vicinity of the ramparts as could be covered and protected by the artillery of early days; and various parts of the colony by purchase. He admitted all land belonged to the people that had not been acquired by other parties by specific process, such as cession, purchase, exchange, or inheritance. "Consequently such general appropriation by the Crown as was contemplated by the Land Bill of 1897 is, in my view, out of question."[62]

There had been great alarm about the alienation of land, Belfield made a survey of the alienated land and found that the situation was not as threatening as had been described. Therefore his conclusion was much more optimistic: "I am of the opinion that the alienation does not at present threaten to deprive natives of adequate land for raising foodstuffs." The following is the statistics quoted in Belfield Report.

Table I   Land Alienation in the Gold Coast Colony

	Actual Area (sq.m.)	Area Alienated (sq.m.)
Western Province	9,723	7.342
Central Province	4,626	47.490
Eastern Province	9,986	824.245
Total	24,335	879.077

Source: *Cmd6278. Belfield Report.* para.39. Notes of Evidence relating to Parts I & II. para. 22.

As for the protest against the Forest Bill, Belfield made two conclusions. First, the protest originated in the Central Province. Secondly, it came from a small group of people, the Gold Coast Aborigines' Rights Protection Society. Belfield looked upon the opposition as "devoid of any substantial foundation" and advised that "the Ordinance be passed and put into force" after some necessary amendments.[63] However, the Secretary of State decided to set up a West African Land Committee to investigate the whole land issue. The Committee's efforts were interrupted and the Department of Forestry closed during the war.[64]

The Role of the Eastern Province

The protest against the Forest Bill was a widespread movement, which involved three provinces in the Colony. Belfield made the assumption that the movement in opposition to the introduction of the Forest Ordinance had its origin in the Central Province, and historians seem to hold the same view. [65] We have to study carefully the activity in the Eastern Province.

When the Bill was introduced into the Legislative Council in October 1910, it met opposition from the Unofficial Members, including Konor Mate Kole, a Paramount Chief of Manya Krobo, Eastern Province. In March 1911, the Ga *Mantse*, Tackie Obiri, *Mantsemei* and people of Eastern Province presented to the Governor their petition against the Bill, the first petition in the protest movement.[66] Two months later, the Bill was withdrawn. The Government's explanation was that "the procedure laid down in it was inconvenient,"[67] but it would be unreasonable to presume that the protest had no effect on the decision.

A new Bill was reintroduced in August 1911 and again met strong opposition from both within the Legislative Council and outside. The Ga *Mantse*, the chiefs and people of the Eastern Province sent their second petition and appointed C. J. Bannerman, a local lawyer, to represent their interests.[68] He made an eloquent speech against the bill, "If it is for their good, my clients say they do not want it, and if it is for the benefit of any other persons they object to it."[69]

Belfield also maintained that protest only appeared at Cape Coast, "I have no reason to presume that a desire for its withdrawal is general throughout the Colony."[70] This statement is not true. In fact, there did exist a popular protest in other provinces as well. Traveling in Birim District in 1912, the Director of Education found there was an intense feeling against the Bill there. In his report, the Director mentioned something interesting. When he was going to Asante in August, a well-educated former Basel Mission teacher saw him as the train stopped at Bekwai. The ex-teacher came across the platform to the carriage and immediately began speaking to him about the Forest Bill. "He likewise was under the impression that the Government intended taking the land and farms of the people." The Director also mentioned that the Aborigines' Rights Protection Society sent people to the town and informed the people about the situation. He suggested that the feeling against the Forest Bill "is prevalent."[71]

J. P. Robertson, the Inspector of Schools, described the same situation. When he was examining the exercise books of the Basel Mission Middle School at Akropong, he found each of the students in the highest class wrote an essay, in the form of a petition to the King, "asking for the abandonment or modification of the Bill." Some students wrote about their fathers who had borrowed considerable money for the cultivation of cocoa farms and trusted to the further sale of the produce to pay the loans. If the government took of the land, they would become liable to imprisonment for debt. "Rather than endure this they were prepared to have recourse to arms." In some essays, a more militant tone was heard: "The first Government official sent to take over the land would be shot." Although the topic was obviously chosen by the teacher, the contents of the compositions reflected the general feeling of the students. He also noticed that the people were less hospitable than before.[72]

After the September petition, the Governor had to agree to "substantial modifications," which satisfied the three African members of the Legislative Council, so that the Bill was passed in November 1911 without dissent.[73] However, the new version did not pacify the protest outside the Legislative Council. Reporting the petition dated 30 November, the Governor complained that some chiefs did not appreciate the modifications in the new Bill or even read the new version. But the chiefs who signed the November petition without reading it first, made some comments after they read it.

They considered that existing land tenure was fine, since any farmer could clear unoccupied land and chiefs could obtain revenue from the land. But under the new Bill the chiefs were liable to lose their rights over land, as the land would be placed under reservation, and restrictions placed on farming, with consequent loss of revenue to the chiefs. What is more, if this Ordinance was allowed to stand, they feared that a further measure would follow to restrict their control of land. They regarded the new Ordinance as unnecessary, and chiefs' by-laws under the Native Jurisdiction Ordinance would be the proper course to take.[74]

It was also alleged that the Aborigines' Rights Protection Society did not have "much influence in the Eastern Province."[75] This judgment proved groundless. It was revealed that the propaganda in opposition to the Forest Ordinance in the Eastern Province was organized by Attoh Ahuma, the Secretary of the Aborigines' Rights Protection Society and a nationalist who contributed immensely to the building of Ghanaian national consciousness.[76] It was reported that letters had been sent to all ministers of the Wesleyan Missionary Society asking "that one day be set apart as a Day of Prayer for the withdrawal of the Bill," and the African ministers had concurred with the idea. This also originated from Attoh Ahuma.[77] The feeling against the Bill was so strong that people from the Aborigines' Rights Protection Society easily collected money in the Province to send a deputation to

London. A new organization called the "Gold Coast Native Institutions Conservation Society" was also formed in the Province on December 16 1911, which caused great alarm in the government. The Governor noticed the by-laws of the Society reflected a policy very similar to that of the Aborigines' Rights Protection Society.[78]

It is clear from the above evidence that chiefs, teachers, students and even ministers in the Eastern Province joined the protest. Then how could Belfield conclude that there was no opposition in the Eastern Province? The answer lies in the fact that he only met with chiefs of the Central and Western Provinces and did not even bother to see any chiefs of the Eastern Province. His indifference was pointed out by Dr. Papafio, the representative of the Eastern Province in the deputation to London.[79]

The 1911 petition was the first time that the Eastern Province joined the protest. This event was so significant that when the Aborigines' Rights Protection Society celebrated its anniversary in 1941, it was still remembered "In 1911, the Forest Bill was passed at the Legislative Council. In the following year the Aborigines Society sent a delegation to the Colonial Office. This time then the states of the Eastern Province had joined the Central and Western."[80] The participation of the Eastern Province not only strengthened the voice of protest but also indicated the eastward move of the political center.

Consequences of the Protest

Land and labor were two vital factors in the colonial economy; thus a policy of control of land became absolutely necessary in any colony. The debate over whether the government should control land transactions was kept alive during the whole colonial period. As early as 1895, Governor Maxwell sent a dispatch to London complaining about the "ridiculous position" of the colonial government: "unable to erect a building or log out a road on waste land, without having to go through a tedious legal process." He was unhappy that the colonial government usually had to pay for the land to someone or the community.

Why was it "ridiculous"? Because Maxwell presumed that the Queen of the Great Britain was the real owner of the "uncultivated lands;" he, the representative of the Queen in the colony, should have every right to deal with such issues as related to the land. This thinking by no means disappeared with the dropping of the Lands Bill. In 1911, Belfield recommended that the control of alienation should be transferred from the Judicial Court to the Executive government, but he noticed that any endeavor of the government to extend the rights of the Crown would amount to a breach of faith with the people. This worry was obviously the result of the prevalent feeling of resistance.

After the Forest Bill failed, Mr. F. H. Gough, the Senior Puisne Judge of the Gold Coast, still urged the control of land holding by the Executive. In 1924, Colonel Rowe, the Surveyor-General of the Gold Coast, advocated a system of registration, which was rejected by the government. Again in 1927, Ormsby-Gore drew attention to the serious problem of land litigation and suggested that there should be a system of registration.[81] In 1931, Governor Sir Ransford Slater insisted that the development of land tenure should be allowed to evolve from within. Professor C. Y. Shephard called again in 1936 for attention to tenure conditions and for a greater measure of government control over land. As late as 1949, C. K. Meek attacked the Government's land policy as "a policy of non-intervention", and deplored its failure to make it acquainted with tenure conditions, to control alienation and to exercise general forms of control. He argued that the African local authorities should remain the ultimate "owners" of as much land as possible, since the "ownership" or control of land lay at the root of all African conceptions of government.[82] This inconsistency reflected a dilemma under the colonial rule. Hancock pointed out the paradoxical situation: "a government which wished to dispossess a Native people could hardly do better than proclaim the principle of absolute ownership by the Native communities."[83]

Although the "absolute ownership by the Native communities" may not exist, this paradox did exist. The government's reluctance to interfere with the land issue had much to do with the protests against the lands bills. In the Danquah Memorial Lectures in February 1970, Robert K. A. Gardiner argued: "I believe that if the Crown Lands Bill had been enacted in its original form we Ghanaians would have been placed in the same predicament as the Kikuyus in the Kenya Highlands, Congo Africans under Belgian rule and Africans in Southern Africa today."[84]

He is right. The same can be said of the Forest Bill. The Governor once stated that out of thirteen chiefs who signed the memorial only one had "any land which is likely to be dealt with under the Ordinance" and concluded that they had been influenced by somebody.[85] But we can also deduce from this fact that the chiefs were acting as the representatives of their people and were defending the indigenous rights of the community rather than their own. Although the Forest Ordinance was passed, it was never put into practice for various reasons. The West African Land Committee took several years to carry out their investigation, which was interrupted by the World War I. Their recommendations were neglected. But the most important cause of the failure of the Ordinance lies in the unity of the educated Africans and the chiefs in the battle against the government's encroachment on their land system.

The Governor often blamed the manipulation of the chief by the educated African. This accusation implied the joint efforts in the protest by the educated and the chiefs.[86] During the protests against the three Bills concerning lands, two social forces, though different in perspective, fought in solidarity. One had the knowledge of modern politics, the other traditional authority; one knew how to strike, the other where. Since their goal was to defend the chiefly sovereignty and the indigenous land tenure system, the educated Africans were also actively involved in mobilizing the common people; it was common for the Aborigines' Rights Protection Society to send their representatives to towns and villages to win support from the masses.

Conclusion

Some writers have explained land legislation in the Gold Coast as a government effort to protect Africans from their unfaithful chiefs, irresponsible local lawyers and greedy European concessionaires. They suggested that before the end of the nineteenth century the chiefs of the Gold Coast were incapable of protecting the people's land. "No other authority than the colonial government was capable of defending the common interest of all the tribes and of their property."[87] If this assertion sounds obsolete, some contemporary scholars still argue that the general policy of the Colonial Office during this period was to protect Africans' interests against European exploitation, or "trusteeship came before development."[88] Judging from the above dispatches between London and Accra, both arguments are very doubtful, reflecting the paternalistic attitude of the colonial government. Nonetheless, these arguments were used in large measure as an excuse to control African land.

The protest also raises some question about the generalization of African nationalism. The development of African nationalism has been generally divided into five phases: primary resistance, millennial protest movement, the period of gestation and adaptation of new local strata, national agitation for self-rule, and the adoption of social programs for the masses by nationalism.[89] The generalization runs the risk of over-simplification. It is obvious that the protest against the Forest Bill cannot be categorized as either primary resistance or millennial movement; nor does it belong to "new local strata" which specifically reflects the social change during the **inter-war period**.[90] This example shows that a particular historical situation may not fit into an analytical model.

To sum up, the protest against the Forest Bill, the Crown Lands Bill and the Lands Bill, among other factors,[91] made the government reluctant to change "traditional small-scale peasant proprietorship" in the Gold Coast, using Omosini's term.[92] It was the last battle fought and won during the colonial period with the joint efforts of the educated African and the chief, and it prevented the further control by the colonial government over their indigenous land tenure system.

Notes

[1] For example, Francis Agbodeka, *Ghana in the Twentieth Century*, pp.19-25. Kimble, *A Political History of Ghana*, pp.362-366.

[2] See Anne Phillips, *The Enigma of Colonialism: British policy in West Africa* (London: James Currey, 1989), pp. 59-84.

[3] Land laws stem from the belief that living land owners are tenants of the dead and trustees of the land for the dead. D. M. Warren, *The Akan of Ghana: An overview of the ethnographic literature* (Accra: Pointer, 1973), pp.51-52.

[4] Kwamena Bentsi-Enchill, *Ghana Land Law: An exposition, analysis and critique* (London: Sweet & Maxwell, 1964), pp.41-86. See also J. M. Sarbah, *Fanti Customary Law* (London: Frank Cass, 1968[1897]); *Cmd6278*. Sir W. H. Belfield, *Report on the Legislation Governing the Alienation of Native Lands in the Gold Coast Colony and Ashanti; with some Observations on the "Forest Ordinance" 1911* (1912)(Thereafter *Belfield Report*).

[5] Casely Hayford, *The Truth about the West African Land Question* (London: Frank Cass, 1970 [1913]), pp.54-55.

[6] This idea was common in West Africa. A Nigerian chief once said, "I conceive that land belongs to a vast family of whom many are dead, few are living, and countless members are still unborn." C. K. Meek, *Land Law and Custom in the Colonies* (London: Oxford, 1949, 2nd ed.), p.178.

[7] Bentsi-Enchill, *Ghana Land Law*, pp.83-84. See also Nii Amaa Ollennu, *Principles of Customary Land Law in Ghana* (Birmingham: CAL Press, 1985), pp.33-37. But some early writers suggested that there was "no trace of individual ownership" in the Customary Law and stressed "the family in the Customary Law is the unit for the purpose of ownership." Casely Hayford, *Truth about Land Question*, p.56; R. S. Rattray, *Ashanti* (Oxford: Clarendon, 1923), p.230. This disagreement may result from the fact that individual ownership was rare in the old days.

[8] "Opinion on Land Tenure by Mr. Justice Smith and Mr. Bruce Hindle," Appendix I, in Sarbah, *Fanti Customary Laws*, p.273.

[9] Bentsi-Enchill, *Ghana Land Law*, pp.83-84.

[10]Field, *Akim-Kotoku*, p.7. Once land was converted into cash by selling, the Paramount Chief was

entitled to one-third of this extra-ordinary wealth.

[11] Rattray, *Ashanti*, p.231.

[12] R. J. H. Pogucki, *Gold Coast Land Tenure* (Accra, 1955), Vol.2, p.33; Vol.3, p.31.

[13] According to A. B. Ellis, "On the Gold Coast private property in land is not recognised, and the sale or purchase of land is unknown." *Yoruba-speaking Peoples of the Slave Coast of West Africa* (London: Chapman & Hall, 1894), p.189. Sarbah wrote "of all things, land is about the last thing which became the subject of an out-and-out sale." He said that family members even volunteered to be sold to raise money to pay debt, rather than part with family lands. *Fanti Customary Laws*, p.86. Paramount Chief Konor Mate Kole pointed out, "No sale of land took place in former days, because there was no demand, but the custom has grown up and has been recognised by the Chiefs and tribes in order to conform to the requirements of Europeans traders." *Cmd6278. Belfield Report.* p.58. Polly Hill describes the *guaha*, a local ceremony of land deal prevalent in Akyem Abuakwa and Akuapem in the nineteenth century. *The Migrant Cocoa-farmers of Southern Ghana*, pp.138, 141-43.

[14] W. Rodney, "African slavery and other forms of social oppression on the upper Guinea coast in the context of the Atlantic slave-trade," *Journal of African History*, 7:3(1966), pp.431-433. Sarbah suggested after the emancipation of slaves and the prohibition of slavery, the sale of lands became "more frequent occurrence." *Fanti Customary Laws*, p.86.

[15] Reindorf, *History of the Gold Coast and Asante*, p.38. The European companies on the Coast "had paid ground rent to the Coast tribes for the land on which their forts were built." See *Cmd6278. Belfield Report.* Notes of Evidence relating to Part IV. p.103.

[16] G. Mikell, *Cocoa and Chaos in Ghana*, pp.70-78. Demographic statistics are not available, for the 1931 census was first in which population was individually counted. But it could be assumed that because of the abolition of the slave trade and the *Pax Britannica*, population began a steady increase which added to the problem of land shortage.

[17] *CO96/361.* CO 19886. Wassaw District Quarterly Report. Encl. in Gold Coast No 163 of 29 May, 1900. Konor Mate Kole stated in 1912 that he had personal knowledge of a case in which a chief granted thirty-two concessions of four square miles each, "thereby depriving the people of permanent cultivation over the whole of this extensive area." *Cmd6278. Belfield Report.* p.59.

[18] Polly Hill, *The Migrant Cocoa-farmers*, p.16. For the company system, see pp.38-74.

[19] *CO96/377.* No.7682. Botanic Gardens, Aburi, Gold Coast, 18 January, 1901. Encl.(1) in Governor to Chamblain, 4 February 1901.

[20] *CO96/399.* Colonial Office. *Gold Coast Report for 1901*.

[21] For the Akan, see Sarbah, *Fanti Customary Laws*, pp.78-100; Field, *Akim-kotoku*, pp.74-81; for the Adangbe and the Ga, see Pogucki, *Gold Coast Land Tenure*, Vol. 2, pp.32-38; Vol.3, pp.31-36.

[22]*CO96/500*. Acting Governor Bryan to Colonial Office, 9 November 1910. A different figure was presented by Belfield, see Table I. No wonder Bryan said "The total area of all concession lands is very difficult to estimate." *CO96/499*. Gold Coast (Confidential). Bryan to Crewe, 5 October 1910.

[23]H. W. Hayes Redwar, *Comments on Some Ordinances of the Gold Coast Colony* (London: Sweet and Maxwell, 1909), p.68.

[24]*CO96/256*. No.140. Encl. in Brandford Griffith to Secretary of State, 6 April 1985; *CO96/257*. No.196. Encl. in Maxwell to Secretary of State, 11 May and 28 May 1895.

[25]*CO96/525*. Colonial Office. Minutes on Forest Ordinance, June 1912. For a detailed description, see D. Kimble, *A Political History of Ghana*, pp.334-339.

[26]*Cmd 6278. Belfield Report*. Notes of Evidence relating to Part IV, p.102.

[27]The Gold Coast Governor wrote to the Secretary of State on 15 July 1897: "it is intelligible that native Chiefs should be vaguely uneasy when they hear that a law affecting stool-lands is under contemplation." *CO879/48*. No.531.

[28]According to the Constitution, the Society was founded "for the immediate purpose of educating the general public to a clear and proper understanding of the true meaning, purport, and effect of the said Lands Bill." See *CO96/648*. Reference "Gold Coast Aborigines' Rights Protection Society, Founded 1897."

[29]*Report of the Proceedings of the Deputation* (1898). See also Olufemi Omosini, "The Gold Coast land question, 1894-1900: some issues raised on West Africa's economic development," *The International Journal of African Historical Studies*, 5:3(1972), pp.453-469.

[30]*Government Gazette* [Extraordinary] No.8 1900. See also *CO879/109*. No.977. Colonial Office: Memorandum, Gold Coast land concessions, 22 November 1910..

[31]Casely Hayford argued in the criticism of the Forest Bill: "as far as the Gold Coast is concerned, there are no Crown lands, the land question on the Gold Coast having been settled as far back as the year 1898." See *Truth about Land Question*, p.41.

[32]*ADM11/1485*. Case No.1007. Precis of Correspondence relating to the Timber Industry in the Gold Coast Colony; Director of Agriculture to Acting Secretary for Native Affairs, 19 October 1905.

[33]*ADM11/1485*. Case No. 1007. Chief Justice to the Governor, 14 November 1905.

[34]*Cmd 4993*. H. N. Thompson, *Report on Forests* (1910). See also *CO96/525*. Colonial Office. Minutes of Forests Ordinance. June 1912.

[35]Alan McPhee, *The Economic Revolution in British West Africa* (London: George Routledge, 1926), p.140.

[36]In 1900, the export was 536 tons, in 1911, 39,726 tons. *Cocoa Conference, 1951* (London, 1951), p.97.

[37]Colonial Office: *The Annual Report for the Gold Coast for 1902*.

[38] *CO96/380*. Encl. in Despatch Gold Coast (Confidential), 13 May 1901.

[39] R. Addo-Fening, "Asante refugees in Akyem Abuakwa 1875-1912," *Transactions of the Historical Society of Ghana*, 14:1 (1973), pp.39-64.

[40] *CO96/410*. Gold Coast No.111. Encl. in Rodger to Lyttelton, 10 March 1904.

[41] *CO96/417*. Gold Coast No.209. Rodger to Lyttelton, 29 April 1904.

[42] *CO96/481*. (Confidential) Tour in the Eastern Province, Rodger to Crewe, 13 February 1909.

[43] *CO879/57*. No.578. Joseph Chamberlain to Governor Sir F. M. Hodgson, 22 December 1899.

[44] *CO96/498*. (Gold Coast Confidential) Roger to Crewe, 29 August 1910.

[45] *CO96/508*. (Confidential) Thorburn to Harcourt, 19 July 1911.

[46] *CO96/514*. The Humble Petition of the *Amanhin, Ahinfu,Mantsemei, Konors,* and *Amagahs* and other Inhabitants of the Western, Central, and Eastern Provinces of the Gold Coast to His Most Gracious Majesty George V. King, 2 December 1911. Encl. in Ashurst, Morris, Crisp & Co. to the Under-Secretary of State, 27 December 1911.

[47] J. Sarbah, *Fanti Customary Laws*, p.66.

[48] Letter by Members of the Deputation appointed by the Kings and Chiefs of the Gold Coast to oppose the Forest Bill, 1911. *Times,* July 18 1912. See Casely Hayford, *Truth about Land Question*, pp.80-81.

[49] B. Cruickshank, *Eighteen Years on the Gold Coast of Africa*, Vol. I, pp.186-187. See also Mcphee, *Economic Revolution*, p.148.

[50] Quoted from Casely Hayford, *Truth about Land Question*, pp.29-30.

[51] *Minutes of the Legislative Council*, 13 September 1911. p.7.

[52] *CO96/514*. Petition to King George V. 2 December 1911.

[53] *CO96/514*. The Humble Petition of the *Amanhin* and *Ahinfu* of the Central and Western Provinces of the Gold Coast in conference with the Aborigines' Rights Protection Society and other inhabitants of the Gold Coast to His Excellecncy James Jamieson, Thorburn, Governor of the Gold Coast Colony. Cape Coast, 3 August 1911.

[54] *CO96/514*. Gold Coast No.12. Thorburn to Harcourt, 8 January 1912; Petition to King George V. 2 December 1911.

[55] *Cmd6278. Belfield Report*. Notes of Evidence relating to Part IV, pp. 115-17; *CO96/514*. Petition to King George V. 2 December 1911.

[56] *CO97/5. Forest Bill*. Gold Coast Ordinance No.15, 1911.

[57] *Cmd6278. Belfield Report.* Notes of Evidence relating to Part IV. p.117; p.111.

[58] *ADM11/1485.* Case No. 1007. Chief Justice to the Governor, 14 November 1905.

[59] *Cmd6278. Belfield Report.* Notes of Evidence relating to Part IV. p.111.

[60] *Cmd 6278. Belfield Report.* para.166.

[61] *CO96/508.* Colonial Office to H. C. Belfield, 12 September 1911. See also Correspondence (November 1909-September 1911) Relating to Concessions and the Alienation of Native Lands on the Gold Coast. *African West 977,* 1911.

[62] *Cmd6278. Belfield Report.* para.22-23.

[63] *Cmd6278. Belfield Report.* paras. 150-151, 167.

[64] For the later development of forest administration, see W. Hancock, *Survey of British Commonwealth Affairs* (London: Oxford University Press, 1964), Vol II, pp.252-254.

[65] For example, Francis Agbodeka, *Ghana in the Twentieth Century,* pp.19-25. Kimble, *A Political History of Ghana,* pp.362-366.

[66] In a letter dated April 6, the Acting Colonial Secretary acknowledged the receipt of the Petitions. See *CO96/525.* Ashurst, Morris, Crisp & Co. to Colonial Office. 16 July 1912.

[67] *CO96/525.* Colonial Office. Minutes on Forest Ordinance. June 1912.

[68] In a letter of September 22, 1911, the Acting Colonial Secretary again acknowledged the receipt of the petition. *CO96/525.* Ashurst, Morris, Crisp & Co. to Colonial Office. 16 July 1912.

[69] *Legislative Council Minutes.* 13 September 1911.

[70] *Cmd6278. Belfield Report.* para. 150.

[71] *CO96/523.* Director of Education to the Acting Colonial Secretary, 13 November 1912. Encl. in (Confidential) Bryan to L. Harcourt, 10 December 1913.

[72] *CO96/523.* Inspector of Schools to Director of Education, 12 November 1912. Sub-encl. in Bryan to Harcourt, 10 December 1912.

[73] The most important modification consisted in the deletion of all parts of the bill that enabled land to be constituted Crown land or government reserves, and substituted a power to make unoccupied land a native Forest Reserve to be managed at the option of the owner either by the owner under the Forest Department, by the government for the benefit of the owner, or by the government under lease. *CO96/525.* Colonial Office. Minutes on Forests Ordinance. June 1912.

[74] *CO96/515.* Memorandum by the Chief Assistant Colonial Secretary Mr. Robertson. Encl.3 in Gold Coast No.12. Thorburn to Harcourt, 8 January 1912.

[75] *CO96/518.* Encl.1 in Gold Coast 398. Thorburn to Harcourt. 12 June 1912.

[76]See his book *The Gold Coast Nation and Nationalist Consciousness* (London: Frank Cass, 1971[1911]).

[77]*CO96/523*. Gold Coast (Confidential). Inspector of Schools to Director of Education, 12 November 1912; Director of Education to Acting Colonial Secretary, 13 November 1912; Sub-encl. and Encl. in Bryan to Harcourt, 10 December 1912.

[78]*CO96/518*. Gold Coast No.398. Thorburn to Harcourt, 12 June 1912. Unfortunately, the by-laws, enclosure (1) in his letter, was missing from the files of the Public Record Office.

[79]*CO96/525*. Proceedings. Encl. in Ashurst, Morris, Crisp & Co. to Colonial Office, 28 June 1912.

[80]Kobina Taylor, *Our Political Destiny: In commemoration of the 43rd year of the Gold Coast Aborigines' Rights Protection Society* (Winneba: Dapa Printing Press, 1941), pp.4-5.

[81]C. K. Meek, *Land Law and Custom in the Colonies* (London: Oxford, 1949), pp.186-192.

[82]C. Y. Shephard, *Report on the Economics of Peasant Agriculture in the Gold Coast* (Accra: Government Printer, 1936); Meek, *Land Law and Custom*, pp.192-193.

[83]Hancock, *Survey*, p.182.

[84]Robert K. A. Gardiner, *The Role of Educational Persons in Ghana Society*, p.24.

[85]*CO96/515*. Gold Coast No.12. Thorburn to Harcourt, 8 January 1912.

[86]*CO96/499*. Gold Coast (Confidential). Bryan to Crewe, 5 October 1910.

[87]Hancock, *Survey of British Commonwealth Affairs*, Vol II, pp.182-5. See also R. L. Buell, *The Native Problem in Africa*(New York, 1928), Vol.I, p.819 and McPhee, *The Economic Revolution*, p.140.

[88]R. Hyam, "The colonial office mind, 1900-1914," *The Journal of Imperial and Commonwealth*, 8:1(1979), pp.30-55.

[89]C. M. Young, *Politics in Congo* (Princeton: Princeton University Press, 1965), pp.281-298; J. S. Coleman, "Nationalism in Tropical Africa," *American Political Science Review*, 18(1954), pp.404-426.

[90]Anthony D. Smith, *State and Nation in the Third World* (Sussex: Wheatsheaf, 1983), pp.44-48.

[91]A. D. Roberts stated that African issues did not matter much in British policies during these years. A. D. Roberts, "The imperial mind," *Cambridge History of Africa* (Cambridge: Cambridge University Press, 1986), Vol.7, pp.24-40. But it would be more convincing to argue that the Colonial Office did not want to threaten the prosperous cocoa production wholly managed by indigenous efforts, thus kept a less strict policy on land issue. The Colonial Office rejected demands from mining companies in the Gold Coast and Nigeria for control on labor and Lever's proposal of palm oil plantations can serve as another footnote.

[92]Omosini, "Gold Coast land question," p.454.

CHAPTER III

Asafo: Commoners against Chiefs

The 1920s was a very disturbing period both for the government and for the chiefs. This decade witnessed a series of protests resulting from the introduction of several controversial bills.[1] There was a turbulent wave of destoolment (deposition) of chiefs that reflected an active involvement of commoners in local politics.

The 1924 Accra incident was a typical political protest in the Gold Coast at this time. Commoners organized as the *Asafo* company and their leaders *Asafoatsemei* (*sing, Asafoatsei*, captains) declared that they would not eat, drink water or live in the same town with the present Ga *Mantse* (*pl. Mantsemei*, chief) Tackie Yaoboi.[2] They beat the gong-gong, a traditional instrument used only by the chief in emergency, and proclaimed that they had deposed the Ga *Mantse*. Although the committee set up by the government to investigate the alleged deposition reinstated the Ga *Mantse* in spite of strong opposition from the *Asafo*, the protest had its own characteristics, the successful mobilization by the *Asafo*, the active involvement of the women and the clash between the commoners and the educated men, to name the most prominent.[3]

An event can only become meaningful when it is put in a wider context. Destoolment, which happened so frequently in the Gold Coast, can hardly be analyzed individually. By setting the Accra incident in a broader analytical frame, we might be able to reach some tentative conclusions. This chapter will study the *Asafo*, the young men's organization, the change in its function and its involvement in local politics characterized by destoolment of chiefs.

Asafo Company System

J. B. Danquah once pointed out, "A town without an *Asafo* company is theoretically as good as dead." Among the Akan people, the warrior organization known as *Asafo* (*osa*, war, *fo*, people) is found in almost every town or village. This system also exists in the Ga, the Krobo, the Guan and other ethnic groups. It seems to have been introduced to these people during the turbulent period from the sixteenth century to the nineteenth century. J. D. De Graft Johnson, a colonial officer who was a Fante himself, talked about the system: "*Asafu* is primarily a warrior organization and is the name given to all male adults banded together for any purpose, particularly war." He distinguished two kinds of *Asafo*, one in general and one in particular. Our interest is in its narrow sense, "the *Asafu* connotes the third estate or common people, which socially goes by the nomenclature of *Kwasafu*, sometimes also described or referred to, politically, as *mbrantsie*, or 'young men' to distinguish them from the *mpanyinfu*, chiefs and elders."[4]

Several studies have been done on the *Asafo* company system. [5] Generally, historians have been more concerned with its origin or the change of its impact on local politics,[6] while both sociologists and anthropologists have treated it as a social institution, stressing its patrilineal character complementary to the matrilineage.[7]

Originally a military organization, the *Asafo* had its flag, song, drums, horns, caps, emblems and priests. The company also had its own post, a rallying place of the company.[8] All able-bodied males, except the chief and the elders, were members of the *Asafo*. In Ga state, boys' puberty rites were closely linked with the entrance into the *Asafo*. People even performed a special ceremony in order to enable their sons qualify for the *Asafo*.[9] All affairs in the *Asafo* were managed on patrilineal lines. There were women captains, who usually took charge of cooking and domestic arrangements.[10]

There are two major interpretations of the origin of the *Asafo*. One view holds the *Asafo* is indigenous to the Fante society, while the other attributes its origin to the presence of early Europeans. We can draw some conclusions from the available evidence. First, although the contact with Europeans might have some influence upon its formation or adaptation, the *Asafo* company's fundamental characteristics are indigenous.[11] Secondly, *Asafo* seems to have appeared in the Fante first.[12] Chiefs were reluctant to accept the *Asafo* as an indigenous organization, probably because the *Asafo* was claiming political rights that would challenge their authority. Thirdly, since the word "*Asafo*" has many meanings, it is necessary to distinguish different kinds of *Asafo* to avoid any confusion.[13] Fourthly, the *Asafo* in various areas might have different origins. Most important, the *Asafo* must have undergone some changes through different periods; so it would be better to interpret its origin from the perspective of a process of adaptation to social changes rather than a stagnant traditional form.

Although certain basic features are universal, *Asafo* companies assumed a wide variety of institutional forms. Since most accounts are about Fante *Asafo*, differences between *Asafo* companies in Fante and other areas should be noted.[14] In the Eastern Province, for example, since the *Asafo* seems to have been introduced from the Fante, it was less elaborated and developed, and was by definition a system among people of low status.[15] There were also different forms of *Asafo* organization. For example, in Akyem Abuakwa the *Asafo* on the central level consisted of the *Amantoo-miensa* (the Council of Three Counties) lying within a seven miles radius of the capital town. It had the right to criticize all acts of the Executive and was regarded as representative of the common people.[16]

All these features had political implications. First, fewer inter-company conflicts occurred compared with the Fante that had a reputation for fierce fighting between rival *Asafo* companies.[17] Secondly, the unified character gave a favorable condition for the involvement of *Asafo* in destoolment. Thirdly, it was easier for them to adapt to the changing situation and meet the new challenge. But how was this social organization translated into a political force and began to challenge the chiefly power? To explain this, we have to compare its functions before and after the colonial rule.

In the early days wars between states were frequent. To obtain greater mobilization and an effective supervision, all the male members in the state, town or village were organized into fighting groups.[18] The *Asafo* either fought against other states or were responsible for the peace of their own state. Though the *Pax Britannica* rendered the military function redundant, the military origin of the *Asafo* was always stressed. During festivals, the *Asafo* performed in order to show their strength and loyalty.

The *Asafo* played an important role in the ritual associated with installation or deposition of a chief. When he was elected, *Asafo* members went to fetch him. As a farewell to him as a commoner, they gave him a last ceremonial flogging, smeared him with white clay, a symbol of innocence and congratulation, and brought him before the assembly. They also performed the same duty when a chief was destooled. The *Asafo* was important on account of its religious power to affect people's status in the other world at the funeral. Besides fetching the dead body, the *Asafo* also performed at the funeral, accompanied by *Asafo* songs. The *Asafo* was also involved in other activities, such as witch-hunting. In Agona, north of Winneba, people believed in the "great *Aku*" (river god) of the Akora River and only the *Asafo* members could save or retrieve a drowning person.[19]

The *Asafo* played a wide range of social functions. They formed hunting team, fire brigade, search party, communal labor and sanitation supervisor of the town. In some place, the *Asafo* acted as guardians over the morals of their members' wives. A member notified the company of his marriage, who in return offered the protection. When he died, the widow was questioned to see if she was responsible for his death. It was not for the sole purpose of forcing a confession, but showed to the spirit of the dead that the *Asafo* was concerned about his affairs.[20]

The most interesting function of the *Asafo* was their role in the traditional political structure. As an unofficial body, it had an effective way to express its opinion. The *Asafo* leader was officially recognized as representative of commoners; elders would consider any ideas he had for them. The *Asafo* had a say in the election of the chief and all matters affecting the state. Without their approval, a candidate could not be elected as chief. Commoners could oppose any policy issued by the chief, while the elders could not for fear of being accused of disloyalty to the chief.

The title and role of the *Asafo* leader varied. In Fante, the commander of all *Asafo* companies was *Tufuhene* (captain-general), the next authoritative person after the *Ohene* (chief, stool-holder). His appointment was originally by popular choice. In early times, the *Tufuhene* ranked so high that when a paramount stool was vacant, he might perform the duty of regent, or even became a chief. Other *Asafo* leaders were chosen or approved by members of the company. In Akyem Abuakwa, the *Asafoakye* (captain), as an appointee of the chief and elders, was liable to dismissal by them. "From the last quarter of the nineteenth century, however, there is evidence of *asafo* asserting the right to choose their own leaders and merely presenting them to the Chief and his Councillors for confirmation."[21] *Asafoakye* had a constitutional role in the political structure and was recognized as member of the Councils.

Among the Ga, *Asafoatsemei* in origin were hunters. After warfare ceased and population increased, they took over the management of secular affairs. When a Ga *Mantse* was dead, *Akwasontse* (Captain-General) was the first person to be told by the elders that a new chief was needed. In Asante, *Nkwankwaahene* represented the interest of young men (*mmerante*), but not a member of the Chief's Council. He played his role in an informal way. In the 1880s the Asante young men were politically active, notably in their involvement in the coup against the King Mensa Bonsu.[22]

In general, in the pre-colonial period, through the political role of the *Asafo* an individual could make his opinion heard concerning state affairs, and commoners could offer or withhold their support to the chief. After the British government was established, the functions of the *Asafo* underwent a great change, especially in the field of local politics.

At the beginning of colonial rule, the government did not recognize the *Asafo*'s role in traditional society; therefore, it did not interfere with the *Asafo* company as a potential political force while they checked the chief's authority at will. Ironically, the *Asafo*'s power gradually increased whereas the chief's legitimate authority decreased.

Since colonial rule put an end to wars, the *Asafo* transformed its main function from a military one to a "public works department" and acted as a task force in particular situations. But resistance did exist, which caused the

British one particular difficulty of obtaining labor, even paid labor, for public works. To solve the problem, the government issued several ordinances, such as Public Labor Ordinance (1883), Trade Roads Ordinance (1894) and Compulsory Labor Ordinance (1895). A chief could be used as recruiting agent to provide wage labor for public works and workers for the Government.

Compulsory labor became a heavy burden on commoners under colonial rule for several reasons. First, the demand for service now came from the government or the chief, not from the community. It usually had nothing to do with their communal interests, such as the service needed for the battle against the Asante, which met some resistance.[23] Secondly, almost all public works were performed on a compulsory basis with little or no payment.[24] Thirdly, it was common that chiefs required extra-service for their own benefit. Communal labor recruitment became a major source of grievances later. Simensen argues that the main reason for both the 1915-18 rising and the 1932 attempted deposition of the Paramount Chief Ofori Atta in Akyem Abuakwa was the use of communal labor and dissatisfaction with payment for the labor.[25]

Another change of the *Asafo* is that commoners in different companies were now more united and usually acted with one voice. For example, in Kwahu, the *Asafo* of each town and village organized in 1905 in a wider organization, the *Asafo Kyenku* (United *Asafo*), which became very active in local affairs till the 1930s. The government admitted the "movement is well organized and is a visible expression of the desire of the younger generation to take a hand in the control of affairs."[26] In 1920, it was noticed that "*Asafos* have formed themselves into an organized body and have members in nearly every town in this district. Its policy seems to be a consistent opposition to established authority."[27] The "opposition to established authority" was characterized by an increasing number of destoolment.

As early as 1908, the Secretary for Native Affairs warned that "the chiefs have been losing influence of late owing to the growth of the 'Companies'[*asafo*]."[28] The *Asafo*'s influence was so popular that Slater, the Governor, was surprised to find in 1927 that in Akyem rural areas, "the person who has power today is the *asafuakye*, not the *odikro* (chief). In some villages, the *odikro* is not informed what his youngmen have done or intend to do."[29] In the early 1930s, an official noticed that in Kwahu "the *Asafo* were prepared to bring about the destoolment of the *Omanhene* if their demands which are undoubtedly reasonable are not met."[30]

Deposition, or destoolment, was a means of retaliation most frequently used by the *Asafo*. During the three decades before 1920 more than seventy attempted destoolments occurred in Akyem and Kwahu.

Destoolment: Mechanism and History

A stool represents the power, spirit and unity of a community, and the chief's stool is held to be the most sacred. Enstoolment[31] and destoolment are therefore among the most solemn events in a state. Since the stool symbolizes the pride and stability of the state, destoolment, the formal removal of a chief from his position, is a politically significant matter. Danquah once pointed out that destoolment was a procedure to get rid of an unwanted and oppressive chief, an insufficient or incapable chief or an unmoral or easy-going chief at any time when "the governed felt that there were good reasons for deposing and replacing him by a better man."[32]

As a constitutional means to keep power in balance, destoolment is usually the last resort and adequate justification must be provided. Generally speaking, it is the "right of those who placed him thereon to put him off the stool for any just cause."[33] But what constitutes a "just cause"?

According to customary law, the specific offenses generally include the following: (1) Adultery. This must be notorious and habitual. (2) Habitual drunkenness and disorderly conduct as a consequence which degraded him. (3) Habitually opposing the councilors and disregarding their advice without just cause. (4) Theft. (5) Perverting justice when hearing cases, and inflicting extortionate fines and penalties as well as failing to protect his subjects. (6) Cowardice in war. (7) Circumcision.[34] (8) Unwarranted disposal of stool property; extravagance and persistently involving his people in debt contracted. (9) Defiling his stool; inability to uphold the dignity and good reputation of the stool. (10) Insufficient provision for the members of the stool family. (11) General misconduct.[35]

A ruler could be questioned for improper conduct that caused discontent among his subjects, elders or commoners. If a chief constantly made use of his subjects for his own benefits, or ignored the *Asafo*'s warning, he would face destoolment. In Asante, a chief "who was always ordering his subjects to be flogged would soon be destooled."[36] A chief's policy could also bring about discontent or even unrest among his people. Such cases usually happened when a chief's engagement in expensive litigations resulted in increasing taxes, or he collaborated with the government at the sacrifice of his people. This could result in his destoolment.

Personal infirmities were considered "unholy". A chief could be destooled if he became blind, deaf or impotent, or suffered from leprosy, madness, or fits; or if he was disfigured by some injuries. This fault not only indicated that the chief had been punished for his private sin by the gods or ancestors, but also became a sign of weakness of the state as a whole. In this case, the chief was usually asked to resign.

Busia once collected some informative cases from history of the Asante area. Chiefs Kwabena Aboagye of Asumegya, Kwabena Bruku and Kwai Ten of Nsuta were destooled for drunkenness; Kwame Asonane of Bekwai for being a glutton; Kwame Asona of Bekwai for dealing in charms and noxious medicines; and Akuamoa Panyin of Dwaben for his abusive tongue and not following his elders' advice. In Kokofu, Osei Yaw was destooled for being fond of disclosing the origin of his subjects (especially their slave ancestry); and Mensa Bonsu for excessive cruelty.[37]

Under colonial rule several changes occurred regarding the grounds for destoolment. Abuse of power became a frequent cause of deposition, which included a chief's exploitation of his people by means of the tribunal or a chief's collaboration with the government in the application of certain ordinances without consulting his people. In addition, since bribery was increasing, both in legal cases and in the election of chiefs, acceptance of bribery also became a ground for destoolment. Chiefs were also destooled because of their involvement in land dealing or financial misappropriation.

Not only should the grounds be sufficient, the procedure of destoolment is also strictly followed. Generally speaking, there are several principles regarding the destoolment. In the first place, the authority that put the chief on the stool was the only authority that could call for his destoolment. This usually consisted of several parties, such as the elders or councilors and the *Asafo*. In some cases, superior chiefs could destool lower chiefs for a variety of reasons. Secondly, a little misconduct could not result in destoolment. The chief must have done something seriously detrimental to the community, or otherwise displayed a behavior unworthy of his position. Thirdly, except for offenses like cowardice, theft, circumcision or defiling his stool, which were liable to instant destoolment, the chief had to be given several warnings in order to have a chance to correct his wrongdoings. Fourthly, before he could be properly destooled, he had to be given an opportunity to defend himself. Fifthly, he had to be tried by some authority that had the legitimate power to make a fair judgment and to supervise the destoolment. The destoolment was usually carried out by taking off the chief's sandals so that his feet touched the ground, or by the simple ceremony of seizing him and bumping his buttocks three times on the ground, indicating that he was formally destooled.

There remains one question to be answered: who had the right to destool a chief? According to Sarbah, "The right of removing a ruler belongs to the people immediately connected with the stool." More specifically, complaint by the *Gyasi* (royal house) against the superior ruler was heard and decided by the second ruler and the councilors. Complaint against the superior ruler by his own councilors or by the second ruler was heard by the *Gyasi* headmen, and as many of the subordinate rulers as possible could attend. In Asante, one of the four major functions of the Council of the Asante Union was to meet for the enstoolment or destoolment of an *Asantehene*, the King of Asante. Evidence also suggests that commoners played an important role in destoolment.

As a witness in a case, Kweku Atta, King of Axim, once explained what would happen if the townspeople complained. He would go to the meeting of the townsmen accompanied by his family. The townsmen put before the family what he had done and he could make his defense. When his family found that he was in the wrong, the family and himself beg the town to forgive him. "They forgive you, and you pacify them. If you repeat it four times, then, they tell the family they don't want you any more, and that ends it. That is the native law and practice."[38]

In Akyem Abuakwa, the authorization of destoolment was made by the king-makers, *i.e.* Kyebi Executive Council, Divisional Chiefs and *Amantoo-miensa* (Council of Three Counties). *Amantoo-miensa* was formed of the chiefs and people of three towns or counties situated within seven miles of the capital: Apapam, Apedwa and Tete. The council really represented the interests of commoners. Termed as the "*Asafo* on the central level", *Amantoo-miensa* was regarded as the official mouthpiece of public opinion.[39] All these practices show that the commoners had a say in the destoolments.

The commoners' involvement in destoolment seems to have been strengthened during the colonial period. For example, in 1902 the District Chief of Mansu under Chief Enimil of Wassaw Amenfi offended his subjects by drunken habits and other misconduct. The people sent messengers to inform Chief Enimil that they wished to remove him from the stool. Although Enimil did not agree with them, the people still exercised their inherent right and destooled their District Chief. Later, Chief Enimil tried to interfere by suggesting he be given another chance, but without success. In some cases, people destooled their chief without the support of the office-holders. In 1910, the oppressive and unconstitutional behavior of Kwadjo Dei VII in Peki aroused strong popular opposition. When he failed to appear before the people and elders to answer charges against him, he was thrice proclaimed as destooled. But he was supported by several important office-holders, who were the proper persons to perform the final acts of formal destoolment. Their resistance to the people's demand lasted for six months until finally the deposition of the chief was ceremonially completed.[40]

In summary, the authorities who carried out the enstoolment and destoolment proceedings were the royal house including the queen mother, the elders and the commoners. Three parties were expected to reach an agreement. As the fundamental principle was that only those who elected a chief could destool him, commoners could initiate a destoolment by bringing pressure on the elders through the *Asafo* companies, but destoolment itself required the consent of the elders. All these principles and procedures were strictly followed in order to prevent an abuse of destoolment.

For the Akan people, there is a long tradition of destoolment. According to Danquah, "Destoolment, for all that, is not a new thing to the Akan peoples. It has been a part of their constitution since the earliest times."[41] During his reign from 1777 to the end of the century, the Asante King Osei Kwame tried to establish Islam as the official religion. Both chiefs and people rejected this change. The chiefs feared the King would use Islam to strengthen his power that would threaten their own prestige and interests.[42] The commoners also realized that the acceptance of Islam would weaken the very basis of their religious beliefs thus their political and social institutions. As a result they deposed the King.[43]

In 1874, Asante King Kofi Kakari took some gold trinkets and other valuable treasures from the royal mausoleum at Bantama without the consent of his councilors in Kumasi or the chiefs. When the case was discovered, people were very angry. The chiefs of four districts together with Kumasi councilors denounced this action as unconstitutional and sacrilegious. Consequently the King was destooled.[44]

But destoolment did not exist in all societies of the Gold Coast. For example, the Ga people had no custom of destoolment in their history. A *Mantse* was made a *Mantse* by a magical process that could not be undone. He could not be destooled and replaced by another *Mantse*, but he could be removed by killing or desertion, according to the degree of his misconduct. It is told that the usurper Queen Dode Akabi (1610-1635) was trapped inside a well and buried alive by angry subjects for her cruelty. Her tyrannical successor, Okaikoi, held power until 1660 when his warriors deserted him.[45]

In early contact with the Danes, the people in Osu were tired of their *Mantse*. But the Danes continued to deal with this undesirable *Mantse*. Since the people could not depose the *Mantse*, they had to create a new post *Mankralo* in order to negotiate with the Danes.[46] So their way of dealing with an unwanted ruler was quite different from that of the Akan. There is no tradition of destoolment among the Krobo and the Ewe either. It was only under the British rule that the people adopted destoolment procedures as a means of checking a chief's excessive power.

Judging from the relevant evidence, it seems that two facts are certain regarding destoolment in the pre-colonial period. First, destoolment was a rare occurrence. As one chief put it, "In the olden days affairs were not in such a deplorable state as they are to-day, and destoolments were of very rare occurrence."[47] The stool was sacred, and a King or chief could only enjoy the prestige as the stool-holder by performing his duty sincerely. Secondly, chiefs destooled for financial offenses were even fewer. During the colonial period, economic change was so rapid and profound that chiefs were more affected than the commoners for obvious reasons. It was very common for chiefs to make use of their position for their own benefits, such as using state funds, extorting tribunal fees or accepting bribes. Consequently their misdeeds caused frequent destoolment.

Destoolment in the Colonial Period

Under colonial rule there was an increase of destoolments. When a destoolment occurred in Begoro in 1908, the Commissioner of the Eastern Province said, "Destoolments are very rare still, but much more frequent than they were." He suggested that the inland people were probably "taking over the customs of the coastal towns, where destoolments were much more frequent."[48] Early in 1913, Governor Clifford made a tour in Eastern Province. He observed that a chief who "abuses his powers to an extent sufficient to arouse popular indignation against him, is liable to be destooled." He called this "the curiously democratic native constitution" and found it was "by no means an uncommon practice."[49]

Five years later, it was reported that there was "an unusual number of depositions" during the year when the destoolment of no less than **16** chiefs was confirmed.[50] Statistics show that there were about **119** destoolments from 1904 to 1925.

Table II   Deposition of Chiefs (1904-1925)

Period	Numbers
1904-1908	10
1909-1913	22
1914-1918	39
1918-1923	32
1924-1925	16

Source: *CO96/663*. Memorandum by Secretary for Native Affairs for the visit of Ormsby-Gore in 1926. David Kimble used another table, see *A Political History of Ghana*, p.490.

Case studies also indicate that the number of destoolment in Akyem Abuakwa was increasing during the first decade of colonial rule.[51] The Governor complained in 1922 "Elections and destoolments were unfortunately frequent among the

Omanhin and *Ohin*."[52] In 1926-27, there were seven destoolments in the colony.

The Native Administration Ordinance, enacted on April 21, 1927, increased the authority of the chief, especially the Paramount Chief. The Governor's power to withhold recognition of the destoolment of a chief generated some protest. It was described in a local newspaper that, "The time is coming when a Chief once installed will sit firmly on the neck of the people, like the old man of the sea, and rule them in his own way without any lawful means of getting rid of him."[53]

Some scholar argued that this Ordinance did check the tendency of destoolment.[54] The Eastern Province did not support this argument. There were nine and seven destoolments in 1927-28 and 1928-29 respectively. In addition, three Paramount Chiefs in the Province were destooled by their subjects. The deposition of Ga *Mantse* was confirmed in 1930, the *Omanhene* of Kwahu was later allowed to abdicate and *Omanhene* of New Dwaben was re-instated by the Governor on February 12 1929.[55]

During 1931-32, the propaganda for the Native Administration Revenue Measure and the launch of Income Tax Ordinance caused great confusion and protest, followed by a wave of destoolments. For example, in Akyem Abuakwa, all the main Divisional Chiefs were destooled and Paramount Chief Ofori Atta was facing a political crisis.[56] Chiefs took advantage of the power granted by the Ordinance either to seek their own benefits or to keep opposition under control, usually with the support of the Government police. A Chief in Begoro insisted "he ruled the people and not they him." He made a list of twelve persons whom he wanted to be arrested by the government police. An official commented "the chiefs with their autocratic methods have been sowing the seed of unrest ever since the introduction of the Native Administration Ordinance."[57]

The problem of destoolment was so grave that Burns, who became the Governor in 1941, was "struck with dismay" by this tendency. He found within the last ten years no less than twenty-two Paramount Chiefs had been destooled, in addition to twenty-two others who had abdicated, seven stools of Paramount Chiefs were vacant, and few Paramount Chiefs had succeeded in maintaining their positions for more than a very short time. The case of subordinate chiefs was even worse.[58]

Although Burns warned the tendency "will be put down with a strong hand", the situation worsened in the 1940s. From 1940 to 1944, at least **36** chiefs were destooled. Then there was a great increase during the period of 1945-1949 when more than **93** chiefs were removed. One major reason for this increase was the enactment of the Native Authorities Ordinance in 1944, which changed the fundamental element of the Native Authorities system. The Ordinance abandoned the old concept and set up a new one in which both central government and Native

Authorities were parts of one unified government system.[59] The Governor's power was greatly increased and he was responsible to appoint the Native Authorities. The only restriction on his choice was the persons appointed must be African of the areas concerned. This new condition must have upset the shaken balance of power and contributed to the sudden boost of destoolment.[60]

Destoolment became a very popular practice during the colonial period. Generally speaking, there were five types of deposition. First, during the early period, the government deposed chiefs as punishment. The measure usually aroused protest or even rebellion. Sarbah made it clear in 1906 that the right of dismissal "is in the people, not in the Crown," and declared that the government had abused its power in the case of Kwamina Faibir, chief of Tarkwa and Awdua.[61] Secondly, some chiefs were destooled because of the opposition of elders. This kind of deposition usually resulted from internal conflict between candidates in the royal house. Sometimes, abdication also became a solution of compromise between the two parties. Thirdly, after the introduction of the Native Administration Ordinance in 1927, some Paramount Chiefs removed their Divisional Chiefs for various reasons, which indicates the increasing power of the Paramount Chiefs. Fourthly, some destoolments were caused by the protest of the educated, as Kimble and Wight suggested.[62] This occurred more often after the 1930s when the educated no longer satisfied with traditional rulers and became more actively involved in politics. What we are interested here is the fifth type, destoolment caused by the *Asafo*. Obviously, there is no clear-cut division between these types, but evidence suggests that before the middle of the 1930s, the *Asafo* was the major mover in destoolment.

Colonial officers noticed the frequency of destoolment. They either complained of the disobedience of the young men, who they believed were the "rabbles" or the "lazy and discontented part of the population", or attributed destoolment to the "weakness of the native institution." Their complaints were usually accompanied by the criticism of the irregularity of destoolment, especially those with the *Asafo* companies involved.

Asafo and Destoolment: Irregularity and Legitimacy

During the Accra incident in 1924, the Governor gave the reason why the Government should stand firmly in dealing with the *Asafo*. It was the duty of the Government not to confirm a deposition that "has been conducted irregularly and without justifiable cause"; to act otherwise would be to encourage the wholesale destoolment of chiefs, "an evil which is already sufficiently great to be serious."[63]

To analyze this accusation of irregularity, three factors have to be considered.

In the first place, the British did not understand pre-colonial institutions in the Gold Coast, since they considered the young men, or the *Asafo*, as insignificant in local politics. "In the actual management of the little kingdom they hitherto have had no real voice."[64] This judgment is dubious because the young men had to be consulted in enstoolment or destoolment and other important matters of state affairs.

Secondly, after the establishment of British rule, the process of enstoolment or destoolment became less regular because of the interference from the government. The Governor, or even Provincial Commissioners, began to depose disloyal chiefs or punish rebellious elders. For instance, Yaw Dakwa, chief of Pankesi, was removed from his position because of his refusal of the Governor's ruling regarding a land dispute.[65] From 1917 to 1921, several Divisional Chiefs and elders in Peki were either fined or suspended from office by the Governor for their protest against a newly elected chief not entitled to the position.[66] Regarding the right of destoolment, Kimble correctly points out, "The Government had never explicitly claimed this right before 1878, but had often dealt in summary fashion with troublesome Chiefs."[67] In addition, some new practices were introduced, such as the suspension of a chief from his office, a notion totally strange to the traditional system.

Thirdly, for those areas where there was no tradition of destoolment, the people had to resort to this measure to protect themselves. As a new tactic in a new situation, this might be regarded as irregular. A provincial annual report of the 1924-1925 described, "The custom of destoolment which was known only among certain tribes is becoming general throughout the Province, the result being that chiefs of today are faced with the possibility of being destooled for the smallest indiscretion on their part." In Krobo area, destoolment was a new phenomenon. The Paramount Chief of Manya Krobo once stated: "We do not recognize destoolment in Krobo as there are no cases in our history. No *Konor* (paramount chief) has ever had the misfortune of being destooled." In the 1930s, however, districts such as Manya Krobo, Yilo Krobo, Shai and Osudoku all passed the same resolution to adopt the measure of destoolment.[68]

Asafo companies were actively involved in destoolment. In some places, the *Asafo* enjoyed such popularity that they became the real "boss" in local politics. For example, in the early 1900s, owing to complaints about the heavy Oath fines, an agreement was reached between *Asafo* and chiefs in the Kwahu state, which was reaffirmed in 1913. In 1917 the *Asafo* passed a system of by-laws, referred to as the *Magna Carta* of Kwahu. The *Omanhene* and his Divisional Chiefs approved and agreed to observe these *Asafo* laws, which imposed extensive price controls; forbade any stool heir to offer a bribe to any party with power to elect and install a chief; forbade chiefs to apply for gunpowder unless with the permission of the *Asafo* leader, and laid down that any chief who cohabited with the wife of a commoner would be destooled.[69] This agreement shows that besides using destoolment as a weapon to check excessive chiefly power, the *Asafo* even carried out specific reforms. These really became a challenge to both the chief and the government.

In 1928, a protest against the application of Native Administration Ordinance led to the actual running of the Kwahu state by the *Asafo*. The *Omanhene*, who was finally destooled in 1932 by the *Asafo*, described in his letter the condition in Kwahu when he asked the Paramount Chief of Akyem Abuakwa for help. Kwahu *Asafo* was not only entirely different from *Asafos* in Akan, Twi and Fanti states, but also different from the old constitutional *Asafos*, "It comprises the rabble of Kwahu, Commoners of the town and villages headed by desperados known as *Asafoakyes*." The *Asafo*'s object was "to make laws for their Chiefs and oppose the Native Jurisdiction Ordinance of 1883 and the new Native Administration Ordinance of 1927."[70]

His letter illustrated almost all the features of the modern *Asafo* system. First, it was new in organization in terms of both its members and leaders. Although epithets such as "rabble of Kwahu" and "desperados known as *Asafoakyes*" were unpleasant, they did indicate the *Asafo* contained people of lower class in the traditional sense. Secondly, the *Asafo*'s main function was to balance the chief's authority; thus it was independent and feared by the chief. Thirdly, it became such a challenge to the established order that chiefs were desperately looking for help from outside.

In 1919, a report was sent to the Governor claiming that there was "a marked tendency on the part of the *asafo* to usurp powers it was never intended they should possess," and the young men were trying to "destroy the existing form of power."[71] Later, it was said that the *Asafo* had often endeavored both in the Kwahu and other Akan Divisions to arrogate to itself powers which it should not possess.[72] So the frequency of destoolment had much to do with this "irregularity", which calls into question the legitimacy of the destoolment.

Not only does an authority need legitimacy, as Max Weber argues,[73] but also the process of offering or depriving power needs legitimacy. According to customary law, it is the right of those who elected the chief to destool him when they thought him unsuitable for the position. Danquah analyzed the function as well as the legitimacy of destoolment. He thought that it was a "sure safeguard of the democratic element in Akan State Constitution" as a check on the ruling princes "reminding them perpetually that first and last the supreme interest or political ideal before them is the good and welfare of the governed and of the State as a whole."[74]

Once incorporated into the colonial administration, the chief's status underwent several changes. Loyalty to the government now became the essential requirement for chiefs. For example, it was common for the government to appoint the *Omanhene* for important areas in Asante after 1900. According to the Chiefs Ordinance in 1904, when the election or deposition of a chief was questioned, the Governor had the final say, not subject to challenge in the courts.[75] This power threw some doubt on the legitimacy of the chief's position. In a report of a case in Bekwai in 1920, the Commissioner in charge of the investigation reported the young men complained that they were not consulted in the choice of the headchief, that they did not respect him at all. The elders were also on the side of the young men. "If we support the Headchief we shall be alone. The whole of the youngmen refuse to serve the Headchief and we support them."[76]

Although the government claimed time and again the traditional political system should remain intact, yet there was a dilemma in their intention and practice. By promoting some chiefs and punishing others, the government had already breached the mechanism of the very structure they wanted to keep. The sacred notion of chiefly power was weakened and a chief was regarded as a mere mouthpiece of the Governor, "a government creature, a quasi-official," rather than as a leader of his people. This image problem was worsened by the abuse of chiefly power.

A more important change occurred in the chiefly power and the institutional channels through which the authority was exercised. Except the loss of power to wage war or to inflict capital punishment, chiefs now enjoyed a more secure authority within the colonial framework. A chief's authority over his people increased, while it became less legitimate and less acceptable. This contradictory situation resulted from two circumstances: the weakening of the traditional checks from the elders and the military backing of the chief by the government. A chief now cared much more about the favor of the Governor than the support of his people.

Decreasing participation of the elders in state affairs also contributed to this "irregularity." An annual report accused the elders of becoming "indifferent to the well-being of their state, regardless of their national welfare and quite obviously antagonistic towards native institution."[77] The "indifferent" or "antagonistic" attitude is understandable considering the changing situation. Economic opportunities affected everybody. Individuals became less concerned about state affairs than ever before, elders were no exception. More important, the elders' authority greatly decreased since the chief, backed by the Government, cared little about their advice. The only choice left for them was to support the chief, thus the Government's decision. The elders were antagonistic not towards the traditional institution, but towards the chief. Their passivity left a political vacuum, which made it possible for *Asafo* companies to play a more active role in local politics.

The *Asafo* leaders seemed to take it as their responsibility to represent the commoners and to guard their interests. Also, they were quite confident of their legitimate right. In the 1924 Accra Incident, an *Asafo* leader stated the following theory of the constitution before the Secretary for Native Affairs: "The Stool of Accra belongs to the *Asafoatsemei* and *Manbii* (townspeople). The *Mantse* is merely a caretaker. A *Mantse* reigns, but never rules. A *Mantse* is not responsible for the actions of his people. If his people ask him to do a thing, he has only to do it."[78] This theory seems to be true in the sense that according to custom the chief can only decide matters on which his people have agreed, as is clearly shown in the oath and ceremony in his election.[79]

In those areas where the *Asafo* company gained power, their function in local politics was no longer questioned. In Akyem Abuakwa, the *Asafo*'s constitutional role was no longer a subject of debate in 1932. It was settled during the earlier risings against the chiefs when the Paramount Chief Ofori Atta and the State Council failed to deny young men the right to organize for political action independently. Finally, the *Asafo* leaders gained the right to sit on the councils of the Divisional Chiefs as representatives of the commoners. In Kwahu, the Paramount Chief compromised to some extent by encouraging the wing chiefs to bring their *Asafo* leaders to the State Council meetings, where they had the opportunities of advising them in matters before the Council. These *Asafo* leaders even refused to sit with their chiefs and tried to speak for themselves and to vote as though they were equal with the Council members.[80]

There have been various interpretations of destoolments brought about by *Asafo* companies. Governor Clifford suggested that chiefs were destooled because they were "more enlightened and progressive than their subjects."[81] Governor Guggisberg thought that it showed the "weakness of the native system."[82] Some considered it as the result of the younger generation's demand for share in power. According to Martin Wight and W.M. Macmillan, the cause of destoolment was "the struggles to control stool wealth and to enjoy the perquisites of office."[83] F. Crowther, the Secretary for Native Affairs, treated this issue more systematically. He attributed the increase of destoolment to spread of education, increase of wealth, change of the chief's duty and lack of co-operation and mutual respect.[84] Without consideration of administrative defect, all these interpretations have a common problem: they ignored the impact of the colonial policy on local politics.

Establishing the chief as administrative agent, the government now could back him with warrant, order, police or even military force. Whenever there was a conflict between the chief and the people, the government would try to support the chief if it was possible. Governor Clifford once emphasized his determination to support chiefs. He also mentioned the threat of the *Asafo* to chiefly power: if the

Asafo was allowed to exert its authority in opposition to that of the chiefs, "it will be impossible for the latter to carry out the administration of the tribe."[85] In order to avoid this situation, it had been the endeavor of the government "to strengthen the position of the Chiefs and to support their authority over their subjects."[86] The government assured this policy to chiefs time and again. If a chief was deposed because of carrying out a government order, this deposition "could not automatically be recognized." In his words, "After all we must claim to govern."[87]

The chief knew how to take advantage of this promise. A District Commissioner once complained of the difficult situation. Whenever a chief heard of any rumor that his opponents intended to do anything "to which he can take the slightest objection", he rushed to the District Commissioner. He usually exaggerated the importance of the intended action, and asked the government to send the police. The police would rush to the spot and the opponents had to postpone or even abandon their action. But the impact was devastating. First, it showed that the chief had the full support of government in anything he may do, the chief was therefore regarded as "little more than a Government servant." Secondly, many abuses would "creep in to his administration and the opinion of the people will be set at naught," and the chief became "a complete autocrat." To make the matter worse, the government was bound to assist the chief in upholding his position.[88]

Besides consolidating chiefly power, the government was also trying to incorporate chiefs into local administration by increasing government control. This attempt, however, was less successful for three major reasons. First, the Bond of 1844 had its impact on the colonial government. Under the Bond, the government, often reluctantly or unwillingly, tried to leave some room for traditional authorities. Secondly, neither the Native Jurisdiction Ordinance (1878) nor the amending bill of 1910 mentioned the appointment of chiefs. Thus the right to appoint a chief was not vested in the government but in traditional institutions. Thirdly, the elimination of educated Africans from high government positions since the end of the nineteenth century and the decision in 1910 to depend solely upon the chief for local administration created an educated group who became increasingly critical of the colonial rulers.[89] Paradoxically, this constant pressure from the educated put the chiefs in an extremely advantageous bargaining position while dealing with the government to preserve their power.[90]

Colonial rule not only rendered the religious authorities politically impotent, but also eroded the checks and balances within the indigenous power structure. This is truly a "necessary precondition for establishing the chiefs as effective administrative agents." The breakdown of traditional political mechanisms resulted in serious abuses of chiefly power. More importantly, misconduct in financial matters, such as the expropriation of stool land and money or extortion in local tribunals became very serious.

This problem was worsened by two other factors. First, there was neither a distinction between the chief's personal income and the stool revenue, nor any system of control to ensure that their expenditures should be on public purposes, thus their position became "an office of profit." In the 1930s, various reports revealed that many disturbances resulted from the dissatisfaction that the *Asafo* "felt at not being consulted before any expenditure, for the payment of which they may ultimately become responsible."[91] Secondly, owing to the lack of normal incomes and adequate funds to maintain their prestige, chiefs continued to depend on fines from indigenous courts and revenue from stool lands. It is little wonder that the majority of the destooled chiefs were charged for financial misconduct, extortion and corruption.[92]

The new condition under colonial rule had a psychological impact on both commoners and chiefs. To meet this challenge, the *Asafo* with its traditional duty to balance the political power took the lead to protect commoners' interests. Up to the 1930s, it was common for the *Asafo* to destool unpopular chiefs. Thus the situation became paradoxical. On the one hand, the chief felt quite secure under the protection of colonial rule. On the other hand, since destoolment was unpredictable and meant total loss of power, the chief had a sense of insecure possession of authority. A **vicious cycle** developed: fear of losing privileges led to an excessive use of power, more abuse of power meant quick destoolment.

Conclusion

Traditional historiography holds that there were only two indigenous political powers in the Gold Coast, the chief and the educated elite. The evidence of this chapter supports a different view; namely, that the *Asafo* company was the third political force. The *Asafo* demanded that their voice be heard by fighting against the unpopular chief or, as the last resort, by destooling the chief.

This chapter has pinpointed the problem caused by colonial local administration policy. Owing to their ignorance of the traditional system, the British accepted the chief as an autocrat who enjoyed absolute power in the indigenous system, thus taking no notice of the role played by the *Asafo*. Later, when the *Asafo* clashed with the chief, the government tried to support the chief in order to strengthen local administration. Thus while they set up chiefs as the local agents of the colonial government, the British sacrificed the democratic elements in the traditional political system.

In 1932, Kwahu *Asafo* destooled their Paramount Chief, a destoolment that was later confirmed by the government. However, the official in charge of the investigation strongly suggested the abolition of the office of senior *Asafoakye* and the repeal of *Asafo* laws.[93] Then in 1936, the chiefs in the Asante area voted unanimously the abolition of the position of *Nkwankwaahene*, *Asafoakye* and *Asafo* from the whole of Ashanti "in view of the fact that they are the cause of political unrest in Asante."[94] From then on, the influence of the *Asafo* gradually decreased, but it by no means disappeared. Up to the 1950s, they were still involved in local politics. [95] In other parts of the colony, the *Asafo* company was also frequently involved in destoolment or petition in Krobo state and attracted a lot of attention from the government.[96]

More importantly, the change of the political climate provided different conditions for people in the Gold Coast. The educated gradually gained a more influential position in the arena of local politics. In addition, more and more social and political organizations appeared to take the role that the *Asafo* used to play. As a result, young men's protests began to assume different forms. Destoolment, however, continued to be a conspicuous phenomenon in the Gold Coast right up to the 1950s. Besides the commoners' fight against the chiefs, another conflict occurred between the lesser chiefs and the big chiefs, which will be discussed in next two chapters.

Notes

[1] Such as the *Native Jurisdiction Bill* (1922), the *Municipal Corporations Ordinance* (1924), the *New Constitution* (1925) and the *Native Administration Ordinance* (1927).

[2] Born in Accra in 1879, he was educated at the local Wesleyan School. He worked as a blacksmith in the Cameroon and the Belgian Congo, and an assistant engineer on a ship. From 1900 to 1908, he learned automobile engineering in Germany, then came back and worked for foreign companies. In 1917, he set up his own business as a motor engineer and general mechanic. Two years later, he was installed Ga *Mantse*. As early as 1920, his action in leasing land at Korle Lagoon was severely criticized and there was an attempt to depose him. His misconduct caused such discontent that during his reign four attempts were made to destool him. In the 1929, he was finally destooled. See *ADM11/1/1676*. Notes of evidence of enquiry, 1921; *CO96/659*. Gold Coast CO48671. See also I. S. Ephson, *Gallery of Gold Coast Celebrities* (Accra: Ilen Publications, 1969), pp.212-215.

[3] D. Fortescue, "The Accra crowd, the *Asafo* and the opposition to the Municipal Corporations Ordinance, 1924-25," *Canadian Journal of African Studies, 24:3 (1990)*, pp. 348-375; Anshan Li,

"Colonial Rule and Social Protest in Rural Ghana: A study of the Eastern Province in the Gold Coast," (PhD dissertation, University of Toronto, 1993), Chapter III.

4 J. D. De Graft Johnson, "The Fante *Asafu*," *Africa*, 5:3(1932), p.308.

5 For original documents, see *ADM11/1/712*. Case No.56/1918. Kwahu-Agogo Land Dispute. *ADM11/1/738*. Case No.11/1919. *Asafo*. origin and the powers of. *ADM11/1136*. Kwahu *Asafo*. *ADM11/1311*. Case No. ANA9/1920. Banbata Native Affairs (This file contains materials of the *Asafo* in Asante Akym.). *ADM11/1/1393*. Case No. 88/1913. Destoolment *GNA. CSO1174/31*. Kwahu *Asafo* Company Papers.

6 A. Datta and R. Porter, "The *Asafo* system in historical perspective," *Journal of African History*, 12:2(1971), pp.279-297; J. Simensen, "Commoners, Chiefs and Colonial Government: British policy and local politics in Akim Abuakwa, Ghana, under colonial rule"(PhD. Thesis, University of Trondheim, 1975); T. Johnson, "Protest: tradition and change," pp.164-193; R. Stone, "Protest: tradition and change: a critique" and T. Johnson's reply, pp.84-105.

7 M. Field, *Akim-Kotoku   An Oman of the Gold Coast*(London: The Crown Agents, 1948), pp.27-34; M. Manoukian, *Akan and Ga-Adangme Peoples of the Gold Coast*, p.46; K. A. Busia, *The Position of the Chief in the Modern Political System of Ashanti*, pp.9-10; I. Chukwukere, "Perspective on the *Asafo* institution in Southern Ghana," *Journal of African Studies*, 7:1(1980), pp.39-47.

8 Arthur Ffoulkes, "The Company system in the Cape Coast Castle," *Journal of the African Society*, 7(1907-8), pp.261-277.

9 M. Field, *Religion and Medicine of the Ga People*, p.186.

10 J. B. Christensen, *Double Descent among the Fanti* (New Haven: Human Relations Area Files, 1954), pp.107-126; Christensen, *Double Descent*, pp.111-112; Kwame Arhin, "The political and military roles of Akan women," in Christina Oppong, *Female and Male in West Africa*(London: George Allen & Unwin, 1983), pp.91-98.

11 J. S. Wartemberg, *Sao Jorge d'El Mina, Premier West African Settlement* (Ilfracombe, n.d.), p.53; E. J. P. Brown, *Gold Coast and Asianti Reader* (London: Crown Agents, 1929), Book I, pp.197-217; Kwame Arhin, "Diffuse authority among the Coastal Fanti," *Ghana Notes and Queries*, 9(1966), p.68; Porter and Datta, "The *Asafo* system," pp.279-297.

12 Meyerowitz suggests that the Fante borrowed the *Asafo* system from the Effutu, but others hold different views. See Meyerowitz, *Early History of the Akan State of Ghana* (London: Red Candle press, 1974), pp.93-96; Karikari Akyempo, *Deer Hunt Festival of the Effutus* (Accra: Anowuo Educational Pub., n.d.). R. W. Wyllie, "The *Aboakyer* of the Effutu: a critique of Meyerowitz's account," *Africa*, 37(1967), pp.81-85.

13 For example, the Christian congregation and dancing and playing clubs formed by Youngsters are all called *Asafo*. See Danquah, *Akan Laws*, p.224; Kwame Nkrumah, *Ghana, The Autobiography of Kwame*

Nkrumah (London: Thomas Nelson, 1957), p.36.

[14]For Fanti *Asafo*, see Ffloulke, "Company system," Johnson, "Fante *Asafu*" and A. Datta, "The Fante *Asafo*: a re-examination," *Africa*, 42(1972), pp.305-314. For Asante, see Busia, *The Position of the Chief*, pp.9-13; I. Wilk, *Asante in the Nineteenth Century*, pp.535-43. For Akyem Abuakwa, see J. B. Danquah, *Gold Coast Akan Laws and Customs and the Akim Abuakwa Constitution* (London: George Routledge, 1928), 119-124; Addo-Fening, "Akyem Abuakwa," pp. 447-459; Simensen, "Rural mass action." For Kwahu, see Y. Twumasi, "Aspects of Politics in Ghana, 1923-39," pp.39-44; Simensen, "*Asafo* of Kwahu." For Winneba, see M. Owusu, *Uses and Abuses of Political Power* (Chicago: University of Chicago Press, 1970), pp.40-44. For Accra, see D. Fortescue, "The Accra crowd," pp.348-375. See also I. Chukwukere, "Perspective on the *Asafo* institution in southern Ghana," pp. 39-47; J. E. Casely Hayford, *Gold Coast National Institutions*, pp.85-92; J. M. Sarbah, *Fanti National Constitution* (London: Frank Cass, 1968[1906]), pp.231-232.

[15]*ADM11/738*. Case No.11/1919. *Asafo*: origin and powers of; P. Jenkins, "Towards a definition of social tension in rural Akan communities of the high colonial period: the *asafo* movement in the Eastern Province and Eastern Asante" (Seminar paper, University of Ghana, 9 Feb, 1971).

[16]Danquah, *Gold Coast Akim Laws and Customs*, pp.16-20. J. Simensen, "Commoners, chiefs and colonial Government," pp.23a-24.

[17]The letter written by the Mayor of Cape Coast to the Chief Justice, 29 Nov. 1859. See Sarbah, *Fanti Customary Laws*, pp.12-13.

[18]R. Kea, *Settlements, Trade, and Politics in Seventeenth-Century Gold Coast* (Baltimore: The John Hopkins University Press, 1982), pp.136-7, 150, 181. D. Crummey, *Banditry, Rebellion and Social Protest in Africa* (London: James Curry, 1986), pp.109-132.

[19]Owusu, *Uses and Abuses*, p.149, no.2.

[20]Christensen, *Double Descent*, p.120.

[21]J. C. De Graft Johnson, "The significance of some Akan titles," *The Gold Coast Review*, 2:2(1927), p.218. Addo-Fening, "Akyem Abuakwa," p.23.

[22]I. Wilks, *Asante in the Nineteenth Century*, pp.534-543.

[23]*CO96/363*. Gold Coast 403. Low (Governor) to Chamberlain, 6 Oct. 1900.

[24]Agbodeka, *African Politics*, pp.135-136.

[25]Simensen, "Commoners," pp.150-152.

[26]*CO98/58*. Report on the Eastern Province for the year 1930-31. Birim District.

[27]*GNA. Adm. 11/738*. Case No.11/1919. Colin Hardings (Commissioner of Eastern Province) to the Governor, April 1920. Quoted from T. Johnson, "Protest," p.177.

[28]*CO96/473*. Ellis memo (n.d.). Encl. in Governor Rodger to Secretary of State, 8 November 1908.

[29]*ADM11/1332*. SS Conf. 2, Slater to Avery, 7 Nov. 1927. Quoted from Mikell, *Cocoa and Chaos*, p.90.

[30]*CO98/58*. Report on the Eastern Province for the Year 1930-31. Birim District.

[31]J. Agyeman-Duah, "The ceremony of enstoolment of the Asantehene," *Ghana Notes and Queries*, 7(1965), pp.8-11; Danquah, *Akan Laws and Customs*, pp.110-115.

[32]J. B. Danquah, *The Akim Abuakwa Handbook*, p.68.

[33]Casely Hayford, *Gold Coast Native Institutions*, p.33.

[34]The Akan custom used to look upon circumcision as a attribute of inferior foreign people. No stool in Akan tolerated it. Danquah, *Akan Laws and Customs*, p.116. But it is no longer regarded as a bar to the office. Agyeman-Duah, "The ceremony of enstoolment," p.8.

[35]J. M. Sarbah, *Fanti National Institution*, pp.22-24; Danquah, *Akan Laws and Customs*, pp.115-117.

[36]Rattray, *Ashanti Law and Constitution*, p.377.

[37]Busia, *The Position of the Chief*, pp.21-22.

[38]Casely Hayford, *Gold Coast Native Institutions*, pp.34-35.

[39]Danquah, *Gold Coast   Akan Laws and Customs*, pp.119-124. M. Manoukian, *Akan and Ga-Adangme Peoples*, p.45.

[40]C. W. Welman, *The Native States of the Gold Coast   History and Constitutions   Part I   Peki* (London: Dawsons, 1969 [1925]), pp.42-43.

[41]Danquah, *Akan Laws and Customs*, p.115.

[42]J. Dupuis, *Journal of a Residence in Ashantee*, p.245.

[43]T. E. Bowdich, *Mission from Cape Coast Castle to Ashantee* (London: Frank Cass, 1966[1819]), pp.238-240.

[44]Busia, *Position of Chief*, p.99.

[45]Reindorf, *History of the Gold Coast and Asante*, pp.29-30.

[46]Since the Danes refused to recognize the *Mankralo*, half the people returned to the *Mantse* recognized by the Danes, and hostility between the *Mantse* and *Mankralo* existed till quite recently. Field, *Social Organization*, pp.76-77.

[47]Busia, *Position of Chief*, p.211.

[48]*GNA. Adm.11/457*. Eastern Province Commissioner to Secretary for Native Affairs, 5 Nov. 1908. Quoted from Simensen, "Commoners, Chiefs and Colonial Government," p.64.

[49] *CO96/528*. Gold Coast, (Confidential). Clifford to Secretary of State, 3 March 1913.

[50] *CO96/601*. Gold Coast 530. Native Affairs Department Report for 1918. Encl in Acting Governor Slater to Viscount Miller, 27 June 1919.

[51] Simensen, "Commoners," pp. 141-160.

[52] *CO98/45*. "A review of the events of 1921-22 and the prospects of 1922-23," Governor Guggisberg's Address to Legislative Council, 27 Feb. 1922.

[53] *The Gold Coast Time*, March 19 1927.

[54] Mikell, *Cocoa and Chaos in Ghana*, p.142.

[55] *CO98/50*. Report on the Eastern Province for the year 1927-8. *CO98/53*. Report on the Eastern Province for the year 1928-9. *Government Gazette*, 1927-29.

[56] *CO96/699/7050A*. Income Tax and protest. Minute. *CO96/704/7260*. G.C. Confidential. Governor to Lister, 31 March 1932; Acting Governor to Lister, 20 August, 1932. See also Stanley Shaloff, "The income tax, indirect rule, and the Depression: the Gold Coast riots of 1931," *Cahier d'etudes Africaines*, No.54, 14:2(1974), pp.359-375; Addo-Fening, ed., *Akyem Abuakwa and Politics of the Inter-war Period in Ghana*, pp.31-57, 90-104.

[57] Quoted form Simensen, "Commoners," p.255.

[58] *Legislative Council Debates*. 29 September 1942. pp.3-4.

[59] W. E. F. Ward, *A History of Ghana* (London: George Allen & Unwin, 1967), p.363.

[60] For the period 1948-51, see *CO554/702*. "Destoolment of Chiefs in the Gold Coast," Governor of the Gold Coast to Secretary of State, 6 December 1951.

[61] Sarbah, *Fanti National Institution*, pp.134-135.

[62] Kimble, *Political History*, pp.469-473; Wight, *Gold Coast Legislative Council*, pp.180-181.

[63] *CO96/654*. Gold Coast Secret, CO18836. G17152/T19212. Guggisberg to L. S. Amery (M.P.), 4 April 1925.

[64] *CO96/567*. Gold Coast (Confidential). Clifford to Secretary of State, 26 May 1916.

[65] *CO96/380*. A land dispute between the Chief of Pankesi under the King of West Akim and the Chiefs of Obo and Obomeng under the King of Kwahu. Gold Coast (Confidential), 13 May 1901.

[66] Welman, *The Native States*, pp.32-35.

[67] Kimble, *Political History*, p.463, no.4.

[68] Busia, *Position of Chief*, p.38 *ADM11/1393*. Acting Commissioner of Eastern Province to Acting Secretary for Native Affairs, 13 August 1930.

[69]*ADM11/1/738.* Case No.11/1919. New orders and regulations inaugurated by the whole Kwahu *Asafo*s at Abetifi on the 6th November 1917. See Appendix.

[70]*GNA. CSO 1174/31.* Akuamoa Boateng II to Ofori Atta I, 30 Dec. 1927. Encl. in Kwahu *Asafo* Company Papers. Twumasi, "Aspects," pp.41-42.

[71]*ADM11/1/738.* Case No.11/1919. Report on the Akim *asafo* by the District Commissioner, Kwahu 1919; *ADM11/1/1311.* A.N.A9/1920. Bompata Native Affairs.

[72]*CO98/48.* Annual report of the Eastern Province for the financial year 1926-27.

[73]Max Weber, *From Max Weber: Essays in Sociology* (New York: Oxford University Press, 1958), trans. & ed. by H. Gerth & C. Wright Mills, p.294.

[74]Danquah, *Akim Abuakwa Handbook*, p.68.

[75]*Chiefs Ordinance*, 1904, Sec. 29.

[76]*Colonial Report: Ashanti, 1920.*

[77]*CO98/55.* Report on the Eastern Province 1929-30.

[78]*CO98/44.* Ga *Mantse* Incident, p.14.

[79]Christensen, *Double Descent*, p.117.

[80]*CO96/718/21755/A.* Annual Report on the Eastern Province 1933-34. Encl. in Gold Coast No.457, 12 Sept. 1934.

[81]*CO96/543.* Gold Coast Confidential (A). Clifford to Secretary of State, 24 Mar. 1914.

[82]Sir Gordon Guggisberg, *Gold Coast: A review of the events of 1920-1926 and prospects of 1927-28* (Accra: Government Printer, 1927), p.238.

[83]Wight, *Gold Coast Legislative Council*, p.36, W. M. Macmillan, "Political and social reconstruction, the peculiar case of the Gold Coast," in C. K. Meek, ed. *Europe and Africa* (London: Oxford University Press, 1940), pp.94-115.

[84]*CO96/593.* Confidential Report of Native Affairs for 1917. Encl. in Clifford to Secretary of State, 9 October 1918.

[85]*CO96/543.* Gold Coast, Confidential(A). Clifford to Secretary of State, 24 March 1914. *CO96/567.* Gold Coast, Confidential. Clifford to Secretary of State, 26 May 1916.

[86]*CO99/33.* "Governor's address to the Legislative Council, 28 Oct. 1918," *Government Gazette*, 1918, No.82 (Extraordinary).

[87]*CO96/614.* Note on conference on Native Jurisdiction Bill with the Legislative Council Chiefs. 24 Feb. 1920. Encl. in Confidential to Secretary of State. 7 July 1920.

[88] *CO96/718/21755A.* Annual report on the Eastern Province 1933-34. Encl. in Gold Coast No.457. 14 September 1934.

[89] Kimble, *A Political History,* pp.98-105.

[90] Addo-Fening, ed., *Akyem Abuakwa and Politics of the Inter-war Period in Ghana,* p.48.

[91] *CO96/711.* Gold Coast No. 468. S. Thomas to P. Cunlifffe Lister, 19 Aug. 1933. A specific case was detailed in *CO96/706.* Northcote to P. C. Lister, 18 Aug. 1932.

[92] Busia, *Position of Chief,* p. 208. See also next two chapters.

[93] *GNA. CSO 1174/31.* "Review of Evidence and Recommendations" in "Kwahu *Asafo* Company Papers." Quoted from Twumasi, "Aspects," p.43.

[94] *Ashanti Confederacy Council Minutes.* Jan. 1936. In 1938, when the Cocoa Farmers' Union began to ask for a recognized position, the colonial official opposed to their claim to be the representatives of the people, a colonial officer suggested that "The *Asafo* movement has seriously impaired the authority of many Chiefs in the Colony, and the present organisation though in no way political in its aims, is in my opinion a potential source of danger in the future unless the Chiefs take control promptly." *GNA.AC/ACC.No.1510/57.* Warrington for Chief Commissioner to District Commissioners Ashanti, Kumasi, 17 February 1938.

[95] E. Meyerowitz, *The Sacred State of the Akan* (London: Faber & Faber, 1949), p.67. In 1955, some *Asafo* company members were among the protesters against the imposition of new property rates. Owusu, *Uses and Abuses of Political Power,* p.217.

[96] *ADM11/1797.* Case No.1501. Yilo Krobo Native Affairs. Petition by *Asafoatse* Narh Dedu III, 21 April 1941; Petition of the *Asafoiatsemei* of Yilo Krobo about the payment of levy, 22 December 1948. Chief Commissioner to Colonial Secretary, 18 February 1949.

CHAPTER IV

Asamankese Affair: The Small against the Big (I)

In February 1919 diamonds were discovered in Asamankese and Akwatia lands in Akyem Abuakwa, a district in the Eastern Province.[1] This led to a change of attitude of the *Ohene* (Divisional Chief) of Asamankese and the *Odikro* (chief) of Akwatia towards the *Omanhene* (Paramount Chief) of Akyem Abuakwa. They both began to claim their independent status and insisted that their relation with Akyem Abuakwa be cut off. The dispute turned into a legal action and lasted for more than fifteen years..

Akyem Abuakwa-Asamankese Dispute

Land Control in Akyem Abuakwa

In the Gold Coast, land tenure varied. The Akan saying "all power rests in the land" shows how the people valued their land. According to tradition, the chief was the guardian of all lands belonging to the town. In practice, the lineages and individual families were in possession of the land they had cleared. All land not under cultivation was regarded as public land or "stool land." Strangers could be admitted to the stool lands, either as tenants or through purchase. But the purchase of stool lands had to be acknowledged by the State Councils.[2]

The relationship between the chief and the Paramount Chief was not entirely clear in matters of land tenure. Among the Akan, although the customary concepts of ownership and land holding were not precisely formalized, the transfer of political authority never meant the transfer of land ownership. According to Casely Hayford, "The paramount King, as such, has no right to exact tribute, nor is his consent necessary to make a grant valid."[3] Akyem Abuakwa, together with other two Akyem states (Akyem Kotoku and Akyem Bosome) was even more extraordinary. Manoukian once pointed out that because of their peculiar history, the three Akyem states differed from other Akan states in their relationship between land and *oman* (state). The nature of each state was rather a military union than a political unity.[4] There was no question that the land should be attached. Margaret Field showed in her study of Akyem Kotoku that "Even when a *Omanhene* virtually forced a defenseless town to come under his banner he never touched or attempted to control its land."[5] Therefore, the relationship between political allegiance and land ownership was casual and informal.

This informality began to change, however, with the establishment of colonial rule and especially with the introduction of the cocoa and mining industries at the end of the nineteenth century. Chiefs began to sell or lease lands to foreigners, without much concern about either their subjects or the paramount stool. The Paramount Chief, on the other hand, tried to control the land deal as much as possible on the ground of the protection of public interests. It seems that chiefs were the main dealers in land. To describe the situation at Akyem Abuakwa, J. B. Danquah emphasized that it was the chief who was the seller, "Our chiefs are very fond of selling lands, especially when they can find a specious reason for it, e.g. to pay for the costs of a Stool land litigation in the Supreme Court, to pay off an old standing debt, or to perform the funeral custom of a deceased Chief."[6]

Polly Hill seems very sure about the right of the chief, rather than the Paramount Chief, to alienate the land of Akyem Abuakwa to the outsiders. "The reckless and unconditional sellers, those who took advantage of the opportunities provided by the flexible traditional system, which tolerated occurrences on a scale which had never been envisaged, were the **sub-chiefs** [my emphasis] in whom the real power resided; there was no disputing that they possessed the right to relieve 'public indebtedness' by selling public lands." She believes that in 1929 as in about 1907, the sub-chiefs acted independently and "quite knew what they were doing."[7]

Although a Concessions Ordinance was passed in 1900, very few people cared about it. The Deputy Governor complained to the Secretary of State in 1913 that "the Ordinance places little or no check on the alienation of their land by the representatives of the native proprietors." He pointed out a real danger existed: "serious wrong being inflicted on the general members of a community by restrictions being placed on their free cultivation of the land which they share in common when the uncontrolled action of their rulers has allowed it to become the subject of concessions."[8] The tendency of selling land had been well under way at the end of the nineteenth century and was still spreading. This trend was clearly shown in the following table:

Table III   Alienation before 1914

Total area of the Gold Coast Colony	24,335 square miles
Total alienation by natives notified in gazette	25,108 square miles
Total struck out by the Courts	10,279 square miles
Total remaining alienated 1913	14,829 square miles
Total area the alienation of which is validated by the Courts up to 1914	1,084 square miles

Source: R. L. Buell, *The Native Problem in Africa*, (London: Frank Cass, 1962), Vol.I, p.822.

The figures show that the Gold Coast chiefs had signed away an area larger than the total area of the Colony. Akyem Abuakwa was already involved in the commercialization of land and there the area formally leased exceeded the total area of the state![9] There was a special form of land deal called *guaha* ceremony. This was the customary act of conveyance necessary for the validation of sales, which existed in Akyem Abuakwa and other areas. The purpose of the ceremony was to placate the spirits who were obliged to move away owing to the transfer of ownership, to inform the permanent spirits of the place, to ask them to help the newcomers, and to provide evidence for future reference.[10] The *guaha* ceremony generally included the presentation of rum, demarcation of the area and payment of the price.[11] Inhabitants of neighboring districts (such as people from Akuapem, Kwahu and Krobo) had gradually acquired ownership of half of the Akyem Abuakwa territory.[12] The process was speeded up by the control of land concessions by the courts rather than by executive authority. Although the colonial government had tried to control land transaction from the very beginning, it never succeeded.

There are various explanations of land control, and different terms were used to describe land deals. In a report of 1938, it was stated that "Land has been in great demand. The custodians of tribal, stool and family lands... have welcomed the opportunity of easy money."[13] Who were those "custodians"? This was the key-point in the Akyem Abuakwa-Asamankese dispute.

The Origins of the Dispute

Since the government was reluctant to impose a land policy, the Paramount Chiefs made the best use of their power. Asamankese was the first capital of Akwamu, which was conquered by the Akyem in the early eighteenth century.[14] Asamankese then was integrated into Akyem Abuakwa State. It was placed under the Oseawuo wing of Akyem Abuakwa. From then on its stool was represented in the State Council; and it participated in the Council's regular meetings and accepted its jurisdiction.[15]

Early in June 1901, the *Omanhene* of Akyem Abuakwa Nana Amoako Atta II told the Colonial Secretary: "It is the fashion and customary from beginning of this Akim throne that whenever any of the Akims had to make a sale of land or happened to obtain a rock of gold or any valuable metal from any part or parts of any land the party is bound by our rule to give up one third of the said product to the stool but nowadays the people are unwilling to do so as it is customary to be done." The following year witnessed the promulgation by the State Council of a new law prohibiting the alienation of land without the consent of the Paramount Chief. With an increasing demand for concessions, land continued to be sold without permission. Soon after his enstoolment at the end of 1912, the *Omanhene* Nana Ofori Atta realized the implicit dangers in all these land deals and decided to control the situation. The State Council passed a series of by-laws in 1914 stating that land alienation be prohibited and the timber and forests be reserved to the stool. The by-laws also prohibited the felling of trees by the purchasers of the land or by their relatives or heirs for the purpose of selling for a profitable use.[16]

Nana Ofori Atta also began to resolve land problems with neighboring districts. In 1915, he had a case with Taffo, another Akwamu town in Akyem Abuakwa. Thanks to intervention by the government, the problem was settled quickly. Ofori Atta showed continued determination to strengthen his control over land.[17] In 1927 when the Native Administration Ordinance was put into effect, he deposed several chiefs for their involvement in land deals.[18]

In July 1913, the *Ohene* Kwahu Amoah wrote to the *Omanhene* to acknowledge the receipt of all the letters concerning or prohibiting the sale of lands. "I have also by your instruction forwarded same to the Chiefs under me so far from here to Akanten and thence to Akwatia and Kade." It seems that the *Ohene* acknowledged the authority of the *Omanhene*, and there was no sign of resistance. But in reality, he had been selling land without notifying the *Omanhene*. In July 1916, the *Omanhene* found out about *Ohene*'s land deals of four years earlier and asked for his share. Kwahu Amoah sent an amount of £86.15 to the *Omanhene* and apologized for the delay in handing over the one-fourth share of the proceeds of a land sale. In a letter to the *Omanhene*, he stated: "Nana it was never my intention to make or order, so far as the laws and customs of this realm are concerned for selling land without your notice; nor can I forfeit any such amount of yours through an illegal practice that had not been before practised [*sic*] by any of my predecessors."[19]

This case revealed the duplicity of the *Ohene*. On the one hand, he acknowledged the by-laws of the State Council and showed his respect to the

Omanhene, on the other hand, he was involved in land deals without reporting them. Although the situation became a bit complicated, it was under control, and the forwarding of the share indicated the obedience of the *Ohene*. An open conflict began in 1919 when diamonds were found in Akwatia, and Ofori Atta insisted that as a Paramount Chief he should take part in the deal of a land concession in Asamankese. *Ohene* Kwaku Amoah resisted this demand and was fined £26 for the contumacy. He admitted that "this was the first act objected to by us and this started the difference between us and the *Omanhene*."[20]

The Conflict

On 27 June 1921, the *Ohene* of Asamankese wrote a letter to the Paramount Chief of Akyem Abuakwa, intimating that he and his elders should not be counted upon by the State Council and that the by-laws and regulations passed by the State Council should not be communicated to them. In October, the stools of Asamankese and Akwatia petitioned the Governor to be allowed to withdraw their allegiance to the Paramount Stool of Akyem Abuakwa. The petition was refused, but the petitioners acted in all matters as if they were independent of the paramount stool. In early 1922 the *Omanhene* brought their behavior to the notice of the government. Governor Guggisberg decided to have an enquiry that the *Ohene* of Asamankese would be required to attend. The *Ohene* failed to appear at the enquiry, the Governor deposed him and the *Odikro* in March 1923 after the charges had been heard by the Executive Council.[21]

In 1927 the conflict gained new momentum when the Native Administration Ordinance was enacted. This Ordinance transferred to State Councils the responsibility for dealing with cases in which persons were charged with undermining the authority or usurping the position of a Paramount Chief.[22] Ofori Atta, who was responsible for the preparation of the draft, made the best use of the opportunity to strengthen his own power by promoting the centralization in his district. He stated that the main purpose of the Ordinance was to provide a remedy against political instability in the form of breakaway or destoolment.[23]

In 1929, Ofori Atta arrested thirty-six people from Asamankese and put them into the local prison. According to their petition, they were "subjected to the most inhuman treatment by Nana Ofori Atta and those acting with him." [24] A Commission of Enquiry was appointed to inquire into the political relationship between the stools of Asamankese and Akwatia and the paramount stool. Commissioner Mr. Justice Hall delivered his award on September 9 1929. It stated that the stool of Asamankese was a sub-stool of the paramount stool of Akyem Abuakwa and a similar ruling was given as to the stool of Akwatia.[25] Regarding the right of alienation, the assent of the paramount stool was "not necessary for the valid alienation of lands held by the stools of Asamangkese and Akwatia," but the paramount stool was "entitled to receive one third equal part share of all rents and profits of lands alienated by the stools of Asamangkese and Akwatia or either of them."[26]

Immediately following the delivery of this award, the *Ohene* took action to have the award set aside in the courts. This action went all the way to the Privy Council in London. In November 1932 the Privy Council delivered judgment in favor of the defendant, the *Omanhene* of Akyem Abuakwa.

In 1930 the government decided to interfere in the case and declared that it would not accept any attempt by Asamankese to separate. Then the *Omanhene* sent to Asamankese for conciliation a delegation headed by *Benkumhene*. But during his stay in Asamankese, two shooting incidents occurred and the rebellious Asamankese became enraged.[27] In December 1932, after the announcement of the Privy Council's decision, the *Ohene* took action against the *Omanhene* and State Council. In April 1933, Chief Justice gave a judgment in the defendant's favor. The *Ohene* made an appeal to the West African Court of Appeal. At the end of November 1933, the case was dismissed by the West African Court of Appeal.

After Mr. Justice Hall's award in 1929, one third of all subsequent receipts in respect of rents and profits from Asamankese concessions awarded to the *Omanhene* was kept on deposit by the government. When the Privy Council delivered its judgment confirming Mr. Justice Hall's award, the Paramount Chief became entitled to the money on deposit. The *Ohene*'s lawyers had endeavored by a series of motions to prevent the payment of this money to the Paramount Chief. The West African Court of Appeal decided the case against them in November 1933.[28]

In 1935, the Asamankese Division Regulation Ordinance was passed and the government decided that stool treasures be established to control the finance of the division. This Ordinance strengthened the central control over the local administration and deprived the Asamankese of the means to continue litigation against the *Omanhene*. However, the dispute lingered on until 1938 when the final decision was made by the colonial government to control the treasures of Asamankese and Akwatia. The *Ohene* of Asamankese and the *Odikro* of Akwatia went to Kyebi to swear their allegiance to the *Omanhene* before the State Council.[29]

The Protest: The Small against the Big

This protest had its typical characteristics: the full use of legal tools and active participation of lawyers, the prolongation and wide involvement of the case, and the direct attack upon colonial rule and the damage to its prestige. Since B. M. Edsman has already studied in detail the lawyers' role,[30] this chapter will concentrate on the other two features.

The Stages of the Protest

The Akyem Abuakwa-Asamankese case began in 1921 and ended in 1938, lasting for seventeen years. During this period, Asamankese and Akwatia sent many petitions for their separation and laid several actions against the Paramount Chief. The victories and losses for both parties caused anxiety, aspiration and expectation. During the dispute, a great variety people were involved, such as commoners, elders, Divisional Chiefs, Paramount Chiefs, colonial officials and lawyers both at home and in Britain. At first, the quarrel was triggered by the rental fee. But it soon developed so dramatically that the protesters began to mount their grievances, and finally it became linked with the nationalist protest against British colonialism.

Asamankese and Akwatia were trying to make clear that they did not come under the authority of the Paramount Chief of Akyem Abuakwa. The *Ohene* was totally against the idea that he was subject to the *Oserwuhene* of Wenchi and thus subordinate to the Paramount Stool in Kyebi, the capital of Akyem Abuakwa. As to the relationship between Akyem Abuakwa and Asamankese, the *Ohene* suggested that originally there was an alliance by marriage which later led to an agreement for mutual defense against a common foe.[31] The *Ohene* later complained that the *Omanhene* had ignored the relationship, and that "he has been subjecting my stool to treatment for which there is no precedent in the tradition of the two stools." The Paramount Stool's attitude was described as "a dominant stool towards a servient [*sic*] stool."[32] The *Ohene* was very strongly opposed to the *Omanhene*'s intention to be a joint-grantor with him. He also objected the *Omanhene*'s decision to increase tax on the Dwaben people in Asamankese.[33]

The most important complaint was against the *Omanhen*'s treatment of arrested Asamankese or sympathetic non-Asamankese. Some were fined, and others were taken to prison and cruelly mistreated. The petitioners listed fifteen grievances and the most important were that on their arrival at Kyebi, they were beaten and humiliated in an obscene way. In a reply to the Governor who wrote to the *Ohene* of Asamankese for conciliation after Mr. Justice Hall's award, the *Ohene* expressed his outrage about the ill-treatment of his subjects and refused the Governor's offer, "All these and several ill treatment made the position very bad that no subject of mine will now chose to follow me to go to Kibi to serve the *Omanhene*."[34]

Although there might be some exaggeration in his response, the anger was evident, and the situation deteriorated. "We were never a conquered people, and none of the *Omanhene*'s predecessors ever attempted to take such liberty with us as he is now doing."[35] The *Ohene* of Asamankese and the *Odikro* of Akwatia sent a petition to the Secretary of State, requesting that they "be freed by legislation or executive order from further service to the Paramount Stool of Nana Sir Ofori Atta."[36]

Finally the incident was carried to London and was used by the opposition in the House of Commons in their attack on colonialism. This case first appeared in Britain in 1923; later the petitions came to London quite often, either directly or through the Governor. On several occasions the anti-colonial wing in Parliament raised questions about the rapid passage of the Asamankese Ordinance of 1935 and the alleged forged letters from Ofori Atta to the government requesting assistance in coercing the rebels.[37]

The West African Youth League, a radical anti-imperialist organization led by Wallace-Johnson, had an active branch in Asamankese, which was also involved in the case. As a nationalist from Sierra Leone, Wallace-Johnson had received training in labor organization in Moscow. He tried to use this dispute to fight against the collaborators of colonial rule. One of the actions of the Youth League was to sponsor a mass protest against the Asamankese Division Bill and against the treatment of the Asamankese people arrested by Ofori Atta's local police. Using his linkage with the left wing in London and the Gold Coast, Wallace-Johnson attacked most severely the injustice suffered by the Asamankese people.[38]

The Impact of the Protest

This case was not a protest against the *Omanhene* alone. The Asamankese's defiance of the government's authority severely damaged the prestige of colonial rule, as shown at least on three occasions.

The first case occurred in 1922. After the *Odikro* of Akwatia was arrested on 24 July 1922, Asamankese filed a case against the *Omanhene* and five government officials who were charged with application of threat of force, false imprisonment and conspiracy with the *Omanhene* of Akim Abuakwa.[39] This might be a bad manoeuvre in terms of tactics, but the direct attack upon the government was a very bold move. In 1925 when the Governor reported to the colonial office the *Ohene's* action, he made it clear that the government should take the responsibility and support Ofori Atta, since the "*Omanhene* has been put to very great expense already over this action which is aimed more at the Government Officials than at him."[40] The alliance between the government and the *Omanhene* made it impossible for the Asamankese to fight against the Paramount Stool without offending the government.

The second example was the Asamankese's attitude towards the government's order. On 28 March 1923 the Governor deposed the *Ohene* of Asamankese and the

Odikro of Akwatia, but Kwaku Amoah continued to be recognized by the elders and people as their *Ohene*, thus making the deposition invalid. According to the District Commissioner in Kyebi who complained of the situation after the deposition, "Whatever may have been the result expected, the order which in effect only prevented the *Ohene* from presiding over his tribunal, has merely served to increase his popularity." In reply to the order, the elders, while questioning the Governor's authority to depose the *Ohene*, stated that they would continued to observe Kwaku Amoah as their chief and would take no orders from the Government except through him. The people of Asamankese "have openly and with impunity defied the authority of government."[41]

The Native Administration Ordinance transferred to the State Council the power to depose and deport chiefs who attempted to separate from their superior chiefs. The *Omanhene* Ofori Atta complained of difficulty in applying the Ordinance to Asamankese. "Under the Ordinance, the State Council can with the approval of government, deport a subordinate chief whenever he sets up a claim of independence of his superior stool. Under the late NJO (Native Jurisdiction Ordinance), the *Ohene* of Asamangkese was deposed by government but, having remained practically as *Ohene* before his people, we cannot deal with him as a chief to be deported under NAO."[42] Later in 1929, in order to clear the way for the final settlement by the Commission of Enquiry, the government had to reinstate the *Ohene* of Asamankese and the *Odikro* of Akwatia![43] The deposition and reinstatement of the two rebellious chiefs showed the indecision and incapability of the colonial government.

The third blow to colonial prestige occurred after Mr. Justice Hall delivered his arbitration award. Although both parties agreed beforehand that they would accept the arbitration, the *Ohene* now found it favored the *Omanhene* and decided to set it aside. In his letter to the Governor, the *Ohene* made his point quite clearly: "The award given by the Arbitrator cannot be considered as a sufficient ground upon which the final and peaceful settlement of the disputes between myself and the *Omanhene* can be arrived at."[44]

Although the Commission was originally suggested by the *Ohene's* lawyers, they now held that it was irregular to trust the case to a colonial officer, who "completely misunderstood and disregarded the evidence of tradition and the evidence of Native Custom, and that he came to an inconsistent conclusion as to tradition and Native Custom." Furthermore, according to Section 34 of the Native Administration Ordinance that prescribed the State Council as the forum for an enquiry into constitutional disputes between a Paramount Chief and his Divisional Chief, the matter should not have been submitted to arbitration by Mr. Justice Hall and hence the award could have no legal effect.[45]

Owing to the repeated defiance of the authority of the government by Asamankese, the government had to change its policy constantly.[46] The protest of the small chiefs against their Paramount Chiefs in order to win their independent status was a very common problem under colonial rule. The settlement of the Asamankese-Akim Abuakwa dispute did check this tendency, but at a high price.

The Causes

There are various interpretations of the cause of the Asamankese-Akim Abuakwa dispute. J. Simensen argues that the essence of the dispute was control of the diamond money.[47] B. M. Edsman holds that after 1927 the Asamankese dispute was "in essence an ARPS campaign against the NAO (Native Administration Ordinance), Ofori Atta, and a constitution which excluded the educated elite."[48] A. B. Holmes blames Kobina Sekyi and those vicious lawyers who intentionally prolonged the case for their own benefits.[49] Addo-Fening has traced its historical origins and suggests that the cause was "a wrangle between Nana Ofori Atta and the two chiefs over matters of title and interest in the Asamankese and Akwatia lands."[50] In order to get a clearer picture, it might be better for us to view the case in its broad historical context.

Traditional Law and British Attitude

Holmes argues in his thesis that the case was utterly hopeless for Asamankese and Akwatia for two reasons: "Not only was the government just as determined to stand by its chief ally in the Colony, Nana Sir Ofori Atta, but also the whole weight of pure native tradition as well as the statutory laws of the land stood squarely behind Ofori Atta."[51]

The first reason is correct, but the second does not seem quite accurate. Neither "native tradition" nor "statutory laws of land" really "stood squarely behind Ofori Atta." As suggested above, in Akyem Abuakwa the seller of the land was not the *Omanhene* himself, but sub-chiefs, the successors of those who had been settled on the land for several centuries.

The fundamental difference between the Akan and western body politic lies in the fact that Akan political system reflected temporary military convenience instead of permanent social needs. This system was decentralized and fostered lesser loyalties from the local communities.[52] Casely Hayford wrote about the subordinate chief paying the "allegiance fee" to the Paramount Chief as a customary present, which was not a tribute in the sense that the latter could exact it as a right. Casely Hayford once said, "Indeed, the custom of the paramount Chief to receive an occasional contribution, be it small or be it large, is in respect of allegiance due to him by a subordinate Chief. Where a paramount Chief happens to receive *abusa*, that is, one-third share, of the proceeds of land, then it is by reason of the fact that the right **to possess** is ultimately traceable to his stool... and the case where a paramount Chief receives a customary present, the extent of it depending upon circumstances, upon the happening of any event in respect of which the subordinate may suitably mark his allegiance to the superior Chief." He also made it clear that allegiance was personal and not territorial.[53]

In his study of Akyem Abukwa history, Simensen points out that at the beginning of colonial rule, the administrative power of the *Omanhene* was weak, mainly because the Akan model of political organization did not admit of strong centralization.[54] This less centralized form of politics could hardly cope with a rapidly changing situation. Even Holmes himself notices that the traditional laws and rules were not able to deal with the massive influence of alien cocoa farmers renting and buying land or large-scale concessions to European mineral exploiters.[55]

The crucial reason for the prolongation of the dispute was the reluctance of the government to deal with it. Its hesitation can be traced to the origin of British rule in the Gold Coast. The Bond of 1844 had an "increasing psychological importance in determining local attitudes towards British protection."[56] Whenever the British tried to interfere in the local affairs, such as the Land Bill of 1897, or the Forest Ordinance in 1911, the Gold Coast activists would cite the Bond as a proof that they were not a conquered people and it was up to them to decide their own business.[57] As a consequence, the colonial government had to care to some extent about the reaction of the people. For example, even in 1929 when the Ofori Atta asked the government to interfere directly, the government refused on the ground that "should the town be brought under the Peace Preservation Ordinance, the Asamangkese people will consider that they have been unfairly treated and that government had been biased by Sir Ofori Atta."[58] Unlike other British colonies where it was common to solve the scarcity of labor by depriving local people of their land, the Gold Coast had its own characteristic. The introduction of cocoa created a new local economy and provided many opportunities for the people. Since the government failed to introduce the land bill at the very beginning, local authorities had more autonomy to deal with land, which contributed to the prosperity of cocoa industry. After the abolition of the slave trade, efforts to develop a plantation system were not successful. Even during World War I, the Empire Resources Committee argued in favor of plantations for the exploitation of the colonial empire, but in vain. Apter suggests that the government preferred that there be no sudden shattering of traditional social patterns.[59] But the more important reason was that the Gold Coast had gradually become the world's leading cocoa producer, and the government feared that any sudden shift towards large-scale production could jeopardize this favorable trading position. This fear may also explain why the government gradually became reluctant to pursue a policy of direct control of land. Another reason for the dispute was British ignorance of traditional institutions in the Gold Coast. In the early period, the colonial government failed to differentiate either in category or in jurisdiction between Paramount Chiefs and Divisional Chiefs. Referring to the settlement of a dispute between Awuna chiefs as to the election of a *Fia* (King) for all Awuna in 1906, the chiefs complained in a letter to the government "The disagreement among the Chiefs of this nation referred to in the first meeting usually occur [*sic*] when a Commissioner inclines a hearing ear to the misrepresentations of one Chief of the others to act upon the same. In fact, some Chiefs, comparatively in a low position having the privilege of frequent access to Commissioner, claim superiority of position over the others, whilst among the natives, practically they are never acknowledged." In other words, without accurate knowledge of chiefs' ranks, the officers could never settle the problem properly.[60]

The same thing occurred in Asamankese. The *Ohene* Kwahu Amoah used to be favored by the colonial government for his experience and capability in local administration. Before the District Commissioner was appointed in Kyebi, Traveling Commissioners from Accra frequently arranged matters in nearby Asamankese instead of going to the *Omanhene* in Kyebi. Land cases were also taken directly to the Divisional Court in Accra for settlement. Hence the *Omanhene* Ofori Atta complained that the British attitude towards local affairs in effect had created the feeling of separateness in Asamankese.

Economic Benefits

The Asamankese were mostly non-Akyems who were left behind after the Akwamus were defeated by the Akyems and fled across the Volta River about 1730. They did not feel that they owed any allegiance to the paramount stool in Kyebi although they had made no demands for independence for two hundred years.[61] As one of the twelve divisions, the Asamankese stool was one of the largest landowners in Akyem Abuakwa, controlling the area between the Apapam and Apedwa tracts to the south. It also had the largest population among the twelve divisions.[62] The Asamankese area was highly attractive to immigrant farmers. Ga and Shai people had early moved in from the south, and by the beginning of World War I, Akuapem and Krobo farmers had reached the Asamankese area from the east. In addition there was a community of Dwabens in the area.

After the discovery of diamonds in Akwatia in 1919, the African Selection Trust started land concessions and mining operations. The high revenue accrued to the stools of Asamankese and Akwatia, which made Asamankese one of the richest stools in the Colony. But the Asamankese *Ohene* refused to admit that the *Omanhene* had any right to a share of the profits. During the period 1925-35 the total revenue of £99,175 had come to the stools of Asamankese and Akwatia.[63] The success of Asamankese secession thus meant that more than £3,000 a year was being withheld from the paramount stool.

Besides the rental fee from the mining companies, the system of rent payments guaranteed a substantial income from immigrant farmers. About one hundred settler villages in the division were put under the supervision of "headmen" or "holders" appointed by the *Ohene*. Those royal members benefited from this position and received *abusa* regularly from the settlers, from £5 to £12 per farmer, or £50 to £200 per village. One third of the rent was kept as remuneration by the headman collector while the rest went to Asamankese. To acknowledge the authority of the paramount stool could mean the loss of these benefits.

The Paramount Chief was no less interested in the profits than the Asamankese. In 1920 the State Council of Akyem Abuakwa decided to increase the paramount share of land money from one fourth to one third. This move was obviously linked to the profitable situation in Asamankese. During the whole dispute, the paramount stool spent about £100,000. However, he made a clever move by persuading the African Selection Trust to advance him a loan equivalent to his share of the concession money until the appeal case had been ended. He began to receive his share after the Asamankese's appeal against the Hall award failed. He received his first payment of £6,900 in 1932 for the three years of 1929-32.[64]

The lawyers involved also benefited financially from the dispute. Several prominent lawyers were actively involved in the case, such as A. W. Kojo Thompson, Thomas Hutton Mills and Kobina Sekyi. Mills took land instead of cash for his service to the *Ohene* of Asamankese and also served as a mediator in negotiating certain gold mining concessions for European firms in Asamankese. Although it was not clear how much Asamankese spent on litigation, up to April 1932, Kobina Sekyi had received as retainer £5,889.[65] But he was not satisfied with the payment. In a letter to the new *Ohene* of Asamankese, he made it clear that he wanted more payment on a regular basis.[66]

Evidence shows that economics played an important role in the Akyem Abuakwa-Asamankese land dispute. No wonder the Secretary for Native Affairs concluded in his report, "Most of the troubles and unrest originated from persons who were financially interested in the continuance of the dispute."[67]

The Native Administration Ordinance

The Native Jurisdiction Ordinance revised in 1919 sought to distinguish the head chiefs from other chiefs; to state the extent of their jurisdiction in land cases; to make the government the arbitrator in stool dispute; and to give Provincial Commissioner more effective control over tribunals.[68] However the Bill was withdrawn because of the strong protest from both the educated people and chiefs. Introduced in 1922, it was again dropped. In 1925, Governor Guggisberg decided to hand over the preparation of the Bill to Ofori Atta. Simensen considers the decision extraordinary, and suggests that this must be a unique event in the history of colonial legislation in the British African territories.

In 1927 the new Native Administration Ordinance was enacted, which offered greater power to the paramount stool. However, the Paramount Chief could hardly exercise the power owing to lack of legitimacy.[69] What is more, since Ofori Atta did not consult with the Divisional Chiefs concerning the draft, many of them laid complaints, causing great disturbance in the Gold Coast.[70] According to a complaint sent to the government after a protest meeting held on March 19 1927 in Accra, the new ordinance would take away "the traditional safeguards of the people against the development of our national system of democratic Monarchical rule into a system of autocratic;" "confers Paramount Chiefs rights which never belonged or could belong to them under the constitutions of our Native State." Moreover, it "reduces the position of the Sub-Chiefs or Chiefs or Head-Chiefs from the position of equals of the Paramount Chiefs in matter affecting the regions over which their responsive Stools are supreme."[71]

The most severe protest came from the Eastern Province. Several Paramount Chiefs resigned from the Provincial Council under pressure from their people. A chief was deposed because he introduced and promulgated to the Oman the Native Administration Ordinance "without first seeking the permission of the Oman or gaining their consent."[72] According to the 1928 petition by the Aborigines' Rights Protection Society, of the sixty-one independent states in the Gold Coast, only twenty-four supported the introduction of the Native Administration Ordinance. Even among these twenty-four, fourteen did not appear to have been consulted at all.[73] Since the Native Administration Ordinance resulted directly from the Akyem Abuakwa-Asamankese dispute, Asamankese became the first target hit by the Ordinance. Immediately, the State Council of Akyem Abuakwa charged Asamankese leaders of committing an act with intent to undermine the authority of the Paramount Chief, to withdraw their allegiance from the stool and to usurp position they were not entitled to. However, the Asamankese fought back by instituting an action in the Divisional Court against the Paramount Chief, declaring that as President of the Tribunal and of the State Council, Ofori Atta's issue of summonses against them contravened the provision of the Ordinance. Kobina Sekyi attributed the deterioration of the situation to the efforts of the *Omanhene* of Akim Abuakwa to apply the Native Administration Ordinance for the settlement of a political dispute of long standing.[74]

The Tendency Towards Independence

The separation tendency, however, was too obvious to be neglected. After the establishment of colonial rule, this movement was evident from colonial annual reports, which indicate the serious problem of land disputes and the conflicts between chiefs and Paramount Chiefs. In 1903, Mate Kole, the Paramount Chief in Eastern Krobo, complained that his subordinates the chiefs Amitei of Dom and Odonkor of Kpong, "have been working in opposition to him." His authority was defied and four of his messengers were killed. Only with the help of the government was the dispute settled.[75] During the first decade, the separation movement occurred in Kwahu, Awuna and Accra areas.[76]

In the 1910s, there were long-time disputes between lesser chiefs and big chiefs in Akuapem, Ada and Keta areas. The relation between *Omanhene* of Akuapem and his chiefs was so tense that the latter even declared that he was destooled. The same thing happened in the Dwaben section where chiefs deposed the *Omanhene*. The *Mantse* of Heowe tried unsuccessfully for independent status while the *Fia* of Aggravey, who was under the jurisdiction of the *Mantse* of Ada, also wanted to claim his independence mainly on the ground that his people did not speak the same language as the people of Ada.[77]

The tendency to separate became more serious in the 1920s. In the Eastern Province for example, the annual report of 1921 stated: "Owing to the gradual growth of prosperity, pecuniary and otherwise, the cry of independence from their Paramount Stools has appeared in several cases."[78] In 1922, besides the action by Asamankese against the *Omanhene*, another case was brought to the Supreme Court by a chief, *Mantse* of Osudoku, against his superior, the *Konor* (Paramount Chief) of Manya Krobo.[79] In 1923, "no less than four Sub-Chiefs have approached government with a view to declaring their independence and severing all connection with their Paramount Chiefs."[80] The next year, "several minor chiefs endeavored to sever their connection with their Suzerain by declaring their independence." These cases occurred in Akuapem, Akyem Abuakwa, Kwahu, Akwamu and Peki, and the government had to warn the chiefs against such actions.[81] In the following years, the government appointed Commissions of Enquiry to investigate the cases of separatist disputes of Prampram-Accra, Anyirawase-Peki and Anum-Peki.[82]

The severe conflicts between lesser chiefs and big chiefs may be explained by the changing conditions. In some cases, such as Akyem Abuakwa, the former state had been based on military function, with the *Omanhene*'s authority very limited in politics and economy. But the establishment of the colonial rule brought changes to this arrangement. Secondly, the *Pax Britannica* made the military role unnecessary while other functions of the states became more important. Struggles for political, economic or judicial powers occurred frequently between big chiefs and lesser ones. Thirdly, because of the ignorance of local conditions, as above-mentioned, the government made a political mistake by elevating some chiefs, thus causing confusion and rebellion. It was not uncommon that lesser chiefs made use of colonial rule to liberate themselves from exploitative authorities. All these factors contributed to a general tendency to separation.

Another reason for the separatist trend was the ambiguity of the government. Before the Native Administration Ordinance in 1927, neither the Paramount Chief nor the government could exercise effective authority to halt this tendency. Even the Native Jurisdiction Ordinance did not provide any concrete measures to handle the problem. Since the economic improvement made it easier and more profitable to gain independent status, a town could enjoy the benefits of its own natural resources and local tribunals after breaking away from the *Omanhene*. Finally, the urge to break away became more serious when the application of the Native Administration Ordinance strengthened the Paramount Chief's position, which brought about grievances of both the educated African and lesser chiefs.

Conclusion

The discovery of diamonds obviously contributed to the Akyem Abuakwa-Asamankese conflict. However, political factors should not be neglected. First, there was a tendency to separation owing to various reasons, as suggested in the chapter. Secondly, the dispute involved the rental fees and the mining revenues, as well as the regular *abusa* paid by migrant farmers. More important, although the dispute concerned the right of the chief to deal with land concessions without reference to the Paramount Chief, land was fundamentally an issue of authority. It involved the conflict between the Paramount Chief who was eager to control land and the local chief who wanted to maintain his authority over land. In the dispute, Asamankese challenged the power of the Paramount Chief and threatened the colonial administration as well. Finally the nationalists used this protest to attack colonialism. R. Addo-Fening correctly points out that in the post-World War II period, the gulf that separated the colonial government and the chiefs on the one hand, and the nationalists on the other, can be regarded as a legacy of the Asamankese dispute and its aftermath.[83]

Compared to other British colonies, the Government of the Gold Coast was less determined to check the disturbance caused by land deals. This difference was probably due to two reasons. First, because of the historical conditions, the Gold Coast was unique in that control over the grant of concessions was exercised by a judicial body and not by the executive authority. Why could this situation continue for such a long time? The prosperity of cocoa production may be the second reason: it prevented the government from a direct interference in the land administration.

The Native Administration Ordinance was issued in order to adjust the local situation. This manifestation of indirect rule had its own problem. The Paramount Chiefs were offered some arbitrary power, but they were reluctant to use it because of lack of legitimacy. They did not want interference from above, but they constantly had to call for the government's help when their authority was challenged. There was a similar anomaly in the government attitude. It encouraged the African chiefs to act independently, yet continuously intervened in their decisions. The government even ignored the Paramount Chiefs' wrongdoing in order to carry out the policy of indirect rule. The Jumapo affair has provided another example, which will be discussed in the next chapter.

Notes

[1] Asamankese, sometimes spelt as Asamangkese, was the largest of the twelve divisions of Akye Abuakwa district while Akwatia was a sub-division under Asamankese.

[2] J. W. deGraft Johnson, "Akan land tenure," *Transactions of the Gold Coast & Togoland Historical Society*, 1:4(1955), pp.99-103.

[3] Casely Hayford, *The Truth about the West African Land Question*, p.66. M. J. Field also stated "It is often said by Akim people 'An *omanhene* has no land.' This is not strictly true, but it is very nearly so." *Akim Kotoku*, p.10. However, the *Omanhene* seemed to be informed of land sales and could expect a certain share of proceeds, either in the form of regular tribute or voluntary gifts.

[4] According to Manoukian, "Each of these *oman* originated, at the beginning of the eighteenth century, as a military union of hitherto independent 'towns' which joined together to defend themselves against the Ashanti. Each such 'town' owned its own land and retained independent control of it." See her *Akan and Ga-Adangme Peoples*, p.48, no.2. M. Field, *Akim Kotoku*, pp.2-11,57-63. This lack of centralization can also be seen from the fact that the *Omanhene* in 1918 admitted in principle that he had no right to intervene in election nor initiate destoolment. *SNA720*. Ofori Atta to Acting Colonial Secretary, 13 August, 1918. Quoted from Simensen, "Commoners, chiefs and colonial Government," p.30.

[5] Field, *Akim Kotoku*, p.4.

[6] J. B. Danquah, *An Epistle to the Educated Youngman in Akim Abuakwa* (Accra, 1929), p.31.

[7] Polly Hill, *The Migrant Cocoa-Farmers*, pp.143-44. She uses "sub-chief" to mean the *Ohene* or the *Odikro*, I prefer using "chief" for the same category.

[8] Letter of April 30 1913. Correspondence and Papers Laid before the West Africa Lands Committee. p.33.

[9] *The Gold Coast Leader*, 17 July 1915.

[10] Polly Hill, *The Migrant Cocoa-farmers*, pp.141-142. The Twi *guaha* has its equivalent in Adangbe *zigigba yibapom*, in Asante *twa dwan*, in Fante *twa guan*, and in Ga *shikpong yibafo*.

[11] Oheneba Sakyi Djan, *The Sunlight Reference Almanac of the Gold Coast and its Dependencies* (Gold Coast, 1936), p.98. J. G. Christaller, *A Dictionary of the Asante and Fante Language called Tshi [Twi]* (Basel: Basel Evangelical Missionary Society, 1933 [1881]), p.153.

[12] Lord Haily, *African Survey* (London: Oxford University Press, 1938), p.828.

[13] *Cmd 5845*. Report of the Commission on the Marketing of West African Cocoa, para. 58.

[14] Ivor Wilks, "The rise of the Akwamu empire 1650-1710," *Transactions of the Historical Society of Ghana*, 2:2(1957), p.132.

[15] Addo-Fening, "The Asamankese dispute," in Addo-Fening, *et al*, ed., *Akyem Abuakwa and the Politics of the Inter-war Period in Ghana*, pp.64-65.

[16] *Arbitration Award*, 9 September, 1929. paras. 22, 23 & 28. Quoted from Addo-Fening, "The Asamankese dispute," pp.65-66, no.17.

[17] Hill, *Migrant Cocoa-farmers*, pp.154-157; Simensen, "Commoners," pp.121-125.

[18] *CO98/50*. Report on Eastern Province, 1927-28.

[19] *Arbitration Award*, 9 September, 1929. Exhibit H, 31 July, 1913. para. 24; Exhibit B6 of 5 May 1916, para. 32 & 33. Quoted from Addo-Fening, "Asamankese," pp.66-67.

[20] *ADM11/1630 Case No.7/1931*. Quoted from Addo-Fening, "Asamankese," p.68.

[21] *ADM11/1627*. History of the Asamankese Dispute. *CO96/713/21613/34*. Affairs of Asamangkese in relation to the Paramount Stoool of Akim Abuakwa State. Minutes. para.9.

[22] Members of the Presbyterian Church in Asamankese organized a company called Kyirem. They refused to pay their customary contributions to the *Ohene* and demonstrated their loyalty to the paramount stool in a provoking manner. The struggle between loyalists and separatists among the *Asafo* companies became serious in 1931. Simensen, "Commoners," p.136. B. M. Edsman, *Lawyers in Gold Coast Politics c. 1900-1945*, p.140.

[23] *CO96/673/5*. Gold Coast 389. CO4308/27/6. Ofori Atta on "Object and reasons" of the bill. Encl.

in Maxwell to Secretary of State, 19 May 1927.

[24]They were given human excrement to eat and made to carry human excrement in latrine cans "filled to the brim with water" and one person had a woman's sanitary towel in use applied to his mouth. *CO96/691/6/6531/29*. Petition from the *Ohene* of Asamankese. Encl. in Governor Slater to Secretary of State, 23 October 1929.

[25]*CO96/698/14*. G.C.490. Gold Coast Law Reports, 1926-1929. Award in Asamangkese Akim Abuakwa Arbitration, 1929. p.291. Encl.(1) in Governor Slater to the Lord Passifield, 30 July 1931.

[26]*CO96/713/21613/34*. Memorandum on the Asamankese Case. Encl. in Governor Thomas to Secretary of State, 19 December, 1933.

[27]On May 5, a man named Philip Afoakwa was shot dead by a member of Kyirem company; three hours later, two British Togolese were shot dead by a follower of the *Benkumhene*. This caused great panic in Asamankese. "Shooting at Asamankese" in *West Africa*, 30 May 1931. "Shooting at Asamankese" in *The Gold Coast Spectator*, May 16 1931; "Echoes of the Kibi-Asamankese Controversy" in *The Gold Coast Spectator*, May 9 1931.

[28]*CO96/713/21613/34*. Gold Coast Confidential. Memo. on Asamankese Case. Encl. in Governor Thomas to Secretary of State, 19 December 1933.

[29]*ADM32/1/15*. Quarterly Report, June 1938. Quoted form Simensen, "Commoners," pp.229-230.

[30]Edsman, *Lawyers*, p.134-147.

[31]*ADM11/1627*. History of the Asamankese Dispute.

[32]*CO96/713/21613/34/5*. Nana Kwahu Amoah II to Colonial Secretary, 17 June 1931. Encl. in Nana Kwahu Amoah II, *Ohene* of Asamangkese to Governor Thomas, 3 February 1934.

[33]*CO98/50*. Report on Eastern Province, 1927-28.

[34]Co96/691/6/6531/29. Petition Encl. In Slater to Secretary of State, 22 October 1929.

[35]*CO96/713/21613/34/5*. Kwahu Amoah II to Colonial Secretary, 17 June 1931. Encl. in Kwahu Amoah II to Thomas, 3 February 1934.

[36]*CO96/691/6/6531/29*. Petition. Encl. in Slater to Secretary of State, October 23 1929.

[37]Simensen, "Commoners," pp.228-229. It was said that two letters were found which were written by the *Omanhene* to the Secretary for Native Affairs, asking the Government's interference with the Judiciary.

[38]The Governor once wrote to London for idea to get rid of Wallace Johnson. "I do wish you could suggest some plan whereby I could get rid of Wallace Johnson. He is in the employ of the *Bolsheviks* and is doing a certain amount of harm by getting hold of the young men for his 'Youth League.' He just keeps within the law, but only just." *CO96/731/31230*. Sir A. Hodson to Sir Cecil Bottomley, 14

January 1936.

[39]*ADM11/1105*. Note of interview with Secretary for Native Affairs, 3 March, 1922. This might be a unique case in British colonies, with government officials were charged by Africans.

[40]*CO96/657*. Gold Coast (Confidential). CO54797. Governor Guggisberg to Amery, 19 November 1925.

[41]*ADM32/4/99*. District Commissioner Kibi Record Book 5, 6/23. Quoted from A. B. Holmes, "Economic and political organizations in the Gold Coast, 1920-1945" (Unpublished Ph.D. dissertation, University of Chicago, 1972), p.488.

[42]*GNA. ACC 32/1/91*. Ofori Atta to the District Commissioner Kibi, 4 September, 1928. Quoted from Holmes, "Economic," p.490.

[43]*ADM11/1627*. Report on the Asamankese dispute by H. Thomas, Secretary for Native Affairs. 9 May 1934. para.16.

[44]*GNA. ACC 334/62*. 17 September, 1929. Ohene of Asamangkese to Governor. Quoted from Holmes, "Economic," p.493.

[45]*ADM11/1105*. Case No.25/29. Thompson's motion on notice, 20/9/29.

[46]The Governor asked to be conferred the power of deportation, as in Serra Leone and Nigeria, then an amendment of Native Jurisdiction Ordinance (1924) gave the Governor the power to deport destooled chiefs. *CO96/713/21613/34*. Memorandum on Asamankese case. Encl. (2) in Gold Coast (Confidential). Governor Thomas to Secretary of State, 19 Dec 1933.

[47]Simensen, "Commoners," p.131.

[48]Edsman, *Lawyers*, p.146.

[49]Holmes, "Economic and political organizations," pp.486-505.

[50]Addo-Fening, "Asamankese dispute," p.65.

[51]Holmes, "Economic and political organizations," p.720.

[52]R. S. Rattray, "Tendencies in the British colonial administration," *Journal of African Society*, 33(1934), pp.29-33.

[53]Casely Hayford, *The Truth*, pp.57-60. The emphasis is mine.

[54]Simensen, "Commoners, chiefs and colonial Government," pp.25-26.

[55]Holmes, "Economic," pp.485-486.

[56]Kimble, *Political History*, p.195.

[57]"[T]he inhabitants submitted themselves to the British Government, not as subjects, but as independent nations, in alliance with, and protected by, the United Kingdom." J. A. B. Horton, *West*

African Country and Peoples (London: Kraus, 1970[1868]). p.243.

[58]*GNA. ACC.32/4/91.* District Commissioner of Kibi to Commissioner of Eastern Province, 5 February 1929. Quoted from Holmes, "Economic," p.491.

[59]See *Land Disputes in the Adansi Division* (mimeographed document, n.p., n.d.). Apter, *Ghana in Transition*, pp.50-51.

[60]*CO96/432.* "Letter of thanks from Awuna Chiefs dated 28th, May, 1906" in Extracts from official correspondence on work done on Gold Coast by C. A. O'Brien, L.L.D, Provincial Commissioner during years 1905-06.

[61]When the Ofori Panin had driven the Akwamu away he gave his sister in marriage to the *Ohene* of Asamankese. This "friendship based on marriage" may explain the long time harmonious relationship. *ADM11/1105.* Note of interview with Secretary for Native Affairs, 3 March, 1922.

[62]*Census Report 1921*(Accra: Government Press, 1923), p.51. By 1921, the population of Asamankese was 5,413, but by 1931 it had increased to 5,900. One reason for the growth was that many people migrated to cultivate cocoa in the area.

[63]*CO96/721/31039.* Maclennan Minutes, 31 August 1935.

[64]*CO96/713/21613/34.* Memorandum on Asamankese case. Encl. in Governor Thomas to Secretary of State, 19 December 1933.

[65]*GNA. Cape Coast ACC 587/64.* Statement of Accounts, 1921-32. Asamankese and Akwatia paid £1,866 to Thompson and Sekyi as "professional fees" between 1932 to 1937; Sekyi received another £497 in the same period. *ADM32/1/29.* Asamankese and Akwatia Stool Debts. File No.16. (1932-37). For the total litigation expense, official sources put them at about £100,000 for each side, while *Gold Coast Independence* indicated that £120,000 for Asamankese and Akwatia, and £60,000 for Ofori Atta. Quoted from Edsman, *Lawyers*, p.143.

[66]*GNA.Accra. ACC571/64.1/4/31.* Sekyi to *Ohene* of Asamangkese. Quoted from Holmes, "Economic," pp.496-497.

[67]Thomas Report, para.20. Quoted from Edsman, *Lawyers*, p.147.

[68]Kimble, *Political History*, p.44.

[69]At an early stage Ofori Atta had admitted his inability to act effectively under the Ordinance and appealed to the government for police support to arrest four Asamankese leaders charged with encouraging insubordination. He even suggested that the National Administration Ordinance should be amended to empower a British Commissioner to arrest on a warrant from a native tribunal when there was a danger of a disturbance. *GNA. Adm.12/5/153.* Eastern Province Commissioner, note 17/1-28. Quoted from Simensen, "Commoners," p.213.

[70]Those complaints include "(A) That Sub-chiefs were not called by the Paramount Chief to

accompany him to the meeting of the Provincial Council. (B) That the Agenda of the Provincial Council is not discussed by the Paramount Chief with his Sub-chiefs before he goes to the Provincial Council. Consequently, he simply speaks for himself. (C) That the Native Administration Ordinance was not discussed by Paramount Chiefs with their Sub-chiefs and that the Sub-chiefs had not been told that the Government had discussed and revised the Bill drafted by the Paramount Chiefs and that it was thus not a law made by the Paramount Chiefs, but a Government measure." *CO96/673/5.* Gold Coast (Confidential). CO4308/24/20. Governor Guggisberg to Secretary of State. 13 September 1927.

[71] *CO96/673/5.* Gold Coast 303. Governor Guggisberg to Amery, 20 April 1927.

[72] *Gold Coast Times,* 14 May 1927, p.8; 11 June 1927, p.4; 13 August 1927, p.2; 14 January 1928, p.2; 7 January 1928, p.8.

[73] *GNA Adm. 11/974.* Protest by A.R.P.S. dated 26 March 1928. Quoted from Addo-Fening, "Asamankese dispute," p.78.

[74] *ADM11/1627.* History of the Asamankese dispute, para.10.

[75] *CO96/417.* Report on the Native Affairs Department for the Year 1903. Encl. in Gold Coast No. 203. Rodgster to Lyttelton, 27 April 1904.

[76] *CO99/20* Native Affairs Department Annual Report for 1907.

[77] *CO98/26.*Report on the Eastern Province 1916. *CO98/28.* Report on the Native Affairs Department for the Year 1917. *CO98/30.* Report on the Eastern Province for the Year 1918. *CO98/32.* Report on Eastern Province for the Year 1919.

[78] *CO98/36.* Annual Report on the Eastern Province for the Year 1921. Encl. in Report on the Native Affairs Department for the Year 1921.

[79] *CO98/38.* Report on the Eastern Province for the Year Jan. 1922-Mar. 1923.

[80] *CO98/40.* Report on the Eastern Province for the period Apr.1923-Mar.1924.

[81] *CO98/42.* Report on the Eastern Province for the period Apr.1924-Mar.1925.

[82] *CO98/46.* Report on Eastern Province for the period Apr.1925-Mar.1926.*CO98/48.* Annual Report of the Eastern Province for the Financial Year, 1926-27. *CO98/50.* Report on Eastern Province, 1927-28. Detailed reports of the Commissions can be found in *CO98/47. Legislative Minutes and Sessional Papers.* 1926-27, VII, "Anyirawase-Peki Inquiry;" VIII, "Anum-Peki Inquiry."

[83] Addo-Fening, "Asamankese dispute," p.88.

CHAPTER V

Jumapo Affair: The Small against the Big (II)

With the introduction of the Native Administration Ordinance in 1927, the authority of Paramount Chiefs was greatly increased. The ordinance not only brought about the change of political structure, but the abuse of power by the Paramount Chief. Economic benefits made forest, land, mines or market tolls a source of revenue, thus causing great contention. In some areas, big chiefs adopted arbitrary measures to extract the benefits from their subjects, and lesser chiefs constantly asked for independence. The Asamangkese diamond affair is a good example. In another case, the Paramount Chief even tried to use his power to take over the resources that belonged to the lesser chief, thus causing great resistance.

In October 1940, a conflict occurred between the *Omanhene* of New Dwaben District and the *Odikro* of Jumapo, a small town within the district. The *Omanhene* destooled the *Odikro* without consulting the elders or people of Jumapo. The *Odikro* protested against this imperious action by a series of petitions. The government interfered and the *Odikro* returned to his position. In June 1943, the *Odikro* was again deposed, this time by some "elders" of Jumapo, with the *Omanhene* behind the scene. The government finally confirmed the deposition because of certain changes in the situation. This chapter will analyze the linkage between politics and economy in the conflict. It shows how the introduction of the Native Administration Treasuries Ordinance changed the government's attitude towards local politics.

Dilemma of the Chief

Colonial rule not only changed the traditional political structure, but also reshaped the system of distribution of resources. Traditionally, the chief's economic position was completely merged with his office. He was wealthy in goods and services since he could order his subjects to provide services in fieldwork or domestic work, and he received tribute from his subjects. In return, the chief had to be generous towards his subjects.

Under colonial rule, nobody would be willing to provide free labor for or send tribute in kind to the chief. The traditional privileges such as ferry fees or trade road duties no longer existed. And there were restrictions on the imposition of levies. Without the regular income that they had received before British rule, chiefs' economic conditions became rather difficult, especially in the early colonial period. Busia did an excellent study on the change of chiefs' economic situation. He suggested that although various changes reduced their wealth, chiefs were still obliged to perform their traditional services. They felt it an obligation to continue to dispense hospitality, reward the services of their subjects, distribute presents generously at religious festivals, and make donations towards the building of schools and churches, in order to maintain their prestige.[1]

Addo-Fening gave us a vivid picture of chiefs' difficult situation in Akyem Abuakwa in the late 1800s and early 1900s.[2] In his tour of the Eastern Province in 1913, the Governor heard the complaint of the Akwamu Paramount Chief about the Senchi Ferry. This ferry used to belong to Akwamu and now yielded over £1,400 annually to the government while the Paramount Chief received nothing. The Governor admitted that "the poverty of this Chief is obvious," and both Provincial and District Commissioners were of opinion that he "would be far easier to control if he were in receipt of a small stipend from the Government, which was made dependent upon his good conduct." [3]

Lack of adequate income remained a problem till the 1930s. In 1937, a report on the situation of Akuapem State disclosed that the major misfortune of the state was that there were no regular sources of income for the chiefs, who were "consequently absorbed in devising means for obtaining money for their own personal needs."[4] This was particularly true for the *Omanhene*, since now he had direct control only over the property of his stool. Deprived of all traditional sources of services and goods, he did not receive regular income from either his state or the colonial government. Having limited income, he had to provide service to all the districts of which he was in charge.

This problem resulted from the fact that the Gold Coast was one of the few colonies in tropical Africa where no direct taxation was imposed for a long time.[5] Whenever there was an attempt to introduce the tax, there was a protest. As early as 1852, the government issued a Poll Tax Ordinance. Chiefs and people refused to pay and the Ordinance was formally repealed in 1866. Strong protests against increases in customs duties took place in 1874, 1877 and 1892. In 1897, the Governor introduced proposals for direct taxation on houses, but abandoned the idea later. No tax was collected until the 1930s.

The 1927 Native Administration Ordinance aimed at defining and regulating "the exercise of certain powers and jurisdictions by native authorities, and to assign certain functions to the Provincial Councils." But it failed to introduce the local treasury system, the "most essential feature in indirect rule."[6] In 1931, in order to increase revenue, the government put forward a proposal to collect a direct tax, which aroused a protest. The protest intensified when it was announced that part of the tax proceeds would go to the government.[7] Two years later, the government tried to impose it again, but in vain.[8]

In 1936, the government decided to put chiefs in charge of the collection of direct tax, but the Governor knew that the introduction of direct taxation "will be bitterly opposed and that serious disorders in connection therewith are not unlikely to occur."[9] He was right. Protest occurred in Awuna State when the State Council passed the "Levy Bill" to collect an annual tax to provide an income for the head chief and for public purposes. The *Omanhene* of the Akwamu state was destooled for the introduction of the same "Levy Bill."[10]

Owing to the lack of normal incomes and adequate funds to maintain their prestige and living standards, chiefs had to rely on other means to collect money for survival: they could either depend on fines from traditional courts or misuse the state fund since there was no strict division between the state fund and the chief's own property. The worst part of the system of Native Tribunals was that fines and costs formed a principal part of the income of the chiefs and their councilors, who tried hard to extract enough money from litigants in order to get a share of the spoils.[11] In 1918, the Secretary for Native Affairs reported "The commoner causes of complaints are the excessive charges for fees and penalties and the inability of a Tribunal to enforce its own judgment."[12] In Accra District, thirty-four appeals from the Native Tribunals were granted by the District Commissioner's court. Complaints and grievances were all "directed against the Native Tribunals."[13]

Not only the Paramount Chiefs took advantage of the Native Tribunals, Divisional Chiefs were also likely to abuse that power. *Adikrofo (pl.* of *Odikro*) set up their own courts in the interior or small villages while the District Commissioner could do nothing since the Native Jurisdiction Ordinance made the authorization of tribunals for sub-chiefs the sole prerogative of the Paramount Chief.[14] In 1924-25, it was reported that "Minor Chiefs look upon their tribunals as their sole source for providing their incomes irrespective of carrying out justice" and "the situation was not encouraging."[15]

Chiefs also misused the state funds and state lands for their own benefit. It is little wonder that the people constantly accused chiefs of extortion, corruption and malpractice in financial matters, and attempted to destool them. During the 1920s, there were thirteen cases of deposed chiefs whose charges were detailed in *Government Gazette*.[16]

Table IV   Charges against the Deposed Chiefs (1925-1929)

Categories	No.	%
Habitual drunkenness	10	17.5
General misconduct	7	12.2
Misconduct concerning financial issue	8	14.0
Pledging Stool or selling Stool property	5	8.8
Selling Stool land without permission	4	7.0
Misappropriation of Stool monies	5	8.8
Involving the Stool in unnecessary debts	5	8.8
Disrespect towards Elders or Divisional Chiefs	5	8.8
Seduction and adultery	5	8.8
Other charges	3	5.3
Total	57	100

CO99/series. Government Gazette. (1925, 1926, 1927, 1929). The sources limited my choice of this particular period. In other years, charges were not detailed in the *Gazette.*

Among the **thirteen** chiefs, **twelve** were charged for economic offenses. The table shows that financial problems accounted for nearly fifty per cent (**47.4**) of the total charges. In other words, on average, each chief was charged with nearly four financial misdeeds. The chiefs' abuse of power through the Native Tribunals continued right through to the 1930s.[17] In 1933-34, the Secretary for Native Affairs analyzed the unstable conditions in the Eastern Province. One of the reasons was that litigants received harsh treatment from tribunals, the members of which had no other objective than to ensure the highest payment possible for their services, showing a complete disregard of the litigant's financial capabilities.[18] In 1934 people still resented "the squandering of stool funds and the heavy penalties imposed by tribunals."[19]

Chiefs were also involved in commercialization of stools. When stool debt became a serious problem in the Gold Coast owing to the increasing cases of land litigation, it was not uncommon for stools to be offered to those who promised to pay the stool debt. In 1920, a candidate in Asante was offered the Kumawu stool on his undertaking to pay the stool debt. He accepted the offer, but persuaded the elders to sign a document making them responsible for reimbursing him in case he was destooled. When he became a chief he tried every means to get as much as possible by levying fines and fees. As a result, the people refused to serve him and brought him before the Chief Commissioner. Frequent use of bribery in elections also showed the tendency to commercialize the stool, which caused an alarm even among chiefs themselves in Asante.[20]

Lack of regular income, some Paramount Chiefs adopted another measure: the exploitation of lesser chiefs. In Akyem Abuakwa, the *Omanhene* sought the income from Asamankese's diamond mines and succeeded. In Akuapem, the Paramount Chief tried every means to augment his income at the expense of his Divisional Chiefs. He even transferred some cases from other chiefs' tribunals to his own in order to get the litigants' payments, an act which naturally "alienated his Divisional Chiefs' affection and loyalty."[21] The Jumapo Affair was a typical example of how a Paramount Chief tried to bully a lesser chief simply for economic benefit.

The Jumapo Affair

Jumapo is a small town in the New Dwaben District. The establishment of New Dwaben State involved a process of migrations, grant of land and conflicts between different ethnic groups. Dwaben was one of the founding members of Asante Kingdom. But the relationship between Dwaben and Kumasi became sour from the beginning of the 1800s Owing to succession disputes, control of trade roads and a murder case.[22] After the defeat by the British in February 1874, the *Asantehene* (Asante King) blamed the Dwaben King for his individual negotiation with the British and the withdrawal of Dwaben army from the Asante Confederacy.

In 1875-76 a war occurred between the two parties, Asante finally defeated Dwaben. King Asafo Agyei led his subjects in exile to the Gold Coast Colony. Reports estimated some 6,500 Dwabens took refuge in Kwahu and Asante Akyem, while about 8,000 refugees settled in Koforidua of Akyem Abuakwa.[23] The Governor offered the land between Akuapem and Eastern Akyem and the Dwabens settled in the present site of Koforidua in 1876, thus laying the foundation of New Dwaben District.[24] Since the Dwaben's settlements were assigned by the government, there were constant land disputes in the area, either with the Akyems or the Krobos, or among themselves. The fight between the *Omanhene* and *Odikro* also had its origin in land ownership, a typical case in the colonial period.

Jumapo Market Tolls: the Bone of Contention

Jumapo was built after the 1900 Yaa Asantewa War. A market gradually developed in the town that attracted many people from neighboring regions. The Jumapo Market was situated on the land that the *Odikro* had bought as a private transaction. Every Monday, Wednesday and Friday, people came to the Jumapo market to trade their agricultural products, wares and other merchandise. They had to pay a small fee to set their stands. The market tolls, stall fees and other profits increased the wealth of Jumapo town and contributed a great deal to the stool property.

In 1935, Nana Osei Hwiree, the *Omanhene* of New Dwaben, coveted the market tolls and tried to obtain the ownership of this market. He asked Jumapo *Odikro* Yaw Osei to pay him the Jumapo Market fees and the *Odikro* obviously refused. Then the *Omanhene* ordered the gong-gong beaten by his messengers on November 8 1935 and declared that people should stop paying any tolls to the *Odikro* of Jumapo; otherwise they would face fine or imprisonment. Under this pressure, people stopped going to the market.

This action caused confusion in the town and the *Odikro* felt angry and humiliated. Finally he went to court and charged that the *Omanhene*'s action had caused his loss of tolls and claimed from the *Omanhene* £200 damages and also an order upon the *Omanhene* to revoke his gong-gong. The Supreme Court heard the case and made the judgment that the market tolls lay with the *Odikro*. The *Omanhene* consented to the judgment but wished the market tolls to be paid into the State Treasury. [25]

After Nana Yaw Sapon was enstooled as *Omanhene* of New Dwaben, he claimed all lands in New Dwaben as stool property. He told the *Odikro* that he was going to take the Jumapo market to the Stool Treasury. Twice he called the *Odikro* to Koforidua, the capital of New Dwaben, and by threats backed up by the Great State Oath (*Ntamkese*) tried to bully him into handing over Jumapo market tolls. With his elders' support, the *Odikro* refused to give up the market. The atmosphere became very tense and the State Oath was taken. The *Odikro* strongly protested this arbitrary action and replied that he did not serve *Ntamkese* but the law. With these words, he took his stool and went away. [26]

When the direct action failed, the *Omanhene* decided to achieve his goal by deposing the *Odikro* and installing his follower. On October 20 1940, Nana Yaw Sapon dismissed *Odikro* Yaw Osei. [27] He ordered his deputies Kwame Boateng, *Sanahene* Nyampo to beat the gong-gong in the town of Jumapo announcing the dismissal. Then the deputies entered Yaw Osei's premises and removed stool properties, together with all tribunal stationeries and form.

Dismissal or Deposition

The *Omanhene* exercised his power and persecuted the deposed *Odikro*, who was charged with insulting the *Omanhene* and unlawfully detaining stool property after the dismissal. The *Odikro* was found guilty on the first charge and sentenced to a fine of £15 or three months imprisonment with hard labor. After his deposition, the *Odikro* was beaten, imprisoned and was forced out of Jumapo. At the same time his wives and children were molested daily.[28]

The *Omanhene* referred to the incident as the "dismissal" of a headman while the *Odikro* protested against this and called it the "deposition" of a chief. There was an important distinction between the two positions. According to the Native Administration Ordinance, a "chief" should be elected or deposed, a "headman" be just appointed or dismissed. The *Omanhene* insisted that he had the right to dismiss the *Odikro* for refusing to obey his orders simply because the *Odikro* was a headman. And his representative stated clearly in the enquiry: "the Paramount Stool is the sole elector of the *Odikro* of Jumapo. The *Odikro* of Jumapo was dismissed in this wise."[29]

However, the evidence suggests that the government regarded *Odikro* a chief, not a headman. In the Native Administration Ordinance, the definition of "chief" was very explicit: "Chief" meant and included *Odikro, Asafotatse, Amega, and Asafohene*; being the occupant of a stool and elected and installed in accordance with native customary law.[30] The *Odikro* of Jumapo had a black stool. One of the charges against Yaw Osei was unlawfully detaining stool property, including a black stool.[31]

A by-law was passed by the New Dwaben State Council and published in *Government Gazette* No.6 of 1924, implying that the *Odikro* of Jumapo was member of the State Council, an important position that only chiefs could hold. In another by-law passed by the State Council in *Government Gazette* No.73 of 1941, it stated "Native Authorities means and includes the Paramount Chief, Divisional Chief, Chief or *Odikro*." All these show that *Odikro* was treated as a chief, both in definition and in reality.

The Protest from the Odikro

As soon as the *Odikro* Yaw Osei was deposed, he immediately wrote a petition to the Governor protesting against the decision, asked the Governor to nullify the unconstitutional deposition. He claimed that he had been elected "by the elders and councilors of his stool in accordance with native customary law," and "those authorized according to native customary law have not preferred any charge or charges against him, neither had your petitioner been brought before any tribunal on trial for destoolment."[32]

He claimed that the deposition by the *Omanhene* was not valid, since it was not through the proper authority; *i.e.* those who elected him. This was exactly the position of the elders who argued that if the *Omanhene* had any claim to the property, he should use legal procedure, rather than declare the *Odikro* destooled. In their petition, they asked to register the "protest against the said unconstitutional destoolment." They stated the *Odikro* was "undestoolable without our bringing any charge or charges against him," and described the deposition of the *Odikro* as the *Omanhene's* "own whims." They suggested that the *Odikro* had not done anything wrong to merit destoolment and made it clear that "we who have the authority to enstool or destool him have no complaint against him." They asked the Governor to disregard "any report concerning the deposition" they complained of." The *Odikro's* second argument was that there was neither a tribunal nor specific charges regarding his deposition. On December 9, 1940, the *Odikro* sent another petition stating the same fact. Since the government maintained the stand of not interfering with "the proceedings of the New Dwaben Paramount Chief's tribunal", he wrote to the District Commissioner, asking for: (1) a certified true copy of the charges preferred against him by those authorized according to customary law, the signatories to those charges and; (2) a certified true copy of the alleged proceedings and decision of New Dwaben Paramount Chief's tribunal. When he did not get any proceedings from the New Dwaben State secretary, he claimed there never existed such proceedings.[33]

But the proceedings did come on August 29 1941. Two special features are worth mentioning. First, the enquiry was held by the State Council Tribunal five days after the elders sent their petition. However, before the tribunal the elders withdrew their opposition one after another, most probably under the pressure of the *Omanhene*.[34] The *Adontenhene* Kwabena Asante who first opposed the deposition changed his stand even before the enquiry started, followed by *Okyeame* Kwabena Aboagye and other elders. Secondly, the proceedings recorded only the statement of the deposing party since the opposing party gave up their position, but there were still no concrete charges relative to the dismissal of the *Odikro*.

With reference to the proceedings, Yaw Osei wrote another letter to the Governor. He argued that the deposition was contradictory to both customary law and the provisions of the Native Administration Ordinance. He pointed out that the proceedings were not that of his trial, but only of the "enquiry into the alleged dismissal of Yaw Osei *Odikro* of Jumapo", which confirmed his statement that no charges were preferred against him by his electoral body and there was no trial before any tribunal. He asked the Governor to "give direction for the necessary redress to be granted to me by nullifying the so-called decision of the State Council in favour of my dismissal." On October 17, 1941, the *Odikro* wrote to the Secretary for Native Affairs asking for an interview to help him "out of present predicament." He complained bitterly of the "great injustice and maltreatment" at the hands of the *Omanhene*, "who declared me destooled without cause, imprisoned me after beating and forced me to seek shelter away from my town and people." After the interview, the Secretary for Native Affairs decided to interfere, and the deposition was declared void.[35]

After the *Omanhene* destooled Yaw Osei, a man named Kwame Gyebi was installed as the *Odikro* of Jumapo. He agreed to hand the market tolls to *Omanhene* Yaw Sapon. When Yaw Osei returned to his position as *Odikro*, he found that he had already lost control of the Jumapo Market. He decided to file a case in order to regain the market. But when he was preparing the case, he received a letter with charges and a notice of his deposition.[36]

The Deposition by "Elders"

On May 22 1943, *Sanahene* Kwasi Boakye and "five elders of the Gyase Division" laid nine charges against the *Odikro*. When the *Odikro* received the letter, he did not recognize those so-called "elders" and insisted that they were politically unimportant and could not represent the people of the town. Among them only two were position holders and others were seller, produce buyer, and young men. In a letter to *Opanin* Kwadjo Okyere, one of the signatories of the charges, the *Odikro* pointed out the signatories had no political status and the charges were "unworthy to be countenanced."[37] However, the later development of the affair showed that he underestimated the deposing party and the situation was much more complex than he thought.

Although there is no direct evidence, there is reason to think that the *Omanhene* was behind the scene. After *Odikro* Yaw Osei received a letter of charges on June 2 1943, he did not take it seriously. He left Jumapo on June 10 to collect some money for the appeal. When he returned from Accra to Jumapo a week later, he was informed by his elders that "certain persons **deputed by the Omanhene of New Juabin** [my emphasis] with *Sanahene* as president assisted by the very unauthorized persons" held an informal tribunal and gong-gong was beaten declaring his destoolment.[38]

The charges against the *Odikro* also provided some hints to this linkage. The first charge was directly linked with the market. It accused the *Odikro* of claiming ownership of the market for his own use. It is interesting that the deposing party did not call it "Jumapo Market" but "New Juabin Market situated at Jumapo", which indicated a challenge to the *Odikro*'s ownership. The third charge was regarding the *Odikro*'s intent to belittle the status of the sacred stool of New Dwaben by refusing to obey the State Oath, an action that obviously meant his defiance of the authority of *Omanhene* Yaw Sapon. What is more, after Yaw Osei was deposed, the *Omanhene* once promised to re-instate him as *Odikro* on the payment of £20. He did this without consultation with the State Council. The ex-*Odikro*, however, was never reinstated.[39]

As soon as the deposition of the *Odikro* was announced, the *Sanahene* informed the *Omanhene* of the news. The *Omanhene* was naturally happy about this destoolment and reported it to the Provincial Commissioner, stating that "no dispute has arisen" concerning the destoolment. This statement is not accurate. In reality, the *Odikro* immediately wrote to the *Omanhene* the next day after he had received the charges and stated his disagreement. He asked the *Omanhene*'s understanding: "I shall be pleased if Nana will give due consideration to this my report [*sic*] and do the needful to check the occurrence of what may tend to vitiate Juaben affairs as far as Jumapo is concerned."[40] This letter shows that not only there was a dispute about the destoolment, the *Odikro* also asked for the *Omanhene*'s interference.

Several important elders of Jumapo town also protested against the destoolment of Yaw Osei and the installation of the new *Odikro* Kwabena Dente. In their petition to the Governor on March 23, 1944, they stated that Yaw Osei was "still our man and the only choice of outstanding merit" and asked for the re-instatement of Yaw Osei as *Odikro*.[41] Three days later, the electoral body of Jumapo held a special sub-council to discuss the matter. The attendants were from the community who were in favor of Yaw Osei "including the captains with the members of the *Asafo* company and elements of the various tribes of people residing Jumapo and the surrounding villages." At the meeting it was resolved "most vehemently and unanimously" that "the OMANHENE and the HIGH AUTHORITY be informed that *Bafuor* Yaw Osei is still the *Odekro* of the town and has the support of all as such, and that his alleged deposition by the unrecognised few be deemed NULLITY."[42]

Yaw Osei also wrote to the Secretary for Native Affairs, explaining the situation and asked for help. But this time the Secretary for Native Affairs was less enthusiastic. Why?

The Government's Response

From Non-interference to Interference

When the *Omanhene* dismissed the *Odikro* in October 1940, the government did not interfere at first, despite frequent petitions from both the *Odikro* and his elders. This reluctance to intervene in local politics resulted from three factors. First, in the late 1930s, the call for indirect rule became stronger in the Gold Coast. Lord Hailey, who used to doubt whether indirect rule in the Gold Coast Colony was worth trying, agreed when he revisited the Colony that the government must "go forward with a system of Government through native authority."[43] There were a lot of talks in favor of indirect rule.[44] It would be unwise to interfere with local politics in this atmosphere. Secondly, the young *Omanhene* was just put in power. From the colonial perspective, he needed support rather than criticism in order to maintain his power.

The third factor, however, was the bias of the Commissioner of Eastern Province. He received the Jumapo Council's petition to the Governor on October 26 1940, but did not forward it to Colonial Secretary until 23 June 1941, eight months later! He also suggested in the letter the "chief" in the Native Administration Ordinance "being the occupant of a Stool" and the *Odikro* had no stool, which was contrary to the fact. He called Yaw Osei "ex-*Odikro*", indicating his acquiescence of the dismissal. Commenting on the petition presented by Yaw Osei on August 21, the Commissioner said: "Regarding Para.1, Yaw Sei **has admitted that he has no stool** [my emphasis] and therefore he cannot be described as a chief as defined in NAO. He is, in every sense of the word, a headman."[45] But the *Odikro*'s petition did not mention anything regarding the stool and the intent was just the opposite.[46]

Obviously, the Commissioner twisted the petition. The reason why he did so is not clear, but a possible explanation was that he did not want the Paramount Chief to lose in the dispute, thus weakening his authority.

Another piece of evidence is in a case regarding an attempted destoolment of *Omanhene* Yaw Sapon. After Yaw Sapon's enstoolment as the *Omanhene* of New Dwaben, his abuse of power alarmed some of the elders. In an attempt to destool him in 1941, one of the charges was directly linked with the Jumapo affair. The *Omanhene* was accused of having bribed a councilor Julius Sarkodee Adoo in the Jumapo case. In order to win the case with the Jumapo *Odikro*, the *Omanhene* was said to have agreed to pay Julius Sarkodee Adoo fifteen per cent commission on the Jumapo Tolls if the latter could influence the District Commissioner to find in his favor. The *Omanhene* made this offer without the knowledge of his elders and contrary to customary law.[47]

There is no evidence that government officials received bribes from Julius Sarkodee Adoo, but it was probable that Julius Sarkodee Adoo tried every means to persuade the District and the Provincial Commissioners. It was also possible that he more or less influenced colonial officials, since he was an educated councilor and ran a grammar school.[48] His influence may explain why the *Odikro* even failed to get a hearing before either the District Commissioner or the Commissioner of Eastern Province.

After the interview with the *Odikro* Yaw Osei on April 18, 1941, the Secretary for Native Affairs found that the *Omanhene* had gone too far, "the Odekro has been the object of definite persecution by the *Omanhene* of New Juabin." He made it clear that (1) an *Omanhene* cannot destool any of his subject chiefs; (2) if the *Odikro* was to be destooled or dismissed, the charges would have to come from those residing in Jumapo and not from the *Omanhene*; (3) no *Omanhene* had any right to dismiss his *Odekro* for disobeying orders.

He instructed the Provincial Commissioner that the deposition was illegal and contrary to native custom, and asked the Commissioner to inform the *Omanhene* of New Dwaben that his attempt to depose the *Odikro* of Jumapo "cannot be tolerated" by the government.[49] Therefore the government announced that the *Omanhene's* action was null and void.

However, there was a reversal when the *Odikro* was deposed again in 1943. The financial situation in New Dwaben had improved because of the introduction in 1939 of the Native Administration Treasuries Ordinance. The establishment of the Stool Treasury in New Dwaben state effected the change of the Government's attitude towards local politics.

The Native Administration Treasuries Ordinance

The 1927 Native Administration Ordinance provided a new frame for traditional power, but there were some leaks that generated criticism from within. The most conspicuous was its failure to introduce a Native Treasury system. In 1931 an Ordinance was issued that merely conferred power on a Paramount Chief to make by-laws establishing treasuries. In 1936, an amending ordinance to the Native Administration Ordinance empowered the Paramount Chief to place a levy on his subjects under certain conditions. Then stool treasuries were established in some states, including New Dwaben. Owing to the long time stool disputes, the by-law was not carried out in New Dwaben.

Governor Hodson was fully aware of the importance of the Stool Treasuries. In 1938 he delivered a speech with a section specifically on "Stool Treasuries" in the Legislative Council, pointing out "this country could make no real advancement in the absence of a properly organized national fund." He made it clear that if the people of the Gold Coast were "desirous of securing economic and political independence, it would be necessary to institute Stool Treasuries on well organized lines."[50]

The Native Administration Treasuries Ordinance was introduced in 1939 to establish and secure "the financial administration of native authorities." The Ordinance had three effects. First, it gave the African authority other power (such as the right to tax their subjects, etc.) than the usual routine of hearing land cases and disputes over oaths. The power could increase the revenue of the state and provide funds for the government and the improvement of local conditions. Secondly, the educated African now could work as clerks, accountants and other professionals for the African authority other than European firms or the government. Thirdly, there was a long-time suspicion about the financial malpractice of chiefs or councilors. A treasury with well-explained revenue and expenditure would kill this suspicion.[51]

But the application of the Ordinance met with opposition from some vocal chiefs led by Nana Sir Ofori Atta, *Omanhene* of Akyem Abuakwa. The African Chiefs' opposition focused on two grounds. First, they objected to any form of control over the Treasuries by the government and wanted their estimates to be submitted for the Governor's information not for approval. Secondly, they objected to regulations that gave the District Commissioner power to control the working of Native Treasuries.

In 1940, the Governor wrote to London explaining the ordinance met with considerable opposition and he needed "still more propaganda" and "meetings with the Chiefs."[52] However, the condition of the Stool Treasury in New Dwaben was gradually improving. In 1940, for the first time the State Council handed in its "Estimates of Revenue and Expenditure" for the Governor's approval. After the Secretary for Native Affairs read these formal Estimates, he was satisfied with the financial situation in New Dwaben.[53]

In 1941, the New Dwaben State Council decided to collect the head rate under the Native Administration Treasuries Ordinance.[54] In that year, the clerical staff in State Council increased, which also suggested improving fiscal conditions. Although the Secretary for Native Affairs thought some of them to be "unnecessary", he did not conceal his satisfaction over the financial situation in New Dwaben which "promises to recover rapidly from the financial after-effects of its protracted stool dispute."[55]

In 1942, the State Council decided to tax the "strangers", since the local *Zongo* (the migrants' community) had refused to pay a tax and it could not be enforced under the 1941 Resolution.[56] It was revealed that the State Council even wanted to tax the police in the Koforidua district. In that year, the State Council also sent supplementary Estimates for the purchase of a motorcar for the *Omanhene*, which the Governor turned down "in view of the very small amount of traveling."[57] The inclusion of the Jumapo market tolls into state revenue also necessitated the employment of four additional market collectors. In 1943-44 Estimates of Revenue and Expenditure, the chiefs of New Dwaben even decided to increase their own salaries, with the *Omanhene's* reaching £488 annually.[58] All these measures showed that the Native Administration Treasuries Ordinance was functioning well in New Dwaben State. Where did the State Council get the money? The answer lies in the Jumapo market tolls, which became a rich source of the state revenue.

Tolerance of the Intolerable

In dealing with the 1940-41 Jumapo affair, the government had certain principles. On September 22 1941, the Assistant told the Secretary for Native Affairs that the young *Omanhene* did not act with justice. He said although the young *Omanhene's* position was "far from secure" and he deserved "every support", yet the policy of backing up the authority of a Paramount Chief could not be followed where "there has been a miscarriage of justice."[59] Obviously, one of the reasons for the government to interfere with the deposition was the dissatisfaction with the *Omanhene's* "miscarriage of justice."

When the *Odikro* was deposed again in 1943-44, there was a big change in New Dwaben, and consequently, in the government's attitude. The state revenue was greatly increased since the *Omanhene* now controlled the Jumapo market tolls. Meanwhile, the *Odikro* was fighting two losing battles. First, he was still trying to get the market tolls back. Since Jumapo market was handed over to *Omanhene* Yaw Sapon by Kwame Gyebi, the new *Odikro* during his dismissal, Yaw Osei laid a case against both Yaw Sapon and Kwame Gyebi. This suit was for title to Jumapo market and was instituted in the Divisional Court, Accra. Although this case was exactly the same as the one he won in 1935, he lost it this time. The *Odikro* was desperate and subsequently appealed to the West African Court of Appeal, where he lost again.[60]

Secondly, he was fighting for his deposition by some of the "elders," whom the *Odikro* called "unauthorized persons of no political status" and his elders called "unrecognized imposters." The *Odikro* adopted the same strategy: writing to the Secretary for Native Affairs. But this time it did not work. The government suggested that the *Odikro* should follow the formal process, and "remedy lies under Section 24 of the N.A.O. and that His Excellency cannot therefore interfere at this stage."[61] The *Odikro* and his elders considered that the deposition was not carried out constitutionally and Yaw Osei still held his position as *Odikro*. It was unnecessary for the *Odikro* either to appear for trial before an unknown tribunal held at Jumapo on the day when the deposition was announced, or to defend himself afterwards.

But the essence lay in the function of colonial policy. After the introduction of the Native Administration Treasuries Ordinance, and especially with the inclusion of Jumapo market fees in 1942, the financial situation of New Dwaben was satisfactory. Market tolls had become the major source of the state revenue with the Jumapo at the top of the list.

Table V   Market Fees in Estimates of Revenue

(pound)

Financial Year	Estimates	Act.Revenue (Previous Year)	Est.Revenue (Coming Year)
1939-40	100	174	280
1940-41	280	185	300
1941-42	300	310	320
1942-43	320	1,013	841
1943-44	841	1,243	1,450

Table VI   Details of Market Fees Estimated (1944-45)

(pound)

Jumapo Market	1,000
Koforidua Palm Wine Market	250
Nkwanta Market	60
Akwadum Market	20
Effiduase, Asokore and Oyoko Markets	120
Total	1,450

Source: *ADM11/1/1798*. File No.1509/S.F.2. Estimates of Revenue and Expenditure, 1939-45.

As the above table shows, in the financial year of 1939-40, total revenue was £1,840, while the market fees (£174) accounted for less than 10 per cent of the revenue. But in the financial year of 1943-44, revenue increased to £6,104, while the market fees (£1,243) accounted for about 20 per cent and became major source of the revenue. The table shows how important the Jumapo market fee was in the whole revenue.

Since the State Treasury was functioning well, Jumapo market tolls were now paid to the State Treasury and parts of them were used to improve the conditions of Jumapo town itself, there was no reason for the government to hurt the State Treasury by protecting the right and property of a small chief. The Acting Commissioner of Eastern Province made this point quite clear in 1944.[62]

Between March and May, the *Adonhene* (a position holder) and the Jumapo sub-council sent four petitions or letters to the government, protesting the unconstitutional deposition and asking the Governor to interfere.[63] Then on June 28, 1944, after the Secretary for Native Affairs read the Estimates from the New Dwaben and found that the State Treasury was functioning smoothly with the increased revenue brought in by the Jumapo market, he wrote to the Commissioner of Eastern Province that the government did not want to interfere with the case. He asked the Commissioner to inform the petitioners accordingly.[64] This was the last nail in the coffin.

Conclusion

The Jumapo affair lasted for four years and resulted in the destoolment of the *Odikro* Yaw Osei in June 1944. However, ten months later, in April 1945, Nana Yaw Sapon himself faced deposition by his chiefs. On January 31 1945, several chiefs preferred five charges against the *Omanhene* but they were consequently persecuted. Later sixteen chiefs supplemented another nineteen charges to serve the purpose of the destoolment. On March 24, they handed in a second set of supplementary charges.[65] After the final trial began and Nana Yaw Sapon found his deposition inevitable, he pleaded guilty to twenty-one charges and offered his abdication, which was accepted by the State Council.[66]

The Jumapo affair shows a protest of a small chief against the Paramount Chief, who wanted to use political power to extract economic benefits. It was fundamentally on the issue of land ownership. The *Omanhene* adopted high-handed measures to achieve his own purposes. Backed by the government, the Paramount Chief won the battle in spite of his failure at an early stage.

As a matter of fact, the government did recognize the abuse of power by the Paramount Chief. However, indirect rule depended upon the Paramount Chief's authority and prestige, which the government could not afford to jeopardize. As a result, the government tried to pursue a policy of non-interference in local politics. On the other hand, by backing Paramount Chiefs with legal as well as coercive means, the government sacrificed the general interests of the ordinary people.

The *Odikro* was only a small pawn in the whole game of colonial politics. As a result, the high-handed action of the Paramount Chief was left unchecked, the unconstitutional destoolment was tolerated, and the government maintained its policy of non-interference. Concern for justice was secondary to convenience of colonial administration. In other words, the principles of colonial administration were considered much more important than the details of local politics.

Notes:

1 K. A. Busia, *The Position of the Chief in the Modern Political System of Ashanti*, pp.199-200.

2 Addo-Fening, "The Native Jurisdiction Ordinance, Indirect Rule and the subject's well-being: the Abukwa experience c.1899-1912," *Research Review*, 6:2(1990), pp.334-335.

3 *CO96/537*. G.C.746. Tour in Eastern Province. Governor Clifford to Harcourt, 7 October 1913.

4 *CO96/738*. G.C.415. Annual Administrative Reports (Eastern Province). Encl. in Governor Hodson to Ormsby-Gore, 7 July 1937.

5 The year of imposition of the direct taxation for other British West African colonies was 1895 for Gambia, 1898 for Sierra Leone, and 1912 for Southern Nigeria (parts of southern Nigeria in the 1920s). See Michael Crowder, *West Africa under Colonial Rule* (Evanston: Northwestern University Press, 1968), pp.206-208.

6 Lord Hailey, *African Survey*, p.471.

7 *CO96/699/7050A*. Minute. Income Tax and Protest; Governor to Passfield, 16 August 1931. *CO96/704/7260*. G.C. (Confidential). Governor to Lister, 31 March, 1932; Acting Governor to Lister, 20 August 1932.

8 Lord Hailey, *An African Survey*, p.472.

9 *CO96/739/31228*. 1937 Political Administration of the Colony. G. C. Conf. Governor Hodson to Ormsby-Gore, 13 November 1937.

10 *CO96/738/31165/A*. Annual Administrative Reports (Eastern Province). G.C.415. Governor Hodson to Ormsby-Gore, 7 July 1937.

[11]*Native Jurisdiction Ordinance* (1883) empowered the chiefs to make by-laws "for promoting the peace, good order, and welfare of the people" and conferred upon them civil and criminal jurisdiction in the causes and matters approved under the by-laws. Metcalfe, ed., *Great Britain and Ghana   Documents of Ghana history, 1807-1957* (Accra: University of Ghana, 1964), pp.390-93.

[12]*CO96/593*. Governor Clifford to W. H. Long, 9 October 1918.

[13]*CO98/30*. Report on the Eastern Province for the year 1918.

[14]Addo-Fening, "Native Jurisdiction Ordinance," pp.35-36.

[15]*CO98/42*. Report on the Eastern Province for the period Apr.1924-Mar.1925.

[16]*CO99/series. Government Gazette.* (1925, 1926, 1927, 1929). The sources limited my choice of this particular period. In other years, charges were not detailed in the *Gazette.*

[17]*CO96/748*. 1938. G.C.31165/A. Annual Administration Reports, Eastern Province.

[18]*CO96/718/21755/A.* Annual Report on the Eastern Province 1933-34. Encl. in G.C. No.457 of 14/9/34.

[19]*CO96/718/21755/A.* Annual Report on the Eastern Province 1933-34. Encl. in G.C. No.457 of 14/9/34.

[20]Busia, *Position of Chief,* p.212.

[21]*CO96/748*. 1938 G. C. 31165/A.   Annual Administrative Reports. Eastern Province. Encl. in G.C. No.585 of 27/8/38.

[22]Addo-Fening, "The background to the deportation of King Asafo Agyei and the foundation of New Dwaben," *Transactions of the Historical Society of Ghana,* 12:2(1973), pp.213-228.

[23]See Thomas J. Lewin, *Asante Before the British: The Prempean years, 1875-1900* (Lawrence: The Regents Press of Kansas, 1978), p.248, no.21.

[24]The formation of the boundaries of New Dwaben settlements underwent two periods: from 1877 to 1895, and from 1895 to 1934. Between 1877 and 1934, various land disputes caused at least six investigations and redefinitions of the boundaries. *ADM11/1/824.* "A history of the boundaries of the New Juabin settlements" by M. K. C. Tours, Ass. D. C. New Dwaben had a population of 26,526 in 1931, the majority were farmers.

[25]*ADM/11/1/1798*. File No.1509/S.F.1. Supreme Court record dated November 18 1935.

[26]*ADM11/1/1798*. File No.1509/S.F.1. Proceedings of New Juabin State Council Tribunal: Enquiry into the alleged dismissal of Yaw Osei *Odekro* of Jumapo, dated 1 November 1940.

[27]There were different versions of their names, such as Yaw Sapon, Yao Sarpon or Yao Sarpong for the *Omanhene,* and Yaw Osei, Yao Sei or Yaw Sei for the *Odikro.* I use Yaw Sapon and Yaw Osei used

respectively unless they appeared differently in original quotations.

28*ADM11/1/1798*. File No.1509/S.F.1. Eastern Province commissioner to Secretary for Native Affairs, 23 June 1941; Yaw Osei to Secretary for Native Affairs, 17 October 1941.

29*ADM11/1/1798*. File No.1509/S.F.1. Proceedings of New Juabin State Council Tribunal: Enquiry into the alleged dismissal of Yaw Osei *Odekro* of Jumapa, dated 1 November 1940.

30Headman includes an *Opanin, Onupka, Hanua, Hafia*, and *Nokotoma. Native Administration Ordinance* (1927). Sec.2.

31*ADM11/1/1798*. File No.1509/S.F.1. Commissioner of Eastern Province to Secretary for Native Affairs, 23 June 1941.

32*ADM1/11/1798*. File No.1509/S.F.1. Petition of *Odekro* Yaw Osei to His Excellency the Governor Sir Arnold W. Hodson K.C.M.G.

33*ADM11/1/1798*. File No.1509/S.F.1. Jumapo Council to His Excellency Governor, 20 October 1940; Yaw Osei to District Commissioner, 31 July 1941; Petition of *Odekro* Yaw Osei of Jumapo in connection with Jumapo affairs dated 21 August 1941.

34*ADM11/1/1798*. File No.1509/S.F.1. Proceedings of New Juabin State Council Tribunal: Enquiry into the alleged dismissal of Yaw Osei *Odekro* of Jumapo, dated 1 November 1940.

35*ADM11/1/1798*. File No.1509/S.F.1. *Odekro* to Governor through District Commissioner, 29 August 1941; Yaw Osei to Secretary for Native Affairs, October 17 1941; Secretary for Native Affairs to Commissioner of Eastern Province, 23 October 1941; District Commissioner to the *Omanhene* New Juabin, 21 November 1941.

36*ADM11/1/1798*. File No.1509/S.F.2. Estimates of Revenue and Expenditure 1942-43; Yaw Osei to Nana Yaw Sapon, 2 June 1943; Petition of Yaw Osei praying for nullification of his alleged deposition by unauthorised persons dated 19 June 1943.

37 *ADM11/1/1798*. File No.1509/S.F.1. *Odekro* to *Opaning* Kwadjo Okyere, 2 June 1943. *ADM11/1/1798*. File No.1509/S.F.1. *Odekro* to District Commissioner, 3 June 1943.

38*ADM11/1/1798*. File No.1509/S.F.1. Petition of Yaw Osei praying for nullification of his alleged deposition by unauthorised persons dated June 19 1943.

39*ADM11/1/1798* File No.1509/S.F.1. Charges referred against *Odekro* Yaw Osei of Jumapo for his deposition by the undermentioned elders, councillors, linguists, etc. 22 May 1943. *ADM29/1/69*. Supplementary charges of charges preferred on the 31st day of January 1945 for the deposition of Nana Yaw Sapong.

40*ADM11/1/1798*. File No.1509/S.F.1. Quoted from Acting Commissioner of Eastern Province to Secretary for Native Affairs, 24 June 1944; *Odekro* Yaw Osei to Nana Yaw Sapon, 2 June 1943.

⁴¹*ADM11/1/1798*. File No.1509/S.F.1. Petition to the Governor through District Commissioner dated 23 March 1944.

⁴²*ADM11/1/1798*. File No.1509/S.F.1. Jumapo Sub-council to the Governor, 28 March 1944.

⁴³*CO96/767/31228/1*. Discussion No.148. Encl. in Governor Hodson to A. J. Dawe, 31 May 1940.

⁴⁴*CO96/739/31228*. 1937. Political Administration of the Colony. In his letter to the Secretary of State, the Governor agreed that there was "no alternative to the development in the Colony of a system of Indirect Rule." Governor Hodson to Ormsby-Gore, 13 November 1937. *CO96/749/31228*. 1938. Political Administration of the Colony. Summary of proposals in connection with the introduction of indirect rule into the Gold Coast Colony. *CO96/767/31228*. Political Administration of the Colony. Governor Hudson to M. MacDonald, 12 April 1940.

⁴⁵*ADM11/1/1798*. File No.1509/S.F.1. Commissioner of Eastern Province to Secretary for Native Affairs, 30 August 1941.

⁴⁶The first paragraph is as follows: (a) That the *Omanhene* misdirected himself when he submitted to Government that he had dismissed Your humble petitioner when *de jure et de facto* Your petitioner is not a headman but an *Odekro* recognized as a "Chief" as defined on page of the N.A.O. and is included in Schedule C of the N.A.O. page 67 wherefore he cannot be dismissed by the *Omanhene* at will without charges having been preferred against him by those authorized according to the provisions of the N.A.O. and tried before any tribunal of any competent jurisdiction. *ADM11/1/1798*. File No.1509/S.F.1. Petition of *Odekro* Yaw Osei of Jumapo in connection with Jumapo affairs dated 21 August 1941.

⁴⁷*ADM29/1/65*. Case No.1916/1941. New Juabin Native Affairs. *Gyasenhene* of New Juabin and three other Chiefs to Commissioner of Eastern Province, 14 July 1941; Charges against Nana Yaw Sapon, *Omanhene* of New Juabin.

⁴⁸Julius Sarkodee Adoo was a very dubious character. In the election and installation of the Paramount Chief of New Dwaben in 1940, he boasted that he had confidential dealings with the authorities. He asked a candidate to give him £200 to fulfil certain arrangements he alleged to have concluded with the Commissioner of Eastern Province and the Secretary for Native Affairs. *ADM29/1/65*. Supreme Court records dated October 4 1940.

⁴⁹*ADM11/1/1798*. File No.1509/S.F.1/50. Secretary for Native Affairs to Commissioner of Eastern Province, 23 October 1941.

⁵⁰*CO96/749/31228*. Political Administration of the Colony.

⁵¹W. E. F. Ward, *A History of Ghana*, pp.362-363.

⁵²*CO96/767/31228*. Political Administration of the Colony. Governor Hodson to M. MacDonald, 12 April 1940.

[53]*ADM11/1/1798*. File No.1509/S.F.2. Secretary for Native Affairs's comments on the Estimates for 1940-41.

[54]*Government Gazette*, 1941, No.73. Resolution. p.671.

[55] *ADM11/1/1798*. File No.1509/S.F.2. Secretary for Native Affairs to Eastern Provincial Commissioner, 26 August 1941; S.N.A to the Governor, 18 August 1941.

[56]*Government Gazette*, 1942, No.41. Resolution; *ADM11/1/1798*. File No. 1509/S.F.2. Commissioner of Eastern Province to Secretary for Native Affairs, 23 May 1942.

[57]*ADM11/1/1798*. File No.1509/S.F.2. Acting Secretary for Native Affairs to Commissioner of Eastern Province, 19 August 1942.

[58]*ADM11/1/1798*. File No.1509/S.F.2. Superintendent of the Gold Coast Police Eastern Province to Commissioner of Police Headquarters, 27 June 1942. Commissioner of Eastern Province to Secretary for Native Affairs, 14 May, 1943; Assistant Secretary for Native Affairs, 4 August 1943.

[59]*ADM11/1/1798*. File No.1509/S.F.1. Assistant to Secretary for Native Affairs's draft letter, 22 September 1941.

[60]*ADM11/1/1798*. File No.1509/S.F.2. Commissioner of Eastern Province to Secretary for Native Affairs, 24 June 1943. Unfortunately the *Odikro* lost his appeal.

[61]*ADM11/1/1798*. S.F.1. *Odekro* to Secretary for Native Affairs, 19 June 1943; Secretary for Native Affairs to Commissioner of eastern Province, 18 September 1943. The part of Section 24 relating to the stool dispute was as follows: "any dispute arising thereout shall be enquired into and determined either by a Divisional Chief's Tribunal, or by the Paramount Chief's Tribunal; and the decision therein of the Paramount Chief's Tribunal shall be final. *The Native Administration Ordinance, 1927*.

[62]*ADM11/1/1798*. No.1367/2490/41. Acting Commissioner of Eastern Province to Secretary for Native Affairs, 16 May 1944.

[63]See petitions of March 23 and March 28, letter of March 29 and the supplementary letter of May 19. *ADM11/1/1798*. File No.1509/S.F.1.

[64]*ADM11/1/1798*. Secretary for Native Affairs to Commissioner of Eastern Province, 28 June 1944.

[65]Their charges covered various aspects, such as misappropriation, dictatorial action, neglect of duty, discourteous act, corruption, receiving bribe, etc. *ADM29/1/69*. Supplementary charges by Principal Chiefs, Chiefs and Elders for the deposition of Nana Yaw Sapon, *Omanhene* of New Juabin dated May 12, 1945; Second supplementary charges against Nana Yaw Sapon *Omanhene* New Juabin dated 24 March 1945.

[66]*ADM29/1/65*. Case No.1916. New Juabin Native Affairs. District Commissioner to Commissioner of Eastern Province, 9 April 1945.

CHAPTER VI

Swollen Shoot: Politics against Science

After the socio-political crisis in February and March 1948, the British government appointed a special Commission headed by Aiken Watson to investigate the situation in the Gold Coast.[1] The Commission summarized seventeen factors, political, economic and social, that had contributed to the outbreak of the disturbances. According to the report, one of the underlying causes was "The Government's acceptance of the scientists' finding that the only cure for Swollen Shoot disease of cocoa, was to cut out diseased trees, and their adoption of that policy combined with allegations of improper methods of carrying it out."[2] This chapter will discuss the spread of swollen shoot and the history of control measures, questioning why cutting-out, the only effective method to control the disease, caused such strong resistance, and trying to trace the linkage between the protest movement and modern nationalism.

Swollen Shoot: Enemy Number One

The value of cocoa to Ghana cannot be overestimated. In 1891, the export of prepared beans was 80 lb. From 1911, the Gold Coast was the world's leading producer of cocoa, reaching its pre-independent peak in 1936-7. The export of cocoa represented more than 90 per cent of the country's agricultural exports and between two-thirds and three-quarters of its total domestic exports right up to the 1950s.

Discovery and Spread

The year 1936 witnessed the peak of cocoa exports in the Gold Coast, and it reached 311,151 tons. In the same year, a cocoa disease was discovered in Koforidua. It was called swollen shoot because the only diagnostic symptom was smooth swellings of young shoots. Eventually the tree was killed. It was found later that the disease first appeared between 1910 and 1915 in Nankese area and had been responsible for the extensive "die-back" reported, but it was not treated as swollen shoot.[3]

Swollen shoot was caused by a group of viruses that were carried from one infected tree to another by small insects known as mealybugs. Control was more difficult since the infected trees continued to produce healthy-looking pods for some time. There was a period between a tree being infected and the visible signs of symptoms, from six weeks to about six months. Unlike other cocoa diseases, swollen shoot could not be cured. The only way was to abandon it and make a protective belt for the healthy cocoa. To destroy the virus, it was necessary to destroy the infected trees.

At first, the outbreak was confined along a line running Koforidua-Jumapo-Maasi-Apedwa-Nankesi-Koforidua. The swollen shoot dispersed rapidly throughout the old cocoa area of the Akyem Abuakwa and Manya Krobo. Very soon it began to spread westward and northwestward. In 1940, the disease was only known in part of the Eastern Province and the government tried to set up a protective belt between Kwahu District and Asante in order to prevent any further spread.[4] In 1943, swollen shoot was found south of Konongo, the first case in Asante. Next year, five outbreaks were discovered in four other regions. From August 1944 to July 1945, a survey was carried out in Asante and about 113 acres of diseased cocoa trees were found in 20 villages.[5] At the same time the disease was also discovered in the Central Province and Western Province. However, those outbreaks were only found in a belt, leaving the main areas of Asante, Central Province, and Trans-Volta/ Togoland untouched by the disease.[6]

After World War II, swollen shoot spread so rapidly that in a few years it reached almost all the cocoa production areas. An intensive survey of all areas became a necessary complement to swollen shoot control. The general plan was to control first all limited outbreaks in the Eastern Province, Asante and Trans-Volta while the control of infection in Western Province was next to follow. In one year, 39.3 per cent of cocoa trees were intensively surveyed in the three areas, but control measures were not taken in the Western Province because of shortage of staff. The damage of swollen shoot became more serious year by year. From 1932 to 1939 the disease killed trees at an average rate of one million a year. From 1939 to 1945, the figure rose to five million. The output of cocoa in 1936-1937 year was 300,000 tons, and 1946-1947, 192,000 tons, representing a loss in production of 108,000 tons valued at £6,480,000.[7]

By 1945, swollen shoot had devastated 200 square miles. Based on the data in 1948, there was a proposal to cut out an area of mass infection estimated at 160 square miles in the Eastern Province.[8] Up to 1948, the yield of cocoa in the

Eastern Province alone had dropped in ten years by over 60,000 tons. At the price paid that year, the loss amounted to about £4,500,000 per annum.[9] During a ten-year period, the whole country lost 707,000 tons. Allowing for the low price during the war years, there was a loss of £20,000,000. These figures show the reason why the Ghanaians named swollen shoot "the cocoa industry's Enemy Number One."[10]

Wrong Diagnosis and Inefficient Control

It would be wrong to suggest that the government's neglect or irresponsibility resulted in the rapid spread of swollen shoot.[11] The government did make a wrong diagnosis at the beginning and an inefficient policy afterwards, which caused a lot of confusion and suspicion. When the disease was found in 1936, it was named "Swollen Shoot and Die-back." A pathologist of the Department of Agriculture W. F. Steven proposed to cut out all the diseased trees.[12] By April 1937, 49,000 trees were cut out and destroyed.[13]

In 1937, the Colonial Office, under the pressure of Cadbury Brothers Ltd., sent H. A. Dade of the Imperial Mycological Institute to the Colony to investigate the disease. After the visit, he concluded that the real killer of the cocoa trees was not swollen shoot, but drought die-back, that occurred when cocoa farms were deprived of protective shade. Therefore, the effective control of the deterioration of the cocoa trees should be forest preservation.[14]

The Colonial Secretary also made it clear that the dispersal of swollen shoot was a result of environmental conditions rapidly growing worse for many years. Therefore the so-called swollen-shoot disease was "a secondary affection of minor," the real disease was "drought die-back." As a result, the cutting-out was abandoned and Dade suggested the planting of shade trees as the control measure. An ordinance was passed in 1937 to implement this policy. Important cocoa areas were later planted with shade trees, especially in New Dwaben, Manya Krobo, Akyem, Akuapem, Togoland and Kwahu.[15]

In 1939, it was discovered that swollen shoot was a virus disease, not a physiological one as Dade had suggested. In dealing with the outbreaks, it was necessary to cut out diseased trees so that they would not remain a source of infection. In July 1940, a regulation was issued, and the transport from the Eastern Province of any cocoa plant was prohibited.

On December 21 1940, the government formally acknowledged the death of cocoa trees was not caused by a form of die-back for lack of shade and shelter but by "a virus disease."[16] However, this discovery of the cause of swollen shoot seemed to have shattered both the credibility of the government and the confidence to combat the disease. The government now began to concentrate on a more effective way to prevent the spread of swollen shoot to the healthy areas rather than controlling the disease in the infected areas; or using an official's words, the general policy was "to delay the spread of the disease rather than eradicate it."[17]

To implement this new policy, the government decided to set up a safety belt between Kwahu and Asante. In May 1941, the government declared a specific area as "in danger of infection by disease" and occupiers of a farm lying wholly or partly within the area should remove all cocoa plants from his farm.[18] These measures did not seem to satisfy some African members of the Legislative Council. Nana Sir Ofori Atta complained of the measure and suggested "everything should be done to see that the disease is prevented from spreading" and the government should "spare no money, spare no effort."[19]

J. B. Danquah also complained about the delays after he made a study in 1947 of the legislation concerning swollen shoot. He found that "between 1940 and 1946 nothing happened by way of legislation" except that a Swollen Shoot Disease of Cocoa Regulation was issued in 1940 and a Swollen Shoot Disease of Cocoa Order was issued in 1941.[20]

The dilemma seems to be caused by three factors: no precedent, no concrete plan and no resources. Swollen shoot was discovered for the first time and nobody could understand it. The government could do nothing definite since research was still going on. The World War II resulted in "lacking sufficient staff and funds to undertake comprehensive and direct control work." The government had to cut all expenditure, including the money for research and control measures. That is why both the Central Research Station and the West Africa Cocoa Institute complained about the shortage of staff. This lack of resources continued after the war.

The Cocoa Rehabilitation Department was established in 1949 to award compensation to farmers whose cocoa trees were being cut down, and in general was responsible for the Special Area, which covered the belt and surrounding zone of scattered outbreaks in the Eastern Province. Its purpose was to make the campaign against swollen shoot more efficient.[21] However, the outcome seemed to be opposite. The Department spent a lot of money to build roads and bungalows for the employees, £120,000 on buildings, £17,800 on road construction, £34,000 on tractors and other road making machinery.[22]

This move caused suspicion among farmers, especially when the bungalows were built on plots where the cocoa trees were cut out. The farmers were "obsessed with the old fact that the white man is bent upon taking away their land from them."[23] The fact that a large staff concentrated in a small area also resulted in a lack of confidence in the work by the Cocoa Rehabilitation Department. Under the recommendation of the Korsah Committee, the Cocoa Rehabilitation Department was finally disbanded after the investigation.[24]

All these facts suggest that the government lacked a systematic policy for control of swollen shoot. However, the most notorious measure was that of cutting-out, which elicited a strong protest from local farmers.

Protest against Cutting-out

Protest: Four Phases

The 1948 disturbance was a result of an accumulation of grievances. As a matter of fact, the protest against cutting-out began early and took various forms. Generally speaking, there were four phases of protest after cutting-out was formally resumed in early 1941. As early as 1936, it was proposed by the government to cut out and burn all diseased trees, together with a few of the apparently healthy trees at the edge of diseased areas in case of infection. The government knew from the beginning that farmers' cooperation was essential. Therefore farmers were requested to report without delay any case of cocoa suffering from the disease.

Farmers were also reminded of the provision under the Native Administration Ordinance (1927) for punishment of anyone who neglected to report a crop-disease to his chief, or who did not apply such treatment advised by the Department of Agriculture. Since New Dwaben, Akyem Abuakwa, Akuapem, Manya Krobo and Yilo Krobo all had by-laws under the Native Administration Ordinance, chiefs of these districts were asked to take every step to ensure that "their farmers report cases in order that Government may help the farmers to take action." [25]

At the start of cutting out, work was proceeding steadily, and no opposition by farmers was encountered. But the policy was obviously not welcomed, and the Governor observed that this would eventually become a source of discontent.[26] In 1940 and 1941, experiments were carried out by the Department of Agriculture in the Kwahu and New Dwaben Districts. It was decided that the cutting-out should be done by farmers themselves, assisted and guided by government personnel. In February 1941, in order to check the spread of the swollen shoot disease, the government decided to create a safety-belt about ten miles between Kwahu and Asante, which meant the removal of some 250 acres of healthy cocoa trees in a two-mile strip.[27]

The decision raised a strong opposition from the Kwahus, who naturally protested against the sacrifice that they were to make to save Asante. Although both the Paramount Chief of Kwahu and the Provincial Commissioner explained the purpose, the people believed the Government wanted to destroy the cocoa trees, which "was to be carried out under the guise of checking disease." The Kwahus were given 28 days to think over their attitude, "should they be still stubborn, the Government would use its power under the law in carrying out the work." Finally the Commissioner had to threaten to use police to carry out the cutting-out. [28]

In 1942, the Governor complained that the control of the disease had lacked assistance and co-operation from the farmers.[29] Farmers were generally afraid that once agricultural officers entered a cocoa farm in the process of combating the disease, the farm would be confiscated by the government. In 1944, the West African Cocoa Research Institute was formed and acquired another 640 acres for experimental sites. A more systematic survey in the same year confirmed that the disease was not only widespread throughout the oldest cocoa areas in the Eastern Province, but also had obtained a foothold in the Western Province and Asante.

The second phase of protest followed the government's launch of a cutting-out campaign right after World War II. The Watson Report indicated that between August 1945 and December 1947, no physical opposition occurred. Only from January 1948, did serious opposition begin.[30] The evidence, however, suggests the opposite. In 1945, the Department of Agriculture drew up a plan to deal with the disease. By explaining the damage and conducting visits to the devastated areas, the government tried to persuade farmers to cut out the diseased trees by themselves. The reaction from farmers was disappointing.

From August 1945, the government paid laborers to cut out infected trees with the individual farmer's approval. At the end of 1946, the Swollen Shoot Disease of Cocoa Order (No.148) was passed, which made it obligatory for every owner or occupier of cocoa farms to remove all infected cocoa plants from his farm. In January 1947, the Department of Agriculture started a more direct and effective method: the compulsory cutting-out of diseased trees by government-paid labor.

In October 1945, the swollen shoot disease control campaign was started in Asante. By June 1946, 100,000 diseased trees had been cut out. Then the campaign met with resistance from farmers. The protest was so serious that the government had to stop its measures. The cutting-out only resumed with the support of the Asante Confederacy Council. According to Mr. Hyslop, the Agricultural Survey Officer in charge of the campaign in Asante, "farmers still did not like their trees being cut down."[31]

There were also particular grievances. At a Legislative Council meeting on September 18 1947, J. B. Danquah gave an example of individual complaint. A

Krobo cocoa farmer came to him "in a state of great trepidation." The farmer complained that the "Agriculture people" were destroying his plantation by cutting cocoa trees in full bearing. Before the labor gang came in, the farmer received no notice in writing. The man had invested a fortune in a big cocoa plantation at Bosuso and lived in it with his wife and family. The cutting-out obviously upset him, and without legal help he would have a total loss.[32]

During the disturbance in February and March 1948, farmers were actively involved in the protest. Farmers of Akyem Abuakwa, Akyem Kotoku, Akuapem and Kwahu held meetings to discuss several issues affecting farmers, including swollen shoot. Danquah recalled his visit at Tafo Research Station on February 26. Before leaving Accra for Tafo, reports reached him that the Tafo farmers had planned to meet him with their *Asafo* companies and drums, and "to beat me up for having 'signed' the Beeton Report agreeing that their cocoa trees should be cut down." When he arrived at New Tafo, he met some farmers, who were "dangerously hostile" and in "the ugly temper." They questioned Danquah why he should have signed the Beeton Report.[33]

The third wave of resistance occurred after the government began the policy of "compulsory by consent" at the end of 1949. After the disturbance in February 1948, the government stopped the compulsory cutting-out. Suggested by the Watson Commission, three international experts were sent by the United Nations to the Gold Coast to study the disease and control measures. After six week's investigation, they drew a conclusion: the cutting-out of diseased trees was the only measure known for the control of swollen shoot and should be resumed as promptly as possible on a greatly increased scale.[34] As a result, compulsory cutting-out was resumed in 1949 and was carried on in face of strong opposition.[35]

Many farmers believed this control measure meant the destruction of all cocoa trees, diseased or healthy. The farmers were most unhappy about the cutting-out of mature cocoa trees carrying well-developed pods. For example, in 1950, a high price offered for the coming crop made farmers strongly opposed to cutting-out. According to the monthly report of July 1950, "such protests will increase in number and intensity as the main crop matures." Two months later, it was reported that farmers had "continued to protest against the cutting-out of diseased trees bearing maturing pods" and had asked that treatment be delayed until the main crop had been harvested. Physical opposition was encountered during the treatment in some areas and police had to be called in. [36]

The fourth phase followed the government's announcement of a committee to enquire into the existing organization and methods for the control of the disease by compulsory cutting-out. Leader of Government Business Kwame Nkrumah made the announcement of a "temporary suspension of compulsory cutting out" on April 4, 1951.[37] However, the policy was considerably distorted by rumors, and all cutting-out, compulsory or voluntary, stopped in most areas shortly afterwards. In Suhum, Kyebi, Osiem, Adukrom and other places, physical confrontations occurred and field staff were threatened or assaulted. In some regions, survey gangs had to be withdrawn owing to "the pugnacious opposition of the villagers." Many farmers feared the survey was just the prelude to mass destruction of cocoa trees.[38]

The more serious assaults occurred in the first few days. Government field workers were "molested and assaulted by bands of hooligans who maintained that government had ordered all treatment to stop." According to the monthly report of Cocoa Disease Control and Rehabilitation of April 1951, serious opposition occurred in a few days in many places.[39] In **Asante**, farmers' opposition interrupted intensive survey continually and little progress was made in the Berekum district. Re-survey continued on a limited scale and with some difficulty particularly in the Konongo and Efiduasi districts; 288 trees were cut out compared with 4,472 trees in March. In the **Western Province**, all survey and treatment work had to be stopped in the Sefwi Bekwai district on April 23, two days after the Committee of Enquiry held a public meeting. Initial treatment and re-treatment were hindered at some places. Because of opposition all work had to be stopped around Odoben in Akroso West district.

The strongest resistance occurred in the **Eastern Province**. Re-treatment of outbreaks was, however, considerably reduced in the Kpeve district in Trans-Volta/Togoland; although the attitude of farmers generally became very antagonistic towards the Department of Agriculture following the suspension of compulsory cutting out and the public meeting of the Committee of Enquiry. Farmers in Mpraeso East district were particularly hostile. In New Dwaben, opposition was more spontaneous than in Kwahu, and became stronger after the meeting at Koforidua of the Committee of Enquiry; opposition was intensified by subsequent misrepresentation of the announcement. By the end of the month, control work almost stopped except in the perimeter and the Suhum division.

The compulsory cutting-out was made more oppressive because of three additional factors: the lack of agricultural training of survey officers, the destruction of healthy cocoa trees by the laborers who were paid in proportion to the number of trees they cut down, and the building of those bungalows by the Cocoa Rehabilitation Department right on the place where the cocoa trees were cut out. Owing to the strong opposition and the recommendation of the Korsah Report, the government decided to stop compulsory cutting-out on May 30 1951.[40]

Protest: Different Forms

The control of the disease consisted of three stages: intensive survey, initial treatment and retreatment. The first step was to survey the land to locate all cocoa farms and examine every single tree for symptoms of the disease. The initial treatment was the cutting-out of all infected trees. The retreatment consisted of monthly examination of all trees near the infected trees and cutting-out of those trees of fresh infection.

A considerable amount of opposition existed even at the stage of survey. Farmers did not allow agricultural officials to go to their farms, or refused to give information on farm boundaries. In 1937 some cocoa farmers refused the Government Inspectors to go on their farms."[41] There were various reports that farmers refused to indicate their farm boundaries. This type of protest existed till the 1950s. A survey officer reported his experience in Kade. He visited the village and called on the *Odikro* to inform him of his intention to survey in his district. He was "quite cordial, and raised no objections," but wanted him to meet his elders the next day. The meeting was held, and after the survey officer's speech, the *Amankrado* consulted the village farmers and told the officer that "as their cocoa was healthy, there was no reason to survey it, and furthermore they would not allow me to do it. I reasoned with them, but without success, and the Chief told me if that was the will of his people, he could do nothing, and seemed rather anxious to close the meeting." [42]

Because of the strong opposition, the intensive survey in Ahamansu of Trans-Volta/Togoland region was completely held up from September 1949 to February 1950.[43] In Akyem Bosume, the *Omanhene* refused to withdraw his order to villages of Ofuasi and Brenasi to prevent survey.[44]

Quite often resistance took passive forms. Few farmers went to visit the experimental plots of cutting-out in the Tafo research institute, as requested by the government. There was vocal opposition almost all the time. Euphemisms such as "tolerant of our activities", "un-co-operative", "remained unhelpful" or "a better though still not friendly atmosphere" were frequently used in the monthly report. One of the passive forms was refusal to provide service to the investigation staff. In 1950, the field staff working between Koforidua and Bunsu reported that the opposition took the form of threats and refusing to provide accommodation or to sell foodstuffs to the field staff.[45] In some place, farmers even refused to house the staff, "making life as uncomfortable for staff as possible while not interfering with them when on duty."[46]

From the end of 1950, another unique form of indirect resistance appeared. Farmers began to show their disobedience by removing or destroying survey pegs or boundary posts. In December 1950, some survey pegs were removed by farmers in most newly opened district in Oda/Swedru area, Western Province.[47] This practice quickly spread to other areas. In February 1951, the same case appeared in the Eastern Province. At first it was not considered as "serious opposition." Very soon "the general childish habit of removing of boundary pegs" became so annoying to the staff that there were complaints almost every month. This practice caused serious damage to the disease control work. In some areas it was on such a scale that "it will mean many weeks will have to be spent in replacing such as are essential to enable work to continue." The practice continued until 1952. [48]

At the same time, various rumors spread around during the protest. A chief said in a meeting: "I am inclined to infer that cocoa has been planted somewhere in Europe; otherwise government would not persist in cutting down our cocoa trees."[49] One rumor went around that the Government had arranged to cut away all cocoa on the Gold Coast because Americans were coming to offer high price for cocoa.[50] Other rumors directly attacked the British government. All the rumors had one explanation in common: the vicious intention of the British colonial administration.

Physical confrontation was not uncommon. There was some armed resistance even before 1950.[51] In October 1950, some trouble appeared in Kwahu/North Birim area and the police was called to restore order. It was also reported that shots were fired and one laborer was wounded when farmers in British Togoland clashed with laborers sent by the government to cut out the infected trees.[52] In November 1950, a serious disturbance occurred in the Wiawo area in the Western Province, "there has been some opposition in all districts. Police assistance was required in one district in order that work could proceed." The situation became more serious in December, when opposition occurred at Bompata and the police made several arrests before the unrest quieted down.[53]

The sittings of the Korsah Commission in April 1951 seemed "to produce only further misunderstandings" instead of clearing up the point. By the end of April, cutting-out had almost totally ceased except in a few places. Some of the assaults committed on the field staff were serious. In one case, several staff members were critically injured while doing their duty in fields. One man suffered a broken arm and another lost some of his teeth. After the police interference, the opposition turned more to intimidation and threats.[54]

There were few examples of collaboration with the government probably because of the unpopularity of cutting-out. Although some Unofficial Members of the Legislative Council and educated Africans knew how serious swollen shoot was, they did not want to be isolated or to be the target of attacks. After the 1948 disturbances, there was a rumor that the Asante King and his chiefs were signing papers ordering the cutting out of cocoa. The Asante King caught an opportunity to clarify himself in a broadcast, stating that the rumor was "wholly untrue." Since everybody in the country benefited from coca, there was no reason that "persons who benefit from cocoa desired that cocoa should be cut down to kill the industry."[55]

Protest and Nationalism

Various Explanations
The Watson Report attributed the protest against the control measures to the "innate conservatism" of the Gold Coast farmers.[56] This judgment, however, needs justification.[57]

First, as mentioned above, the government policy was so inconsistent and changeable that it caused confusion and suspicion, passivity or hostility. The inefficient policy also hindered the effective control of the swollen shoot disease. Secondly, the traditional cure for any crop disease was very simple: to abandon the piece of land infected and start again.[58] Farmers and their chiefs made by-laws regarding plant disease as early as 1910.[59] The previous experience against cocoa disease also contradicted the interpretation of "conservatism." During 1914-18, there was a serious cocoa disease and "the farmers nearly cut down all their cocoa trees." Cocoa industry was saved thanks to some Africans who went around to farmers, explaining the condition and encouraging the control measure. [60]

Thirdly, the people of the Gold Coast could hardly believe that the government would think of their well-being after all they had suffered under colonial rule. They still remembered the fact that during cocoa hold-ups the government stood by the side of European merchants. Later in the boycott of February 1948, Nii Kwabena Bonne III found there was a "gentleman's agreement" between the government and foreign firms, which served as another example of the government's intention.[61] "When a man is ill, we send him to hospital. Why should we cut the cocoa trees when they are diseased?"[62] The people could hardly trust the government, when they saw survey officers with very little knowledge about cocoa gave orders to cut down cocoa trees and then built bungalows right on the place.

R. H. Bates suggests that the farmers' resistance against cutting-out resulted from lack of compensation.[63] From 1936, the government offered compensation for the healthy trees cut to prevent the spread of the disease.[64] The Plants and

Disease (Amendment) Ordinance was made in 1941. It improved upon the previous provision as to the payment of compensation to farmers whose plants had been destroyed, "it shall be lawful for the Governor to authorize payment out of the general revenue to any such person of such sum as to the Governor shall seem fit."[65] However, in application, it seemed that there was compensation only for the healthy trees cut down. Compensation was not paid for diseased trees "as their life was very limited."[66]

After the war, the cry for reasonable compensation rose. In 1947, William Ofori Atta, a prominent leader of United Gold Coast Convention and Chief Farmer in Akyem Abuakwa, once suggested that the government should pay the cost of the diseased trees that were being cut out. He argued that in some cases the diseased trees were actually bearing and were capable of bearing for two or three years. But these trees had to be cut in order to save the cocoa industry, which meant that the owner was deprived of two or three years of living income. Therefore the government should compensate him for the estimated income. The owner of diseased farms should have ready funds not only for living but also for starting new farms of cocoa or other crops. The compensation system should also reflect the rise in prices of other goods, the deterioration of the prices of agriculture products and other related factors.[67]

By the end of April 1947, as many as 1,334,809 trees had been cut out, which covered an area of 5,180 acres. Farmers suffered a lot and the cry for "adequate compensation" became louder.[68] On September 18 1947, the Legislative Council decided that a Committee of Enquiry should be appointed to review the legislation concerning the swollen shoot disease, to consider appropriate legislation to provide for payment of compensation, and to make recommendations.[69] After the Committee's recommendation, the government announced the scheme that allowed for payment of an initial grant of £5 for every acre of cocoa lost and a further grant of £7 for every acre replanted.[70]

This change of policy did not produce a similar result throughout the Colony. For example, in New Dwaben, farmers were happy about the change, while in the areas of scattered outbreaks where an amount of healthy cocoa trees remained untouched, there was very little change in the farmers' attitude towards the cutting out.[71] Some were also worried about the form of the compensation. In the Editorial "Lost Farms," it was suggested that compensation should be in the nature of "grants" controlled and utilized by a competent authority for the replacement of specific cocoa trees, for some money lenders took advantage of the farmers' "illiteracy or ignorance of the complexity of modern economy."[72]

Although the compensation was a major grievance, it was not the only one. Even after the government decided to pay compensation, the farmers still opposed cutting-out. For example, although the Beeton Committee recommended generous compensation, farmers were not happy about it. Farmers of Akyem Abuakwa blamed J. B. Danquah for allowing his name to appear on the Beeton Report list of witnesses. "You are the only man we have in Abuakwa to speak for us in these matters, and now you have gone and signed the paper that they should cut down our cocoa trees."[73] In 1950, a sum of £9,000,000 was allotted for compensation. According to the Chairman of the Cocoa Marketing Board, the choice was simple. "Why then the apathy, the non-co-operation, the opposition? Does it make sense?" He could not understand why the farmers still refused the cutting-out.[74]

What the farmers were concerned about was not the compensation, but the simple fact of cutting-out, the fact of destroying their cocoa trees. That is why when they were asked about the methods of cutting-out, some witnesses declared: "The payment of larger grants would have no effect on their opposition to cutting-out. They wanted to see the money which was used for grant payment spent instead on the improvement of the social services and communications and on industrial development."[75] In some cases, farmers not planting cocoa stood together with cocoa farmers against cutting-out. The Chief of Mo in Asante made his attitude clear in the Asante Confederacy Council: "We plant no cocoa in Mo. But I feel I should side with the group who are protesting against the cutting down of diseased trees."[76] Why? What was the reason for taking this stand?

Political Inspiration

In the Watson Report, it was stated that the opposition "was to a great extent politically inspired."[77] This statement is only partly true. On the one hand, the protest against cutting-out had long existed and was therefore simply an expression of farmers' economic grievances. On the other hand, there was a relation between nationalism and opposition against cutting-out. There were constant reports concerning the connection of "the educated" or "those who did not have any interest in cocoa" with the protest movement.

In an article published in *The Gold Coast Observer*, William Ofori Atta vehemently criticized the government's policy on the control of cocoa disease. Actively involved in the activities of the Akyem Abuakwa Farmers Union, he tried to relate the cocoa farmers' complaint against cutting-out with their living standard, arguing that cocoa farmers had the same right as civil servants, teachers and people in other businesses who had all asked for raise in salary. "But what of the farmers?

What of the persons who support the Agriculture Industry which mainly supports the entire country?" "Don't they buy in the same market with the Civil Servants and the Teachers and the Mercantile Clerk?" He looked at the problem from a broader perspective, linking the cocoa industry with the future of the colony: "But what of the FUTURE? I am not here concerned solely with the future of the cocoa trees, but also and principally of Gold Coast agriculture and of Gold Coast itself."[78]

Another nationalist leader J. B. Danquah also offered his expertise as a lawyer to those farmers opposed to cutting-out. When the Executive Committee of the Farmers' Union asked his opinion about whether it would be proper to bring a test case in the High Court against the agricultural officers for cutting down their cocoa trees, he thought it was uncertain that they could win the case. Instead he advised them to take other measures, to bring their grievances to the notice of the Colony Farmers Union meeting and that "when general agreement was secured they could do one of two things: present a Petition to the Governor, or present a Petition to the Legislative Council."[79]

On February 13, 1948, two editorials appeared on the same page of *The Gold Coast Observer*, one entitled "More trouble with swollen shoot", another "Nationalism in the Gold Coast." Then in half a month, the political disturbances occurred in Accra and spread to other areas. In November 1950, it was found that some meetings were called to discuss opposition to treatment. These meetings were organized "by politically minded people not by true farmers." The Government officials worried about the fact: "It is unfortunate that we are not getting the full support of all sections of the educated community in the effort. Some people apparently for political ends continued to spread fake rumors regarding the objects and methods of the disease control campaign; most of these people have no direct interest in cocoa farming."[80]

In July 1951, the Governor revealed his worry about the political implications of the opposition to cutting-out. He told the Secretary of State in his confidential telegram: "Since abolition of compulsion was announced on 30th May there has continued to be in a large measure of opposition to cutting out. This has been most marked in the Eastern Province where there has been organized opposition mostly by non-farmers and numerous incidents of interference with cutting out where this was being undertaken with the consent of the farmers concerned." Some report suggested that the "fear of intimidation from political sources is keeping farmers from allowing treatment."[81]

The government organized some village meetings to explain disease control measures. However, those meetings turned out to be an occasion for nationalists to carry out their propaganda. It was revealed in the annual report of cocoa disease control and rehabilitation that "large meetings served little useful purpose as they invariably attracted people who had no interest in disease control but apparently considerable interest in upsetting any Government policy however beneficial."[82]

Another sign that could suggest the connection between nationalism and protest lay in the mobilization of farmers against control measure by some organizations.

Organizational Linkage

During the protest, some organizations were formed and systematic actions were taken to oppose the treatment. In February 1948, a Farmers' Union was formed in Akyem Abuakwa named as "the core of the resistance of cutting-out" by the Press.[83] The resolution of the Akyem Abuakwa Farmers' Union made very clear the purpose of the organization: "the present Government policy of cutting down cocoa trees in the swollen shoot campaign is a certain cause of destruction of the cocoa industry and consequently of the ruin of the entire economy of the Country and of individual farmers and whole families." It was unanimously resolved at the meeting on January 28, 1948: (1) the Farmers of Akyem Abuakwa were opposed to the present government policy of cutting down cocoa trees in the swollen shoot campaign; (2) in the interest of the Gold Coast Agriculture and of Cocoa Industry, treatment and retreatment gangs engaged in cutting out cocoa trees should be withdrawn.[84] Other farmers' organizations were also active in the protest. For example, the government blamed "continuous propaganda from a farmers' organization opposed to disease control" in New Dwaben District.[85]

Most actively involved in the protest campaign was the Ghana Farmers' Congress, which was founded after the mass meeting at Nsawan on December 13 1949, based on three farmers' organizations. The Farmers' Congress was based on the Gold Coast Farmers' Association Ltd., the Mandated Togoland Farmers' Association Ltd. and the Farmers Committee of British West Africa. But according to the Governor, "This body is not (repeat not) representative of the cocoa producers in the Colony and Ashanti. It is composed largely of farmers in the Suhum Nkawkaw and Akyem Abuakua areas."[86]

After its conference in October 1950, the Congress sent a telegram to the Colonial Secretary, raising several issues regarding cocoa production. It complained that the peasants could no longer continue to live under the yoke of "economic slavery." It questioned the very existence of the Department of Cocoa Rehabilitation and declared that the Department was "wasteful," since its services "are in no way commensurate with expenditure it entails." Responsible officers in charge of its operations had "little or no scientific training", which had "resulted in ruthless destruction of healthy cocoa trees with ripe pods on them by its treatment and retreatment gangs." In November the Congress sent another cable to the Colonial Secretary asking for the government to immediately stop the "present manner in which cocoa trees are cut down by laborers of department of cocoa rehabilitation headed by Europeans with no scientific training."[87] Besides the issue of cutting-out and rehabilitation, the Congress also addressed other problems, such as the relation between the Cocoa Marketing Board and the Gold Coast farmers, and even the direct political representation for farmers in the forthcoming legislative assembly.

In January 1951, ten branches of the Ghana Farmers' Congress sent cables to the Secretary of State protesting the action of the Department of Agriculture to "apply force in cutting down cocoa trees." They warned that the action could provoke "peace loving farmers into riot not benefiting a trustee Government." One cable from Adeiso Branch stated despite the government's threats of arrest and prosecution, serious protests against destruction of cocoa farms "still continues," and "country will be thrown into confusion and chaos as farmers can no longer stand provocation under disguise of keeping law and order." [88]

The Secretary of Ghana Farmers' Congress Ashie-Nikoi was in fact Chairman of the Convention Peoples Party Eastern Region branch and was supported by Kwame Nkrumah, Bankole Awooner Renner and other nationalist leaders. Naturally, the Governor Sir Arden-Clarke was greatly alarmed by the situation. In a letter to the Secretary of State, he disclosed his worry: "C.P.P. will exploit any local grievances that can be found in its endeavor to win adherents in rural areas. It is, therefore, likely that C.P.P. would [use] Ghana Farmers Congress as a useful auxiliary in election campaign if it appeared to be gaining influence."[89]

Kwame Nkrumah made no secret of his strategy of exploiting all useful resources: "in all fairness it must be said that in our agitation for self-government, we would not have been against taking advantage of any grievance that presented itself if by so doing it could further our political purpose."[90] He did exactly what he said. And the overwhelming victory of Convention Peoples Party in the 1951 election was a clear sign.

Conclusion

An editorial in *The Gold Coast Observer* on February 13 1948 disclosed the difficult situation of the cocoa farmer: "There is debt due to advance received; there is the loss of income for himself and dependants; worse still, he is faced with ruin for an unknown period. He blames Government, he blames the Agricultural officer, he blames the Cocoa Marketing Board" and he became "a potential source of discontent."

The potential source of discontent soon became the reality by the end of February 1948. The cocoa farmers took an active part in the political disturbances all over the country. After the riot, the nationalist leaders became more and more conscious of the strong force of the cocoa farmers. It was reported in 1949, "Unfortunately the only people who were prepared to lead were those who opposed treatment, not on any scientific knowledge of the nature and spread of the disease, but apparently only because of a desire to embarrass Government in every possible way."[91]

This observation shows how political roles functioned in the protest. The "people who were prepared to lead" clearly meant nationalist leaders. The interests of the farmers and those leaders were not exactly the same. But it was easy for nationalists to establish a connection between protest against colonial rule and opposition to cutting-out, which in turn resulted in the mobilization of the farmers by the political leaders.

Since cutting-out was, and still remains, the only effective method to control swollen shoot,[92] the campaign against cutting-out evolved into a battle of politics against the approach to science.[93] The nationalists used the opposition to cutting-out as a means to fight the colonial government. However, this battle against science was only a makeshift in the nationalist movement. Ironically, the colonial government adopted the same attitude when its rule was threatened. Facing conflict between politics and science, it was in a dilemma. If it had stuck to the cutting-out policy, cocoa trees could have been saved. But the victory of science could have resulted in political chaos, and the colonial government could not afford this outcome. Instead it preferred to sacrifice science for politics. Twice, in 1948 and 1951, it relinquished the compulsory cutting-out, the only effective control measure, for fear of political crisis.

The Convention Peoples Party government did overcome this dilemma. Soon after CPP won the election and took office in 1951, the Government began a new campaign of cutting-out. After the "New Deal" scheme was announced in August, the reaction from farmers was still not encouraging. Then the government resumed cutting-out in September with strong determination, with fourteen days' notice and generous compensation. The peasants gradually accepted the reality, and the cutting-out made great progress. The annual report of 1953-54 pointed out, "The good progress being made in the last quarter of 1952-53 was maintained throughout 1953-54."[94]

The farmers were always suspicious of the colonial intentions. This suspicion materialized when their interests were threatened. Suspicion developed first into passivity or hostility, then to popular protest. The cutting-out lasted more than fifteen years, so did the protest. The resistance played such an important role in local politics that it caused constant changes in colonial policy. Together with other factors, it put colonialism on the edge of crisis and speeded up the movement to self-government.

Notes

[1] In January 1948, Accra chief Nii Kwabena Bonne III led a boycott against imported goods and high living standard, which lasted more than a month. After negotiation, the boycott ended on February 28. In a peaceful demonstration on the same day to demand for better treatment after their demobilization, a group of ex-servicemen marched to the Governor's residence. On the way a clash with policemen left two dead and four or five injured. Angered by this, people attacked foreign shops. In the end 29 persons lost their lives and 237 injured. See Kwame Nkrumah, *The Autobiography of Kwame Nkrumah* (London: Thomas Nelson and Sons, 1957), pp.62-63; Nii Kwabena Bonne III, *Milestones in the History of the Gold Coast: Autobiography of Nii Kwabena Bonne III Osu Alata Mantse*, pp.63-88.

[2] *Report of the Commission of Enquiry into the Disturbances in the Gold Coast, 1948*. Colonial. No.231. para.20. (Thereafter *Watson Report*.)

[3] A. F. Posnette, "Pathology," in Department of Agriculture, *Report on the Central Research Station*, compiled and edited by M. Greenwood (Accra: Government Printing Department, 1943), p.56; D. H. Urquhart, *Cocoa* (London: Longman, 1956), p.145.

[4] *ADM11/1799*. Provincial Council (Eastern Province). Minutes of the 35th Session of the Provincial Council of Eastern Province, 23 September 1941, p.29.

[5] *Minutes of the 13th Session of the Ashanti Confederacy Council on 18th-26th February, 1948* (Accra, 1953). Appendix III. Mr. Hyslop's Address, p.35.

[6] K. B. Dickson, "Cocoa in Ghana" (Unpublished PhD thesis, University of London, 1960), p.267.

[7] "Data on swollen shoot," *The Gold Coast Observer*, February 6, 1948. pp.486-487.

[8] The damage by swollen shoot also caused the migration of the population, mainly Krobos and Akwapims from the Eastern Province, to the less densely populated and more heavily forested areas in the north and west. According to K. Arhin, the main reason for 41 per cent of the migrants was shortage of suitable cocoa farmland in a previous farming area, and the reputed availability of farming land in the settlement areas. Kwame Arhin, *The Expansion of Cocoa Production: The working conditions of migrant cocoa farmers in the Central and Western Regions* (Accra, 1985).

9 *Minutes of the 13th Session*, Appendix III. Mr. Hyslop's Address, p.34. The export of cocoa rose in 1946/47 to £9,500,000, and £41,000,000 in 1947/8 owing to the increase of the world prices.

10 Information Service Department: *Golden Harvest The story of the Gold Coast cocoa industry* (Accra, 1953), p. 28.

11 Nana Ofori Atta blamed the government for not making the maximum efforts to control the disease. *Legislative Council Debates*, Session 1942, No.1. p.108. In 1949 *The Spectator Daily* was impatient with Government's "excuses" about shortage of staff. *ADM1/2/313*. Saving No.2433. Governor to Secretary of State, 24 December 1949.

12 *The Gold Coast Farmer*, 5:8(1936), p.144. Dickson suggested that the first method used to control swollen shoot was the planting of shade trees, the cutting out was first tested in 1939. This seems to be inaccurate. Dickson, "Cocoa in Ghana," p.270.

13 *The Gold Coast Farmer*, 6:2(1937), p.23.

14 *CO96/741I*. File. No.31265. F. A. Stockdale to G. C. Auchinleek (Gold Coast Director of Agriculture), 8 December 1936. Stockdale to Cadbury, 6 May 1937. H. A. Dade arrived on June 2 1937, together with another mycologist F. Deighton who was from Sierra Leone; Report of H. A. Dade on Swollen Shoot, 1937.

15 Dickson, "Cocoa in Ghana," p.272. It was possible that this policy helped the spread of the disease.

16 *Gold Coast Gazette*. No.80, 21 December 1940.

17 *Legislative Council Debates*, Session 1941, No. 1. p.17.

18 *Order in Council Made under the Plant Pests and Diseases Ordinance, 1937. Order No.12 of 1941.*

19 *Legislative Council Debates*, Session 1942, No.1. p.108.

20 *Legislative Council Debates*, Session 1947, No.2. p.80.

21 *ADM1/2/316*. Governor to Secretary of State, 26 November 1949.

22 *Korsah Report*. para.21.

23 *ADM5/3/76. Report of the Committee of Enquiry into the Existing Organization and Methods for the Control of Swollen Shoot Disease by the Compulsory Cutting Out of Infected Cocoa Trees, 1951.* para.22. (There after *Korsah Report*).

24 *ADM1/2/316*. Extract from a speech broadcast by Leader of Government Business on Thursday, June 28 1951.

25 *The Gold Coast Farmer*, 5:7(1936), p.122; 5:8(1936), p.144; 5:9(1937), p.165.

26 *CO96/741*. A. W. Hodson to W. G. A. Ormsby-Gore, 4 December 1937.

[27] *Legislative Council Debates*, Session 1941, No.1. p.55.

[28] *ADM11/1799*. Provincial Council (Eastern Province). Minutes of 35th session, September 1941. p.41.

[29] *Legislative Council Debates*, Session 1942, No.1. p.4.

[30] *Watson Report*, para.264.

[31] *Minutes of the 13th Session*, Appendix III. Mr. Hyslop's Address. p.35.

[32] *Legislative Council Debates*, Session 1947. No.2.

[33] J. B. Danquah, *Journey to Independence and After (Danquah's Letters)* (Accra: Waterville Publishing House, 1970), compiled by H. K. Akyeampong, pp.56-57.

[34] Colonial Office: *Annual Report on the Gold Coast for 1948* (London: HMSO, 1950). Appendix IIA. Report of the Commission of Enquiry into the swollen shoot disease of cacao in the Gold Coast. p.178.

[35] *ADM1/2/316*. Governor to Secretary of State, 26 November 1949.

[36] *ADM36/1/114*. File No.19. Cocoa Disease Control and Rehabilitation Monthly Progress Report, July 1950(Thereafter Monthly Report); Monthly Report, September 1950.

[37] *ADM1/2/316*. Statement by Leader of Government Business and the Minister of Health and Labour in the Legislative Assembly on the cutting-out of diseased cocoa trees.

[38] *ADM36/1/114*. File No.19. Monthly Report of Oda District, April, 1951. Divisional Office. Akim Oda; Monthly Report, May 1951.

[39] Department of Agriculture, *Monthly News-letter*, May, 1951.

[40] *Korsah Report*. para.13.

[41] *Legislative Council Debates*, Session 1937, No.2, p.36.

[42] *ADM36/1/115*. Kade Survey dated 15 March 1950 by Acting Survey Officer.

[43] Department of Agriculture, *Monthly News-letter*, September 1949 to February 1951.

[44] *Monthly News-letter*, May 1950; April 1951. *ADM36/1/114*. Swollen shoot. Monthly Report of Oda District. June 1951.

[45] *Report of a Conference on Cocoa* (London, 1950), p.52.

[46] Department of Agriculture, *Monthly News-letter*, January 1950.

[47] *ADM36/1/114*. File No.19. Swollen shoot. Quarterly Progress Report of Oda Division, December 1950. Department of Agriculture, *Monthly News-letter*, January 1951.

48 *ADM36/1/114*. File No.19. Swollen shoot (Eastern Province). Cocoa Disease Control and Rehabilitation Progress Report of April 1951. Dated 6 June 1951; Monthly Report of Oda District, January 1952.

49 *Minutes of the 13th Session of the Ashanti Confederacy Council on 18th-26th February, 1948.* p.10.

50 *The Gold Coast Observer*, April 9 1948, p.599.

51 According to Mr. MacDonald-Smith: "The opposition, so far as I know, has not been armed as it was previously." *Report of a Conference on Cocoa* (London, 1950), p.52.

52 *CO96/830/31709/1950*. Shots. Gold Coast, Accra, October 28 1950, Reuter, Department of Agriculture, *Monthly News-letter*, November 1950.

53 Department of Agriculture, *Monthly News-letter*, December 1950, January 1951.

54 *ADM36/1/114*. File No.19. Swollen shoot (Eastern Province). Cocoa Disease Control and Rehabilitation Monthly Progress Report, April, 1951 dated 6 June 1951.

55 *The Gold Coast Observer*, April 2 1948, p.585.

56 Farmers in the Gold Coast like most farmers throughout the world tend to an innate conservatism." Watson Report. para.264.

57 Peasant's culture has been constantly described as conservative by many scholars. See K. Dobrowolski, "Peasant traditional culture" in Teodor Shanin, *Peasants and Peasant Societies* (Oxford: Basil Blackwell, 1987), pp.261-77. However, it would be better, or at least more important, to notice two fundamental characteristics of the peasant's culture: materialism and pragmatism.

58 W. S. D. Tudhope, *Enquiry into the Gold Coast cocoa industry, Final Report. Minutes of the Legislative Council and Sessional Papers*, Session 1918-1919. IV, p.14.

59 *CO96/647*. Bye-Laws as to Cocoa Farms. Dated 19 November, 1910. Encl. in the Gold Coast No.426. Acting Governor to Secretary of State. 24 May 1924.

60 *Legislative Council Debates*, Session 1937, No.2. p.39.

61 Nii Kwabena Bonne III, *Milestones in the History of the Gold Coast*, p.64.

62 I would like to thank Dr. Addo-Fening of the Department of History, University of Ghana, for his mentioning of the situation at his hometown in Akyem Abuakwa. He recalled that during those days, farmers were alarmed about the government's intention. "One day my father took his gun and went to the bush. He said that the government men were coming to cut the cocoa trees. I was at school at that time and did not understand what was happening."

63 R. H. Bates, *Essays on the Political Economy of Rural Africa* (London: Cambridge University Press, 1983), p.96.

[64] *The Gold Coast Farmers*, 5:8(1936), p.144; 5:9(1937), p.165; 6:1(1937), p.3.

[65] *Legislative Council Debates*, Session 1947, No.2. p.80.

[66] *ADM11/1799*. Provincial Council (Eastern Province). Appendix S. Minutes of a meeting held at the Director of Agriculture's Office, Accra, on 3rd October 1941.

[67] *The Gold Coast Observer*, July 25 1947, p.146.

[68] *The Gold Coast Observer*, September 5 1947, p.222.

[69] This Committee is usually refereed to as Beeton Committee.

[70] *ADM5/1/124*. Report on the Department of Agriculture for 1947-48. p.8.

[71] Colonial Office, *Annual Report on the Gold Coast for 1948*. p.37.

[72] *The Gold Coast Observer*, January 30 1948, p.474.

[73] Danquah, *Journey to Independence and After*, p.58.

[74] *ADM1/2/316*. Address by the Chairman of the Cocoa Marketing Board, Mr. S. MacDonald-Smith, to the Joint Provincial Council at Dodowah on the 24th January 1950.

[75] *Korsah Report*. para.16.

[76] *Minutes of the 13th Session of the Ashanti Confederacy Council*, p.10.

[77] *Watson Report*. para.265.

[78] William Ofori Atta, "Our Country's Agriculture," *The Gold Coast Observer*, July 25 1947.

[79] Danquah, *Journey to Independence and After*, pp.58-59.

[80] *ADM36/1/114*. File No.19. Monthly Report. November 1950.

[81] *ADM1/2/316*. Saving No.948. Governor to Secretary of State. 6 July 1951. *ADM36/1/114*. Swollen shoot. Monthly Progress Report of Oda District. June 1951.

[82] Department of Agriculture, *Monthly News-letter*, June 1949.

[83] *ADM1/2/313*. Governor to Secretary of State, 24 December 1949.

[84] *Minute of the 13th Session of the Ashanti Confederacy Council*. Appendix IV. Resolution II. The Akyem Abuakwa Farmers' Union, 28 January, 1948. p.38.

[85] Department of Agriculture, *Monthly News-letter*, June 1951.

[86] *CO96/830/31709/1951*. File No.174. Police Special Branch Report: Ghana (Gold Coast) Farmers' Congress. Encl. in Governor to Secretary of State, 24 January 1951. See *CO96/830/31709/1950*. Inward Telegram. Confidential. No.989. Governor to Secretary of State, 14 November 1950.

[87] *CO96/830/31709/1950*. Ghana's Farmers Congress to James Griffiths (Colonial Secretary), 27 October 1950. Ghana's Farmers Congress, 1950. Cable to Colonial Secretary, 28 November 1950.

[88] *CO96/830/31709/1951*. Cable from Ghana Farmers' Congress. 11 January 1951. Encl. in Fenner Brockway (M.P.) to Secretary of State, 15 January 1951. See also Cable No.8. 18 January 1951. Cables from Ghana Farmers' Congress to Secretary of State, January 1951.

[89] *CO96/830/31709/1950*. No.989 (Confidential). Inward Telegram. Governor to Secretary of State, 14 November 1950.

[90] Kwame Nkrumah, *Autobiography*, p.62.

[91] Department of Agriculture, *Monthly News-letter*, June 1949.

[92] "There is no chemical cure for diseased trees and the only possible method of control is to cut out infected trees." L. A. Are and D. R. G. Gwynne-Jones, *Cocoa in West Africa* (Ibadan: Oxford University Press, 1974), p.83.

[93] There were always protests against whoever was violating peasants' interests, long term or short term, during the colonial period. The anti-cattle-dipping in South Africa and opposition to anti soil-erosion in Malawi were other two cases of the same kind. See W. Beinart, *Hidden Struggle*, pp.191-221; Elias C. Mandala, *Works and Control in a Peasant Economy: A history of the lower Tchiri valley in Malawi, 1959-1960* (Wisconsin: Wisconsin University Press, 1990), pp.219-237.

[94] *Annual Report on the Department of Agriculture, 1953-54*, p.4. See also J. D. Broatch, "The progress of the Gold Coast swollen shoot control campaign," *Report of the Cocoa Conference 1953* (London, 1953), p.78.

CONCLUSION

Colonialism and Rural Protest

J. F. A. Ajayi points out that colonialism was only an episode in African history.[1] The originality of his assertion lies in its challenge to the prevalent belief that the dawn of African history began with the arrival of the European. Ajayi's statement is obviously correct regarding time and space, but not in terms of the effect. The colonial "episode" was so important that it changed the process of African history and brought it into the modern capitalist system. As another distinguished African historian put it, "Never in the history of Africa did so many changes occur and with such speed as they did between 1880 and 1935."[2] If we study the history of Africa, the hundred-year colonial period should be treated equally with other African experiences, in the long process of the development of African civilization. But if we study African history under colonialism, the impact and legacy of colonialism cannot be overemphasized.

Colonialism and the Question of Class Formation

Under colonialism, the Gold Coast underwent various changes, one important change occurred in its social structure. It is difficult to make a clear-cut analysis of class formation in the Gold Coast society, especially in rural areas. This difficulty results from both theoretical confusion and African reality.

Although class analysis is believed to be a Marxist method in social science research, Marx himself never gave a clear definition of class. It was Lenin who gave a definition in his pamphlet *A Great Beginning* that was published in 1919: "Classes are large groups of people differing from each other by the place they occupy in a historically determined system of social production, by their relation (in most cases fixed and formulated in law) to the means of production, by their role in the social organization of labor, and, consequently, by the dimensions and mode of acquiring the share of social wealth of which they dispose. Classes are groups of people one of which can appropriate the labor of another owing to the different places they occupy in a definite system of social economy."[3]

Here, the emphasis is on the separation between those who own the means of production, and those who must sell their labor. The ownership of the means of production decides almost everything about classes: their place in the system of social production, their role in the social organization of labor and their share of social wealth. In theoretical analysis, the attention has been usually shifted to two other related aspects. Capitalists could mean those who do not work but live on the exploitation of others; or could mean those who employ hired labor. This different focus has obviously brought confusion to the study of rural community in the Gold Coast. A wealthy farmer employed laborers, who could be his wife, sons or daughters, or relatives. This farmer would not be regarded as capitalists in the first case, but he was a capitalist in the second.[4]

The history of African capitalist development also contributed to this difficulty of analysis. Unlike European society where capitalism evolved from the soil of feudalism, capitalism was transplanted to Africa without being rooted in the internal evolution of African societies. The transformation was sudden and abrupt, not gradual and evolutionary. However, older political structures, economic systems and social values still persisted, inhibiting the new capitalist system, which was advancing cruelly with the support of the colonial government. This duality made the situation in the Gold Coast more complicated than that of modern Europe, where money had simplified every social relation.

The study of the class formation in Africa, or in the developing countries for that matter, usually emphasizes the role of capitalism. The general argument is that capitalism speeded up the process.[5] This is only one side of the picture. I would argue that the imposition of capitalism and colonialism from outside also hindered the process of class formation. First, the former basis of power (such as the state or the control of trade routes) was broken down, and the traditional ruling class was stripped of its economic benefits. However, it is remarkable that no coercion was needed to make the dominant group accept cocoa production during the early colonial period. The reason was that there had already been an experience of cash-crop production (palm oil and rubber) in the Gold Coast after the abolition of the slave trade.

Secondly, the government used various ways to control land and cocoa production, such as the attempt to stop the outright sale of land by chiefs to outside farmer-traders; the introduction of a state-controlled cocoa marketing co-operative system; and the establishment of the Cocoa Marketing Board in 1947/48 which "slowed down considerably the process of class formation."[6]

Thirdly, although land became increasingly important as a means of production, the traditional idea of communal ownership still lingered on and inhibited development of capitalist relations. The acquisition of land by purchase did not prevent it from becoming family property. The means of production were owned by family, lineage or state; private ownership did not enjoy its sacred position as it did in capitalist society. Consequently, the relationship of production was less clearly defined. The modern force of production was not clearly formed; thus it did not reveal itself as vigorously as traditional ones. Proletarianization was limited, and a national capitalist class hardly existed. This peculiar situation blurred the rigid line of class.

Most important, theoretical synthesis should follow the study of reality, not precede it. In other words, "simply to prescribe class analysis" or the "mechanistic application of preconceived class divisions" does not in itself clarify the pattern of the Gold Coast's rural politics; nor does it help us to understand the linkage of social protest within either the traditional context or modern nationalism. Only through historical analysis of African societies, can we get a clearer picture of its social structure. Moreover, the argument that rural class formation was delayed by the peculiar situation of colonialism should not prevent us from studying the differentiation or stratification of various social groups in rural areas.

In Akan society, there existed two major social groups: *Ahenfo* (office holders) that included secular and religious authorities and *Akoa* (a commoner, *pl. nkoa*). This stratification, however, only reflects the existence of "minor contradictions in the system of wealth distribution", and the formation of class did not occur because of "illiteracy, ignorance, lack of modern science and technology", the "small volume of surplus production", and "lack of an adequate communication system."[7] But the nineteenth century witnessed a growth of tension between commoners and rulers. "We want no more cruelties, or taking off of heads, or taking of other men's wives... we want a good King, peace, open roads, and trade."[8] This was a commoners' call for political reform, not only in Asante, but also in other Akan areas. Conflict increased with the establishment of colonial rule and the introduction of cash crops.

There are various interpretations of the formation of classes in the Gold Coast. Based on her study of migrant farmers in southern Ghana, Polly Hill concluded that the migrant farmers of southern Ghana should be regarded as "capitalists engaged in the business cocoa-farming." She used three factors to support her argument. First, the migrant farmers had been functioning within the framework of "market economy" or "money economy." Secondly, the activities during the expansionary period, which included ever-increasing land acquisition, output of cocoa and labor employment, seem to justify some degree of analogy with capitalism. Thirdly, the farmers made money because they were enterprising, not because they were obliged to do so in order to survive.[9] These factors are definitely capitalistic, but they do not support the argument.[10]

Although her study claims to be "essentially historical", her research indicates no polarization between poor and rich in capitalist development, a phenomenon that is inevitable in this process. Neither does she provide any evidence to suggest that there was a striking difference of life style, technology and economic behavior between those "capitalist farmers" and their neighbors. There did not exist a serious division of labor either.[11] It is correct to suggest that cocoa farmers contributed greatly to the development of capitalism in the Gold Coast, but it is less convincing to conclude that they themselves were capitalist farmers.

Rhoda Howard has presented another view. She has divided rural community into four groups. The rural petty bourgeoisie was the wealthiest. The second was a middle peasantry comprised of families who worked only one farm, using their own labor. The third was the indebted peasantry who had to borrow money from the rural petty bourgeoisie and often in order to pay their debts, had to either engage in sharecropping arrangements with the creditors or give up usufruct entirely. The final group was a class of landless migrant laborers from the Northern Territories and the French colonies, who worked for the petty bourgeoisie. In an article on peasantry, she made her criteria more clearly in the analysis of stratification of peasantry: "A perhaps more succinct way of observing stratification among peasants would be to observe their debt relationships as well as their relationship to buying and selling labor power." [12]

The two criteria, however, have their own limitation. First, in the Gold Coast, many cocoa farmers bought and sold their labor power at the same time. Konings' fieldwork strongly indicates this fact. According to Konings, poor farmers often leave their newly established, low-producing cocoa farms to share-croppers, while they themselves either sell their labor to rich peasants or devote their own labor time to food production and other economic activities.[13] Secondly, the debt is an unclear factor. We have to ask an important question: debt for what? Some farmers may have to borrow money in order to survive whereas others may do so simply to expand their cocoa farms. There is a world of difference between these two cases. To make the matter more complicated, the laborers from the Northern Territories usually retained access to land in their homelands, which R. Howard herself correctly points out.[14]

An excellent study of social stratification and class formation in Ghana is made by P. Konings. His contribution lies in his conclusion that class consciousness and action based on exploitation in the process of exchange seems more explicit than in that based on the exploitation in the process of production. His classification resembles Mao Tse-tung's analysis of the Chinese peasantry in the 1920s,[15] but less explicit. The peasantry was divided into three categories: a stratum of rich peasants, that is able to accumulate capital and producing at least 200 loads per year, a stratum of middle peasants which is generally able to sustain itself and its household members, producing about 50-200 loads a year, and a stratum of poor peasants producing under 50 loads a year.[16] Simply using loads of cocoa as a measure seems to be rather arbitrary. Two questions have to be asked regarding this criterion.

First, was the cocoa the only produce of the family? Evidence suggests that in some areas it was far more complicated than that. In those areas close to food markets, farmers were usually involved in food production. G. Austin has provided us with an extreme example: Kwame Akowuah produced 52 loads a year from his cocoa farm, which were worth about £35 according to 1930s prices, yet his lawyer claimed that he had thirty foodstuff farms, from which he made at least £600 a year.[17] Secondly, if the load was used as the only criterion, did the size of the family have any effect upon the life style? A family with two members producing 195 loads would live a much better life than a family with ten members producing 205 loads a year. But according to Koning's standard, the former was a middle peasant while the latter was a rich peasant.

Cocoa cultivation produced a large group of cocoa farmers, most of them migrants. With the expansion of the production and trading activities, there also appeared a group of businessmen, brokers and peddlers, who formed a chain to link the cocoa farmers on one end and the foreign companies on the other.

Mining, transportation and other industries gradually created a working class. Although they were not a significant percentage of the population, they fought for their own interests as a social force. Their continuous resistance to exploitation by foreign companies and the control of the colonial government made them one of the most militant groups. However, their struggle was usually defined in **occupational** rather than **class** terms. This limitation narrowed their perspective of national politics and hindered the development of a proletarian consciousness. Because of their narrow outlook, they displayed little interest in participating in the national political arena and failed to become a leading force in the nationalist movement.[18]

Another change occurred with the rise of the educated African. In the early period, missionary schools did contribute to this aspect. However, as Agbodeka correctly points out, the zeal for progress among African communities was not only confined to industry and commerce, "Educational development was the first major concern of the Gold Coast people." When the government failed to meet the demands for schools, people began their own projects. [19] There were 204 government-assisted schools in 1918. The Education Ordinance was passed in 1925, which set up a new Board of Education. This year also saw building of Achimota College, which was formally opened in 1927. According to the 1948 census, of the 4,111,680 Africans enumerated in the Gold Coast, 98,935 had attained the school standard of III-VI and 64,717 standard VII or higher. A greater percentage of educated persons were in Accra, Akuapem-New Dwaben and Ho than in other districts. [20]

For the sake of analysis, the rural society of the Gold Coast can be divided into three social groups: the educated Africans, traditional leaders and commoners. [21] Although these groups could also be divided into sub-groups either politically or economically, each one had its own characteristics, and was viewed by other groups as distinctive. As a social group, educated Africans' strength and weakness both lay in the fact that they were a mixture of African and western cultures. They were pioneers in the building of national consciousness, but some of them looked down on their own people and tried every means to separate from commoners. For this reason, they sometimes enjoyed less popularity than chiefs. [22] Beginning from 1920, there was a conflict between the educated Africans and traditional leaders. Later, the educated Africans became increasingly involved in the nationalist movement.

Under colonialism, the traditional leaders, including chiefs, elders or councilors, and religious leaders, lost some of their power or advantages. Since the British only recognized the authority of the chiefs, their position underwent great changes. As suggested in this work, their economic situation worsened during the early period owing to the lack of regular income. This situation, together with the decline of checks and balances in traditional society, resulted in chiefs' abuse of power, followed by much conflict between them and their subjects. In most cases, the government protected their abuse of power in order to maintain indirect rule.

The commoners were a more complicated group. Traditionally, they were called "young men", a term referring to those people of lower class, who held no traditional office but could exercise their political power if dissatisfied with the conduct of affairs. [23] Some of them became rich owing to cocoa cultivation while others remained poor or worked as migrant laborers. Although ownership of property did bring advantages in education and other social benefits, the simple fact that commoners did not hold any traditional position put the rich and the poor together. They did not like the chief's abuse of power, but they depended on him more or less, since he was the only person recognized by the government to represent them. Lacking political participation, they had to voice their grievances through some informal or even extreme means, which caused the deposition or abdication of their chief.[24]

Another phenomenon is that the different attitudes of commoners and educated Africans towards the colonial government and the conflict among themselves indicate a gradual disintegration of the young men. This division, brought about by western education and economic opportunity, made "young men" an obscure term less and less definable.

Colonialism and Chief: A Paradox

Related to the change of the social structure, the most prominent phenomenon was the change of the traditional leader's position and role. It is remarkable that every protest in this study concerns the position and role of the chief. In the *Abirewa* movement, the priest, followed by the commoners, began to question chiefly power. The power of *Abirewa* caused such fear among chiefs that they requested the government to interfere directly with the movement. In the protest against the Forest Bill, a joint force of chiefs and the educated, supported by the people, won a victory in their resistance against the encroachment on the traditional land system. The *Asafo*'s active participation in local affairs greatly challenged chiefs' authority and resulted in many destoolments. This "undermining and usurping" also caused much concern from the colonial government, which had to adjust its policy in order to maintain control.

Lesser chiefs' rebellion against their respective Paramount Chief not only confronted the *Amanhene*'s authority but also defied the colonial policy of indirect rule. Although the resistances failed, the impact remained and the Paramount Chief was usually destooled afterwards. Finally, in the protest against the cutting-out campaign, farmers adopted different attitudes towards different chiefs. Those chiefs who took a lead in the resistance were respected, while those who supported the government's measures were attcked. Even the *Asantehene* had to make a speech to deny the allegation of his collaboration with the government.

Divide and rule, as a universal feature of colonialism, was practised by the British in the Gold Coast. Whenever educated Africans collaborated with traditional leaders, colonial officials cried "bad influence", "control" or "usurping the leadership." The protest in 1911 against the Forest Bill marked a notable unity between the educated African and the chief. The government was alert to this "tendency of the educated classes to control the actions of uneducated chiefs" and considered this "a less healthful sign particularly as it cannot be wholly disassociated from a spirit of personal gain."[25] After the 1920s, the British relied more upon chiefs rather than educated Africans. The educated were often accused of knowing their own people less than Europeans. In fact, they were made the "scapegoat" in colonial West Africa.[26]

The gradual erosion of legitimacy of chiefly power made administration more and more difficult. The result was the extension of British indirect rule in an effort to bolster chiefs and make them more effective intermediaries. This change of policy caused some tension as well. In the Gold Coast, the issue of the Native Administration Ordinance in 1927 increased the power of the Paramount Chief, which caused anger and resistance from the chiefs, the educated and the commoners. The more important factor was that with this increased authority, the Paramount Chiefs doubled their efforts to use or abuse their power, usually with the government's support. However, the result was clearly shown in this work: more abuse of power, more destoolments.

The paradox of chiefly power lies in the fact that the chief had to fulfill various functions within the indigenous institutions and yet at the same time occupied a position in the imported institutions.[27] Under colonialism, the stool was no longer sacred and the chief no longer "father of his people." Approved or even appointed by the government, he had to obey the government before he took any action. Usually he was caught in the middle by his paradoxical position.

On the one hand, the chief was a single authority without any checks and balances, an unusual situation compared to the pre-colonial period. Backed by the government, their power increased and was even feared by the commoners. On the other hand, their installation had to be approved by the Governor, their position and authority became less legitimate, thus less respected by their subjects. As a government tool, he lacked the legitimate means to exercise the power granted to him. Owing to the very nature of colonialism, the more responsible he was to the government, the less popular with his subjects. In other words, the more trust he enjoyed from the government, the less credibility from his people. No wonder people contemptuously called them "the Government made Chiefs."[28]

Another paradox was that the more the colonial government increased chiefly power, the more it weakened the indigenous institution. In the traditional system, the chief never possessed unlimited power, no matter how authoritative. His power was restricted by other factors, such as the religious leaders, the royal house, the councilors, the elders, or the *Asafo* organization. Under colonialism, democratic elements in the traditional system were sacrificed to chiefly power and the practice of so-called indirect rule. Religious leaders no longer enjoyed their authority under colonialism, the elder's prestige was not recognized by the government, and the commoners had no status in the modern political structure. Since the colonial government neutralized traditional checks and balances, there occurred more abuse of power by the chief.

The chief's attitude towards the colonial government was also paradoxical. In the pre-colonial period, a chief could enjoy authority and prestige in his community, or gifts and free labor from his subjects, or tributes from his subjugated territories. Under colonial rule, however, he lost all these privileges. He could no longer expect any presents or demand unpaid labor, yet he was still supposed to provide services for the community or show his generosity at grant occasions. His power was granted and supported by the government. The chief wished to enjoy his own privileges without colonial interference, yet he could enjoy that tranquility only with the help of the government because of lack of legitimacy. Constantly he had to ask for the government's support when he faced difficulties from below.

The fourth paradox was between colonial policy and practice. In theory, indirect rule is about local government: to leave local affairs to the indigenous authority. This was the essence of the British system.[29] Although the government tried to meddle with local affairs as little as possible, and this policy was stressed time and again, yet the local situation usually caused its interference, sometimes at the request of chiefs because of the challenge from below, sometimes to meet the colonial requirement when there was an extreme case of abuse of chiefly power. Whenever the government had to break its own policy and interfere directly, it usually did so at a high price. In some cases, the government had to send police or even troops to preserve order, which often caused open confrontation with local people. Sometimes the Governor even interfered with the legal system in order to support the chief, or to keep indirect rule running. So the dilemma became very ironic: to use direct measure in order to preserve indirect rule.

The Native Administration Ordinance (1927) was an example of such irony in practice. On the one hand, it stipulated that the election, installation or the deposition of a divisional chief or a Paramount Chief should behave "according to native customary law."[30] What is more, undermining and usurping the authority and position of a chief became an offence. All the measures attempted to strengthen the indigenous administrative system. On the other hand, both the unopposed election and deposition of either a Divisional Chief or a Paramount Chief were to be reported to the District Commissioner and the result was to be published in the government *Gazette*. The case of the opposed election or the opposed deposition of either a Paramount Chief or a Divisional Chief was to be reported to the government, and if the State Council failed to decide the matter, the "Governor's decision shall be final."[31]

All these regulations show that colonial rule and its native policy failed to establish an effective authority in the Gold Coast. It can be said that indirect rule uprooted traditional institutions but failed to replace them with a valid system. There were several reasons for the failure. First, the elders who used to play their part effectively in the traditional structure had less influence on the chief under colonial rule. This left the *Asafo* as the only force both legitimate and effective. Secondly, while the government ignored the institutional function of the *Asafo*, the chief no longer cared about their role as checks and balances. The *Asafo* were forced to gain power by more radical means. Thirdly, the hostility towards foreign rule and the grievances towards the chief added more fuel on the flame.

Less legitimate and less sacred, the chief faced more political crises and was constantly threatened by destoolment. Nonetheless his political role was not insignificant. Some of them, like Nana Ofori Atta, remained politically important, and the government depended on them to carry out difficult tasks. The chief controlled both natural resources that could make him rich and political resources that made him powerful. By distributing or redistributing the resources, they kept control of their community and enjoyed trust from the government. Most important, because they were still appointed to the position through the traditional process, especially before 1944, they could rightly claim their legitimacy and authority.

Legitimacy of the Protest

The legitimacy of protest forms a very important part of the ideology of protest. It is important to decide why at a given time some resisted, while others did not; yet it is more meaningful to ask why some collaborated with the government, while others took the risk of protesting. This phenomenon was closely linked with the issue of legitimacy.

Comparatively speaking, the British put more emphasis on the issue of legitimacy than the French in terms of indigenous authority.[32] This study shows once incorporated in the colonial administration, the chief's position gradually lost legitimacy, and he was facing challenges from two directions: common people represented by *Asafo* and the western-educated African. Not only does the authority need legitimacy, but any political power or action including protest needs legitimacy.

The protests discussed above had their own justification respectively, be it legal, traditional or historical.

In any form of political action, one party's legitimacy often implies the illegitimacy of the opposition. Therefore, the most effective way to claim legitimacy is to put the counterpart in the position of illegitimacy. For example, both the Lands Bill and the Forest Bill were based on the British government's claim that it had legitimate authority over land in the Gold Coast, which the Ghanaian people questioned on the basis of the 1844 Bond. Casely Hayford argued that nothing, not even the disputes between the Asante and the British, gave the British government "any additional jurisdiction than that which had been conferred by the Bond of 1844."[33] Its limited degree of legitimacy seems to be the Achilles' heel and some officials claimed that this bond was obsolete. Since the Forest Bill was based on legislation in southern Nigeria, the government argued the similarity between the two areas. But many educated Ghanaians did not agree: "Lagos, the capital of Southern Nigeria, was ceded to the British Government by its King in 1861. The Gold Coast has never been conquered, ceded, or alienated in any way to the British Crown."[34]

In other words, the British government did not have the right to manage the land of the Gold Coast, and the Forest Bill was illegitimate. The chiefs also used indigenous land tenure to oppose the government's intervention. Using Chief Achene's words, "My reason for objection is that I prefer to manage my forest myself."[35] In the protest against cutting-out, farmers questioned squarely the government's authority over their own cocoa crop and stopped the cutting-out several times.

It should be noticed that in the fight against the Land Bill in 1897 and the Forest Bill in 1910, there was an important connection between chiefs and educated Africans, while the *Asafo* played a very limited role. One reason was that in regard to these two issues, both the educated and chiefs represented the interests of the whole, fighting against the colonial government's attempt to encroach upon the traditional land system. After the founding of National Congress of British West Africa in 1920 and the open split between the educated and chiefs, there came a struggle for the representation of the people, which in reality promoted the integration of the mass with either the educated or the chiefs. Both the educated and chiefs claimed that they could best represent the people of the Gold Coast. However, both claims needed justification. From the perspective of the commoners, the educated could not represent them and the chiefs had betrayed them. The educated Africans, though they used to be young men, were no longer part of the common people.[36] The chiefs had simply become British agents working for the government to the disadvantage of the common people. In the 1924-5 Accra incident, the *Asafo* leaders sent a letter to the Ga *Mantse*, stating: "we have lost confidence in you as Ga *Mantse* and have therefore unanimously come to the conclusion that you should be suspended from the exercise of your office as Ga *Mantse* pending the result of our investigation." [37]

The tone really shows that the *Asafo* leaders believed in their role in the traditional power structure. Some colonial officials' liberal attitude also contributed to this sense of legitimacy. The Secretary for Native Affairs F. G. Crowther suggested there was nothing serious about *Asafo*. On the contrary, the commoners' participation in destoolments showed their demand for a higher standard of integrity in their rulers, which was a democratic sign. He stressed that this popular movement was an effect of changing conditions rather than the changing of political ideas; it was directed more to an individual ruler than to the colonial system.[38] No wonder that some chiefs complained time and again that District Commissioners sympathized with the *Asafo*, which made the government fail to understand the real situation.[39]

As for the conflict between the religious leaders and the chiefs, the priests often used tradition to justify their action against the chiefs. However, in order to make their activities acceptable, they had to meet two standards of legitimacy: that of the people and of the government. As is shown in this study, religion was a major part of life for Gold Coast people, and the priests used to enjoy privileges and power. However, under the influence of both Christianity and colonialism, the priests gradually lost their power and status. It was natural the language of religion was transformed into the language of protest in local politics. In some cases, the priests purposely challenged the chiefly power by gathering a large group of followers; in other cases, the rebels united under the leadership of religious leaders who thus became a threat to the established authority. The priests' protest in an attempt to regain a share in political leadership was always echoed by popular grievances caused by abuse of power.

Unlike other religious movements in colonial Africa, *Abirewa* was by no means a syncretism,[40] but an indigenous religious movement. However, besides the legitimacy in terms of acceptance by the common people, the priests also wanted to make local religion more acceptable to the government. Usually they tried to take forms or procedures from Christianity. We can observe some similarities between *Abirewa* and Christianity. For example, some of the commandments in the decalogue, the suspension of the male figure and the rite of confession all seem to indicate that the priests of *Abirewa* were not unacquainted with Christianity. The religious leaders were obviously trying to make their activities more legitimate by imitating Christianity. This practice partly explains why it took some time for the government to make up its mind to suppress *Abirewa*.

In West African colonies, there was a tendency for subordinate chiefs to achieve separation, as M. Crowder and O. Ikime point out in their work.[41] This claim resulted from different situations. First, the nature of paramountcy needs elaboration. The authority of some superior Chiefs such as *Asantehene* was well established before colonial rule. But there was always a tension between local towns and the larger state. Colonial rule did provide a better opportunity for the lesser chiefs to liberate themselves from the higher authority. In some cases, because of either ignorance or favoritism, the British elevated a chief who was originally *primus inter pares* to the position of the Paramount Chief. For example, the Ga *Mantse* used to be merely *Mantse* of Accra. Owing to the misunderstanding of the government, he was made Paramount Chief of the Ga people. This wrong recognition caused confusion and conflict.

Secondly, some states were originally established on a military basis and the Akan political institution did not admit of strong centralization. Therefore, in the pre-colonial period, towns and villages of these states enjoyed considerable independence in both political and economic matters. The *Pax Britannica* made wars less impossible and the military role became obsolete while the introduction of the modern state system made political, judicial and economic functions more important. From the informal allegiance in the pre-colonial period to the formal submission in the colonial period, this structural change in the mechanism of local administration obviously caused frustration and anxiety on both the chief and the Paramount Chief. While the big chief tried every means to increase his power that had not belonged to him before, the lesser chief reacted by protesting or trying to break away.

In addition, the tendency to separation was in some ways promoted by colonial administration. At an early stage, the government's failure to distinguish different levels of indigenous rulers obviously encouraged separatists. After the establishment of colonial rule, the Akan doctrine of "all power rests in the land" seemed to have changed to "all interest rests in power." With the support of the government, chiefly power was greatly augmented. Mining industry and cash crops brought about a rise in land values. In order to maintain their control over land, the lesser chiefs naturally tried to keep their independent position or break away from their Paramount Chief. An independent status meant economic benefits. In some places where fortune did not increase the resources of the local chiefs, the possibility of setting up their own tribunal also encouraged separation.

Rural Protest: Forms, Strategy and Significance

Protest takes different forms. We can categorize them into two major types: passive and active.[42] In the first type, there are many forms of daily-life protest, such as gossip, rumor, theft, slow down of work, and withdrawal or exit. Active protest includes violent and non-violent response. Violent resistance has two major forms: rebellion or uprising, and guerrilla wars. Non-violent protest has various forms, such as appeal and petition, legal action against the authority, deposition of unpopular chiefs, sabotage, boycott of European goods or hold-up of cash crops. Religious movement is another from of active resistance; sometimes it is non-violent, but it can turn out to be armed struggle.

In southern Ghana, almost all the forms existed. People showed less or even no respect to their chief when they were under the influence of priests in the *Abirewa* movement, and defied the authority of the government by ignoring official orders. Other forms of protest included the cocoa farmers' refusal to visit the experimental sites of cutting-out at the Tafo research institute, as requested by the government. They did not show up when the inspection team came to investigate their farms and refused to provide accommodations for the staff. Some of them even pulled up and destroyed inspection posts. Verbal confrontation was not uncommon.

The people spread rumors that were damaging the government's image or discrediting the chief's authority. James Scott argues that rumor is a powerful form of anonymous communication that can serve particular interests, especially in a situation when events of vital importance to people's interests are occurring yet no reliable information is available.[43] In other words, rumor is an attempt to provide structure in an uncertain situation. This explanation is true, but not complete. The important precondition for making and spreading rumor is the disadvantageous position of the rumor-makers or transmitters and their distrust of their superiors, whose reputation the rumor is intended to damage. This could happen even in a situation when reliable information is available.

For example, in 1927 absurd rumors as to the seizure of lands and crops by the government acting under the Native Administration Ordinance were disseminated among the people who could not read the Ordinance themselves.[44] In the protest against the Income Tax Ordinance in 1931-2, rumors were spread that there would be a tax on every door and window, that first born children would have to be given up and that every wife would have to spend the first three months of her marriage in the *Omanhen's* palace.[45] In the resistance against cutting-out, there were wild rumors, such as Britain intended to sell the Gold Coast to the United States but wished to ensure the death of the cocoa industry to avoid subsequent competition; the large importing firms, such as the United African Company, were starting big plantations in the Far East or in East Africa, and were anxious to reduce West African production.[46]

The rumor syndrome in the colonial period was extremely complex. Although it is almost impossible to trace its origin, its function in protest cannot be denied. First, in local conditions, rumor always meant the orally transmitted message. Unlike written media, it could worked effectively especially among the illiterate. Secondly, in spite of the varied forms of rumor, its content was usually consistent with the wishes or the worries of the ordinary people. It is difficult to prove that rumors were deliberately spread; however, this consistency in content indicates that they were often spread by those who could most gain from the grievances articulated.[47]

It has been argued that rural social protest usually takes a low-profile strategy or forms of day-to-day resistance, for fear of revenge by the authority or because of the lack of organization. Rural protest in southern Ghana shows that Ghanaians did not follow this conventional wisdom. Their most frequent strategy was non-violent and active. For example, the form of petition or legal actions was frequently taken. In the Forest Bill case, more than fourteen petitions were sent to either the Governor or directly addressed to London. In both the Akyem Abuakwa-Asamankese dispute and the New Dwaben-Jumapo conflict, there were constant petitions sent to the Governor's desk.

Destoolment or deposition was another frequently used measure for the commoners to fight against those corrupted, unpopular or so-called "collaborative" chiefs. Martin Wight once suggested that "Destoolments arise largely from struggles to control stool wealth and to enjoy the perquisites of office, and many of them are the constitutional expression of land disputes, which in the old days would have been settled by going to war. This state of affairs will be remedied when stool treasuries are fully organized and stool revenues are applied to the purposes of native administration."[48]

This is a highly paternalistic perspective. It missed the political implication of those destoolments and the close linkage between the *Asafo* and the destoolment. Popular forces had a say in the traditional system that was not recognized under colonial rule. Moreover, after the state treasuries were established in the 1940s, the situation did not change as Wight had predicted. Administrative problems, the change of the chief's position, the abuse of chiefly power, and economic hardship, all contributed to the frequent destoolment.

Other active forms included hold-ups and boycotts, which were all organized forms. In hold-ups, cocoa farmers had to sacrifice their own benefit to protest against the monopoly fixing of cocoa prices by the foreign companies. The boycott of February 1948 was on such a wide scale that it contributed greatly to the "Accra riot" in March. Because of the interference from the government, the young men sometimes resorted to extreme measure to settle the problem since they knew the government's attitude towards the unpopular chiefs. In 1927, the young men and elders in Techiman killed their chief for his collaboration with the government in the recruitment of communal labor. In the report, they claimed: "If we merely destool the *Omanhene* in the usual way, he will appeal to the government and the latter will support him and put him back to rule over us again. We don't want him ever again." The colonial officer thought that the *Omanhene's* principal offense was "his readiness to help the government."[49] There were similar reports in other districts as well. When they could not find other means to stop the chiefs' wrong-doings, the young men had to resort to the extreme measure in order to protect their interests.

The strategy of protest was usually directly linked to the result. Strategic interaction usually involved two parties, such as the Ghanaians and the colonial government, or three parties, such as in lesser chiefs-big chiefs-government or *Asafo*-chiefs-government conflicts. The protest against the Forest Bill turned out to be a success because the Ghanaian activists used Joseph Chamberlain's acknowledgement of the "validity of the objection" to the Lands Bill in 1898, that the British government found it difficult to refute. In contrast, the Asamankese case provides a negative example. The government at first tried to avoid confrontation with the Asamankese because it found the *Omanhene's* arbitrary measure unable to accept. After the *Odikro* of Akwatia was arrested on 24 July 1922, the Asamankese filed a case against five government officials. When the Governor reported this to the Colonial Office in 1925, he made it clear that the government should take the responsibility and support *Omanhene* Ofori Atta, since the "*Omanhene* has been put to very great expense already over this action which is aimed more at the Government Officials than at him."[50] Now the government had no room to manoeuvre and had to stand by the *Omanhene*. Had the Asamankese tried to isolate the *Omanhene*, the result could have been different.

Another important issue is mobilization. A successful mobilization needs three key factors: a good leader, adequate opportunity, and the compatibility between the mobilizer and the mobilized. Protests frequently used traditional means to organize or mobile, although some modern measures were also applied. The priest's traditional authority fit perfectly in the frame of the protest, yet the more important factor was the discontent of the masses. The *Asafo* company even used gong-gong, that only the chief could use in old times, to make their announcement. But the *Asafo* was most effective when the chiefs abused their power and the elders lost their ability to check this tendency. The farmers' organization could impressively mobilize farmers simply because it represented their interests. In the 1948 boycott, the organizer Chief Nii Kwabena Bonne showed superb skill at mobilization and won widespread support from the people.[51]

The significance of rural social protest during the colonial period was not its success or failure, nor how long it lasted or what scale it involved. Its significance lay in the fact that it challenged the colonial authority, directly or indirectly. Rural protests caused serious problems for the colonial government. Generally speaking, there were three major consequences. First, the protest forced the government to delay or change policy, thus having influenced the process of policy-making. Using Ghanaian historian Agbodeka's words, "the formulation and execution of colonial policies did not depend entirely on the men in Whitehall."[52] The Ghanaian people through constant protest had influenced the process of policy-making and shaped the colonial administration in terms of policy of indirect rule. Their resistance prevented the issue of the Municipal Corporations Ordinance (1858), Lands Bill (1898), the Forest Bill (1910), the Native Jurisdiction Ordinance (1919, 1922, 1924), the Native Administration Revenue Measure (1931-32), among other abortive bills.

Protest also led the government to issue certain laws in order to keep a situation under control. One main flaw in the 1910 Native Jurisdiction Ordinance was that it failed to differentiate either in category or in jurisdiction between Paramount Chiefs and Divisional Chiefs, a failure that more or less contributed to the tendency of the subordinate chiefs to separate from their Paramount Chiefs. After the Governor deposed in 1923 the *Ohene* of Asamankese, the main actor in the case, the elders and people still recognized him as their chief. The District Commissioner suggested that the order of deposition had even increased the chief's popularity. To control the situation, the Governor sought authority to "give orders requiring this chief to reside in another part of the country." The Secretary of State approved his proposal; thus Ordinance No. 10 of 1924 was enacted, giving the Governor power of deporting destooled chiefs.[53]

Secondly, the protest directly undermined colonial rule in various ways by challenging the authority of either the government or the chief. In the *Abirewa* movement, the chiefs were so afraid of the subversion of their power by the priests that they urged the government to adopt more severe measures. Sometimes the protest even changed the colonial officials' ideology regarding African local affairs. For example, after the protest against the Forest Bill, the Governor had to advise the Secretary of State in London: "I do not advise any interference with the rights of the natives as regards their land, since I do not think that such actions can be taken after all that has passed since Sir William Maxwell's Land Bill was dropped in 1900." [54]

The *Asafo* company exercised their authority by making their own laws and regulations regarding local affairs and setting up prices for different local products. Even the chiefs had to ask their permission to purchase certain goods. This became a real threat to chiefly power and weakened the government authority. In the Asamankese case, the *Ohene* defied fifteen years the authority of an *Omanhene* supported by the government and made colonial rule almost void. The message also went to London, causing heated debate on the colonial policy. All these events show that the protest nibbled at the colonial authority bit by bit.

Finally, rural social protest also contributed to the formation of the independence movement. The key to the nationalists' success was their mobilization of the masses, and they made good use of every possibility to achieve their purpose. The significance of social protest was that it provided an excellent opportunity for mobilization and prepared a strong base for nationalism. For the nationalists, destoolment was not only a protest against the chief; it was a protest against colonial administration. In his speech at the CPP (Convention Peoples Party) annual meeting in 1951, Kwame Nkrumah pictured the wave of destoolment of chiefs "as a revolt of the people not directly against the Chiefs but against the system of rule of the imperialists through the Chiefs." [55] His analysis was certainly right in the sense that destoolment obviously weakened the colonial administration. More importantly, this claim justified the young men's move and served the purpose of mobilization.

Owing to the two important factor, time and scale, the resistance to the cutting-out campaign provided a particular content to the anti-colonial struggle and naturally turned out to be part of the nation-wide independent movement. That is why Danquah, in answering the question of the Watson Commission about the swollen shoot disease, said that the government's measure of cutting-out was "scientifically sound but politically inexpedient." The organization of farmers by CPP serves a good example.

Colonialism was by nature a dilemma, and colonial policy was more paradoxical than appropriate in the local situation. When the colonial government co-opted chiefs into its political structure, it created two unsolvable problems in local politics: the legitimacy of the chiefs' authority and their abuse of power. These problems caused constant destoolment, a special form of protest of common people. However, whether or not colonialism should have dominated Africa or whether the Africans should have protested is a moral issue; but to study various reactions towards colonialism, including protests against it, is a historical one. The protest of the Gold Coast in the colonial period, however, was not an isolated phenomenon, but part of a continuum. It inherited the democratic tradition from the pre-colonial period, and continued after the establishment of the nationalist government.[56]

Based on specific cases in southern Ghana,, this study has provided some explanations for the changes caused by colonialism and responses in the Gold Coast. The conclusions drawn from this research on the protest of different communities, which resulted from the hostility between the Ghanaian people and the colonial government, the conflict between the commoners and their superiors, the contention between priests and chiefs, and the confrontation between subordinate chiefs and Paramount Chiefs, may help us understand both the initiative of the Africans and the impact of colonialism as a whole.

Notes

[1] J. F. A. Ajayi, "Colonialism: An episode in African History," in L. H. Gann & P. Duignan, *Colonialism in Africa 1870-1960*(London: Cambridge University Press, 1969), Vol.I, pp.497-509. See also his article "The continuity of African institutions under colonialism," in T. O. Ranger, ed., *Emerging Themes of African History*, pp.189-200.

[2] A. Adu Boahen, "Africa and the colonial challenge" in *General History of Africa* (Unesco, 1985), Vol.VII, p.1. See also his conclusion in the same volume, "Colonialism in Africa: its impact and significance," pp.782-809.

[3] V. Lenin, *Selected Works* (Moscow: Foreign Languages Publishing House, 1961), Vol. 3, p.248.

[4] P. Konings, *The State and Rural Class Formation in Ghana: A comparative analysis* (London: KPI Ltd., 1986), pp.75-83. Rhoda Howard, *Colonialism and Underdevelopment in Ghana*, pp.193-206.

[5] For general studies of African class formation, see Irving Leonard Markovitz, *Power and Class in Africa: An introduction to change and conflict in African politics* (New Jersey: Englewood Cliffs, 1977), pp.153-172; Richard L. Sklar, "The nature of class domination in Africa," *The Journal of Modern African Studies*, 17:4(1979), pp.531-552; P. P. Rey, "Class contradiction in lineage societies," *Critique of Anthropology*,

13 & 14:4(1979), pp.41-60.

[6] Konings, *The State and Rural Class Formation in Ghana*, p.14.

[7] Ansa Asamoa, *Classes and Tribalism in Ghana* (Accra, n.d.), pp.31-32.

[8] Quoted from Ivor Wilks, *Asante in the Nineteenth Century*, p.539. See also Kwame Arhin, "Rank and class among the Asante and Fante in the nineteenth century," *Africa*, 53:1(1983), pp.2-22.

[9] Polly Hill, *The Migrant Cocoa-Farmers of Southern Ghana*, pp.214-215.

[10]For example, the Chinese have been engaged in "market economy" since ancient time, and they invented paper money in Yuan dynasty (1206-1368), but the capitalist class did not appear then.

[11]See also Polly Hill, *Studies in Rural Capitalism in West Africa* (London: Cambridge University Press, 1970).

[12]R. Howard, *Colonialism and Underdevelopment in Ghana*, pp.193-199; R. Howard, "Formation and stratification of the peasantry in colonial Ghana," *Journal of Peasant Studies*, 8:4(1981), p.72.

[13]Konings, *State and Rural Class Formation*, pp.75-83.

[14]Howard, *Colonialism and Underdevelopment*, p.198. Another school deals with this issue from a contemporary perspective. A. Asamoa claims that there were a comprador bourgeoisie, a national and petty bourgeoisie, a rural bourgeoisie, a working class and a peasantry in the colonial Ghana. See his article "Classes in Ghana," *Ghana Journal of Sociology*, 13:1 (1979/80), pp.130-162 and his booklet entitled *Classes and Tribalism in Ghana*.

[15]Mao Tse-tung, "Analysis of the classes in Chinese society," in *Selected Works of Mao Tse-tung* (Peking: Foreign Languages Press, 1965), pp.13-21.

[16]Konings, *State and Rural Class Formation*, pp.75-83.

[17]G. Austin, "Capitalists and chiefs in the cocoa hold-ups in South Asante, " p.72.

[18]For example, Jeff Crisp has noticed that the mine workers' solidarity has always been defined in *occupational* rather than *class* terms and they have traditionally displayed very little interest in participating in the national political arena. See his *The Story of an African Working Class: Ghanaian miners' struggle 1870-1980* (London: Zed, 1984). Don Robotham holds the same view. See his *Militants or Proletarians? The economic culture of underground gold miners in southern Ghana, 1906-1976* (Cambridge African monographs 12, 1989).

[19]Adbodeka described the successful efforts by educated Africans to build their own schools in the country. See *Ghana in the Twentieth Century*, pp.39-43.

[20]*The Gold Coast Census of Population 1948: Report and Tables* (Accra: Government Printing Department, 1950), p.18.

[21]J. F. A. Ajayi's analysis of the present Nigerian society may help us to understand the social structure in colonial Ghana. See his article "Expectations of the independence," *Daedalous*, Vol. 111:2(1982), pp.1-9.

[22]This is a generalization of this group. The best study of this group is by Robert K. A. Gardiner, *The Role of Educated Persons in Ghana Society*. See also Philip Foster, *Education and Social Change in Ghana*(Chicago: The University of Chicago Press, 1965), pp.74-175.

[23]D. Brokensha, *Social Change at Larteh, Ghana* (London: Oxford University Press, 1966), p.106.

[24]Obviously, the division was not so rigid. After receiving a bit of education, some commoners became contemptuous of their fellows and tried to separate from them. There were chiefs, such as Ga *Mantse* Tackie Yaoboi and the *Omanhene* of Akyem Abuakwa Ofori Atta, who received some education and were called "enlightened Chiefs" by the government.

[25]*CO96/532*. Gold Coast Confidential. Native Affairs. 19 June 1913.

[26]E. U. Essien-Udom, "Introduction to the second edition," in Casely Hayford, *Truth about Land Question*, vii-xii.

[27]Lloyd Fallers made an excellant study of this paradox in Uganda. William John Hanna, *Independent Black Africa: The politics of freedom* (Chicago: Rand McNally, 1964), pp.278-296.

[28]*The Gold Coast Leader*, December 23 1911, p.3.

[29]M. Crowder and O. Ikime, *West African Chiefs: Their changing status under colonial rule and independence*(Ibadan: University of Ife Press, 1970), xviii-xxii. For the classic work on indirect rule, see F.D. Lugard, *The Dual Mandate in British Tropical Africa* (London: Frank Cass, 1929).

[30]The establishment of a State Council and a Provincial Council also seemed to have built the power base on local level. Under the constitution of 1925, Provincial Councils were established, consisting of all the Paramount Chiefs of the southern provinces.

[31]*Native Administration Ordinance, 1927*. Sections 3,4,5.7,8. Part III.

[32]Crowder and Ikime, *West African Chiefs*, xvii.

[33]Casely Hayford, *The Truth about the West African Land Question*, p.26.

[34]*Cmd6278. Belfield Report*. Notes of Evidence relating to Part I. p.107.

[35]*Cmd6278. Belfield Report*. Notes of evidence relating to Part I. p.115.

[36]As one old farmer in Nsawam Gold Coast Farmers' Association put it, when asked about the role of the urban elite, "Oh yes, they would come up here once in a while." If this could be said to an area so near to Accra, it would be all the more true for the remote hinterland. A. B. Holmes, "What was the 'nationalism' of the 1930's in Ghana?" in Addo-Fening, *et al, Akyem Abuakwa and the Politics of the*

Inter-war Period in Ghana, p.27.

[37] *CO98/44. Ga Mantse* Incident, p.13.

[38] *CO96/543.* Confidential Report by F. Crowther dated 27 Jan. 1914. Encl. in Gold Coast Confidential (A). Clifford to Harcourt, 24 March 1914. The Colonial Secretary Ransford Slater held the same view. *ADM11/692.* Clifford minute, 5 March 1918.

[39] *ADM11/692.* Note of a meeting of paramount chiefs with the Governor, 5 March 1918. *GNA. CSO 1174/31.* Akuamoa Boateng II to Ofori Atta I, 30 Dec. 1927. Kwahu *Asafo* Company Papers. Twumasi, "Aspects," p.42.

[40] For the study of spiritual churches in Ghana, see C. G. Baeta, *Prophetism in Ghana* (Lonodn: SCM Press, 1962).

[41] Crowder and Ikime, *West African Chiefs,* x.

[42] The two terms, "active" and "passive," are used to describe only the forms of protests, not the attitude of the protesters. What is more, the two forms are sometimes interrelated.

[43] J. Scott, *Domination and the Arts of Resistance* (New Haven: Yale University Press, 1990), p.144.

[44] *CO98/50.* Report on Eastern Province, 1927-28.

[45] *CSO22/32.* Akyem Abuakwa Sate Council minutes. 22 August, 1932. Quoted from J. Simensen, "Crisis in Akyem Abuakwa: The Native Administration Revenue Measure of 1932," in Addo-Fening, *et al, Akyem Abuakwa and the Politics,* p.95.

[46] *Watson Report.* para.268.

[47] It is interesting to compare the function of rumor in slave rebellions in the British West Indies. See for example, Michael Craton, *Testing the Chains: Resistance to Slavery in the British West Indies*(Ithaca: Cornell University Press, 1982), pp.241-253.

[48] Martin Wight, *Gold Coast Legislative Council,* p.36.

[49] *ADM11/1332 MPS.* NA Case 13/21. Slater to Avery, 30 Sept. 1927. Quoted from Mikell, *Cocoa and Chaos,* p.89.

[50] CO96/657. Gold Coast (Confidential). CO54797. Governor Guggisberg to Amery, 19 November 1925.

[51] He made a survey beforehand and found "the poorer classes in the villages could not afford to clothe themselves and the majority went in rags." See his autobiography *Milestones in the History of the Gold Coast,* p.64.

[52] F. Agbodeka, *African Politics and British Policy,* viii-ix.

[53]The Secretary of State replied on May 15, 1923, "A similar power is possessed already by the Governors of Sierra Leone and Nigeria and I approve of the Native Jurisdiction Ordinance being amended without delay so as to give that power to the Governor of the Gold Coast." *CO96/713/21613/34*. Memorandum.

[54]*CO96/528*. Gold Coast (Confidential) Governor Clifford to L. Harcourt, 3 March 1913.

[55]*ADM1/2/318*. Governor to Secretary of State, 17 August 1951.

[56]Maxwell Owusu has contributed several studies on the linkage between Ghanaian tradition and present situation in terms of resistance. See his "Custom and coups: a juridical interpretation of civil order and disorder in Ghana," *The Journal of Modern African Studies*, 24:1(1986), pp.69-99; "Rebellion, revolution, and tradition: Reinterpreting coups in Ghana," *Comparative Studies in Society and History*, 31:2(1989), pp.372-397.

APPENDIX

New Orders and Regulations Inaugurated by the Whole Kwahu *Asafos* on the 6th November 1917

The object of the constitution of this *Asafo* is due to the deaths of our late *Omanhene* Kwami[*sic*] Apeadu who after his death is alleged that left cash amounting to only -/9 in his box as a property. On account of this, the people of the whole Kwahu felt aggrieved and convened a general meeting with intent to have held a property inquiry into the secret but the elders and councilors of the stool did not attend the meeting. Taking close view on the matter and still wandered of the death of the *Omanhene* without leaving a capital in his box in consequence of the large amount of monies he has received from us as a fine for breach of his oaths, and secondly as we could not see or get any of his elders to solve to our understanding how it happened so, we determined to form a company and call it *Asafo* with the object to protest and resist against the imposition of heavy fines for breach of oaths, because nothing worthy of significant or remembrance was left as a result of the heavy fines made by our late *Omanhene* Kwame Apeadu.

When Kwasi Wiredu, the then *Omanhene* and his elders heard of our proposal, he accompanied by his elders, councilors of his stool and people of Kwahu joined us in the meeting at Nkwatia. There the *Asafo* Company was then organized, before the *Omanhene* as aforesaid and his elders and councilors and people and the following rules were suggested and passed as Bye-laws of Kwahu. Viz:--

1. Whoever shall be found guilty of violation *Omanhene*'s oath shall be liable to a fine not exceeding £2.8/- inclusive of pacification to the judgment creditor and 2 sheep @ £1.4/ each fee for arrest 2/-.
2. Whoever shall be found guilty of contravening the *Adontenhene Benkumhene* or *Nifahene*'s oath shall be liable to a fine of £1.12/- with 2 sheep at 16/- inclusive of pacification to the judgment creditor. Likewise fines of £1.12/- is alloted [*sic*] to the chiefs of Pepease, Obomeng, and Nkwatia with 1 sheep each at 13/-. The witness summons fee and witness's fees are left to the discretion of the Tribunal and it is not to be repugance [sic] with the Native Jurisdiction Ordinance.

3. Any person who is a courtier(*ahenquah*) to *Omanhene* Akuamoa and fails or wants to sever his connection in that capacity shall be liable to a fine not exceeding £9 and two sheep before freed. Whoever is courtier to the *Adontenhene, Benkumhene* or *Nifahene* and fails or is desire to resign his post, shall be liable to a fine not exceeding £7 and 2 sheep before such application is granted.

4. Whoever shall wilfully or negligently assault any of *Omanhene* courtier or *Adontenhene, Benkumhene* or *Nifahene*'s such as *Karaguarefo* or a courtier would be liable to a fine of one sheep to *Omanhene* and pacification of 8/- to the aggrieved person. Also one sheep and pacification of 4/- to the ahenquahs belonging to the chiefs respectively.

5. It shall not be lawful for the *Omanhene* and other chiefs and the *odikros* to sort the hands on any girl while she is in her infancy except in the case of a female *rufus* or twine [*sic*] who are according to the Native Custom, if female, are wives to *Omanhene* or the chief in whose division the incident may occur, or the child will be borne.

6. It shall not be lawful for *Omanhene* or any other chief or *Odikro* to have sexual connection with youngmen's wife. Whoever shall be found guilty of this offence, on conviction, will be liable to interment from Kwahu District.

7. Any youngmen who will wilfully or negligently seduce or have sexual connection with *Omanhene*, a chief, or an *Odikro*'s wife shall on conviction, be liable to the same punishment as set forth in section 6 as herein-before mentioned. (both the man and the woman are to be interned).

8. After a deposition, resignation or death of *Omanhene*, a chief or an *Odikro*, if an heir apparent gives out bribes and presents in monies to people to help him to obtain the stool and it comes to the notice of the *Asafos*, such heir apparent is entirely deprived of the stool and the person or persons to whom the bribe was given, if he or they are elders occupying stools, is or are to be destooled.

9. It shall be lawful for a person, if falsely accused of an offence to put himself into fetish to affirm his denial of such an offence and as consequence, the person making the accusation is not to take any further action.

10. It shall be lawful for any tribunal whatever to instruct two litigants standing before it to swear an oath and put themselves into fetishes after they have given their statement.

11. Whoever, on conviction be found guilty of an offence of giving injury to a

girl in her carnal in consequence of sexual connection had with her, or whoever shall have sexual connection with a girl or woman in bush without her consent, will be liable to a fine of £7 for *Omanhene* (or according to the nature of the offence) and compensation (as the Tribunal thinks fit) to the woman aggrieved or the girl so injured.

12. Whoever shall have sexual connection with a wife belonging to *Omanhen*'s messenger such as hammock carriers, gold symbol bearers (*Akrafo*) not possessing the gold symbol is liable to pay only satisfaction rate to the person whose wife the carnal knowledge was had. No sheep is to be cut in either cases [*sic*].

13. The values of sheep to be paid to senior fetish priest or preisess [*sic*] and junior fetish priest or priestess for contravension [*sic*] of any of their fetish rites should be 10/- and 8/- respectively. If a fetish catches anyone, and the fetish priest or priestess to whom does that fetish belong fails to heal the person who the fetish has caught after he or she has received the sheep etc., to the fetish must recover the cost of the sheep and all expenses made to him by person who the fetish had caught or by his family.

14. Whoever engages a girl with a mat or buys a slave without given headrum, is not entitled to claim any satisfaction rate for an adultery committed with her by a person.

15. Any woman who applied to her husband for dissolution of marriage without giving any tangible reason is to make good of double her head money to the man so desired to divorce. Whoever if such an application is [s]upported by proper grounds either by impotency etc., then the woman is to refund her ordinary headmoney to the husband. Any appeal made by a husband to person to intercede with his wife and beg her for re-cohabitation should be made to a chief alone. If such an appeal is made and the woman refuses to accept them she should give one sheep @ 16/- to such chief.

16. Application for civil summonses against persons for payment of debt, monies got as a loan, should be made to a chief whose division the transaction took place and if such chief did not succeed in claiming the money from the defendant them the plaintiff should carry out the action to *Omanhene*'s Court (Tribunal) and therefrom if not again successful then the case should be appealed to the District Commissioner[']s Court. Whoever at the absence of these 3 Courts shall hire any soldier or policeman, or young men to demand him his money, shall be guilty of an offence.

17. All monies chargeable on hearing cocoa farm disputes should not exceed the scale of charges of the oath sworn by disputants.

18. Whoever fall [*sic*] in love with a woman and desires to engage her as a wife should give some of the headrum to an elder of the girl or the woman family. No presentation in money whatsoever should be made to the woman or the girl so desired to engage. All presentations to the woman as well as to her parents, sisters, etc., should comprise of salt meat, tobacco and shea-butter. Whoever shall in default of this order give out money as a presentation to the woman or the girl to be engaged, or to her parents etc., is guilty of *Asafos*' orders and shall be liable to a fine of 3 sheep to the *Asafos*. If a man observes or notices that his wife is being courted by another man, he should caution her to put a stop to such affection but the man is not to be sworn upon.

19. *Omanhene* or any of the Chiefs is not to apply for permission to purchase gun-powder, lead bars etc., without the information of the *Asafoatche* in his town. On the receipt of signed permission from the District Commissioner and when sending messengers to purchase same, *Asafoatche* in the town should be told in order to send his messengers along with that of the *Omanhene* or the Chief for his supply.

20. No rum should be used in celebration of funeral customs. Only palm wine should be used instead with the exception of rum sending to *Omanhene* or a chief to inform him of the death. Whoever shall be guilty of this offence shall be liable to a fine of 3 sheep by the *Asafos*.

21. Any fisher man who shall carry his fishes to other District than Kwahu shall be liable to a fine of 3 sheep by the *Asafos*.

22. The same question applies to hunters.

23. No other summonses for damages etc., other than civil summonses to claim an amount from a person should be permissible.

24. List of Native Foodstuff and Their Scale of Market Prices to be Bought....

25. Whoever shall have sexual connection with any fetish carrier shall be liable to a fine of 1 sheep.

26. Any woman who shall use obsene [sic] words to her husband shall be liable to a fine of one sheep by the *Asafos*. The following are the names of the headmen of the *Asafo* members who suggested the aforesaid rules and have them passes: -- Viz: --

(names and signatures, omitted)

Dated on this 6th day of November 1917 at Nkwatia, 1917 ..
Writer and witness to marks.

(Sgd). D. D. Chansah.

Copied by M. M. Donkor.
           B. M. Station.
                      Abetifi. 15.11.17.

Source: National Archives of Ghana, Accra. *ADM11/1/738*. *Case No.11/1919*. Sub. *Asafo:*
Origin of the Powers of.

BIBLIOGRAPHY

I. Government Records

Ghana National Archives, Accra, Ghana
ADM1/Series (Original Correspondence),
ADM4/Series (Gold Coast Ordinances, etc.).
ADM5/Series (Sessional Papers and Reports).
ADM11/Series (Papers of the Secretary for Native Affairs).
ADM12/Series (Confidential Despatches/Reports).
ADM29-36/Series (Regional Records Office, Koforidua).

Public Record Office, London, Great Britain
CO96/Series (Gold Coast Correspondence).
CO98/Series (Gold Coast Executive Council Debates, Minutes, Departmental
    Annual Reports, etc.).
CO99/Series (Gold Coast Government Gazettes).

Confidential Prints
Correspondence Relating to Land Grants and Concessions in the Gold Coast Protectorate,
    African West 531, 1897.
Further Correspondence (January 1897-December 1898) Relating to Land Concessions and
    Railways on the Gold Coast, African West 531, 1899.
Gold Coast: Further Correspondence (December 1898-December 1900) Relating to Land
    Concessions and Regulations, African West 578, 1900.
Correspondence (November 1909-September 1911) Relating to Concessions and the Alienation of
    Native Lands on the Gold Coast, African West 977, 1911.
West African Lands Committee: Minutes of Evidence, African West 1047, 1916.

Gold Coast Government Documents
Gold Coast Annual Reports.
Gold Coast Census Reports, 1901, 1911, 1921, 1931, 1948.
Gold Coast Legislative Council (Minutes, Debates, Sessional Papers).

Annual Reports on the Department of Agriculture (1937-53).
The Gold Coast Colonial Civil Lists.

Reports of Committees and Commissions

Report on Forests, 1910. By H. N. Thompson. Cd.4993.

Report on the Legislation Governing the Alienation of Native Lands in the Gold Coast Colony and Ashanti; with Some Observations on the "Forest Ordinance, 1911," 1912. By H. Conway Belfield. (*Cmd.6278. Belfield Report*)

Enquiry into the Gold Coast Cocoa Industry, 1918-1919. By W. S. D. Tudhope.

Report on the Economics of Peasant Agriculture in the Gold Coast, 1936. By C. Y. Shephard.

Report of the Commission on the Marketing of West African Cocoa, 1938. (*Cmd.5845. Nowell Report*)

Report of the Native Tribunals Committee of Enquiry, 1943.

Report of the Commission of Enquiry into Disturbance in the Gold Coast, 1948. (*Colonial No.231. Watson Report*)

Report of the Commission of Enquiry into the Swollen Shoot Disease of Cacao in the Gold Coast, 1948.

Report of the Committee of Enquiry into the Existing Organization and Methods for the Control of Swollen Shoot Disease by the Compulsory Cutting Out of Infected Cocoa Trees, 1951. (*Korsah Report*)

Other Published Documents

Minutes of the 35th Session of the Provincial Council (the Eastern Province), 1941.

Ashanti Confederacy Council Minutes. Jan. 1936.

Minutes of the 13th Session of the Ashanti Confederacy Council on 18th-26th February, 1948.

Cocoa Disease Control and Rehabilitation Monthly Progress Reports.

Monthly News-letters, by Department of Agriculture.

The Gold Coast Farmers, by Department of Agriculture.

Report on the Central Research Station, 1943.   Compiled by M. Greenwood.

Golden Harvest, The Story of the Gold Coast Cocoa Industry. By Information Service Department, 1953.

West African Cocoa Research Institute 1944-49, London: Crown Agents, 1950.

II. Newspapers and Weekly

Gold Coast Leader
The Gold Coast Nation

The Gold Coast Observer
The Gold Coast Spectator
Gold Coast Times
West Africa

III. Literature

Books

Acquah, I., *Accra Survey (London: University of London, 1958)*.

Addo-Fening, R., *et al, Akyem Abuakwa and the Politics of the Inter-war Period in Ghana* (Basel: Basel Afrika Bibliographien, 1975).

Agbodeka, F., *African Politics and British Policy in the Gold Coast 1868-1900 A study in the forms and force of protest* (London: Longman, 1971).

————, *Ghana in the Twentieth Century* (Accra: Ghana Universities Press, 1972).

Ahuma, Attoh, *The Gold Coast Nation and Nationalist Consciousness* (London: Frank Cass, 1971[1911]).

Akyempo, Karikari, *Deer Hunt Festival of the Effutus* (Accra: Anowuo Educational Pub., n.d.).

Amin, Samir, *Neo-Colonialism in West Africa* (Penguin, 1973).

Ansah, J. K., *The Centenary History of the Larteh Presbyterian Church1853-1953* (Larteh: Larteh Presbyterian Church, 1955).

Appiah-Kubi, Kofi, *Man Cures, God Heals Religion and medical practice among the Akans of Ghana* (Totowa: Allanheld, Osmun Publishers, 1981).

Apter, David E., *Ghana in Transition* (Princeton: Princeton University Press, 1963).

Arhin, Kwame, *The Expansion of Cocoa Production: The working conditions of migrant cocoa farmers in the Central and Western Regions* (Accra, 1985).

Asamoa, A., *Classes and Tribalism in Ghana* (Accra, n.d.).

Asamoa, Ansa K., *The Ewe of South-Eastern Ghana and Togo on the Eve of Colonialism* (Tema: Ghana Publishing Co., 1986).

Austin, Dennis, *Politics in Ghana 1946-1960* (London: Oxford University Press, 1964).

Awoonor, Kofi N., *Ghana, A Political History* (Accra: Sedco & Woeli, 1990).

Ayandele, E., *African Historical Studies* (London: Frank Cass, 1979).

Bartels, F. L., *The Rise of Ghana Methodism* (London: Cambridge University Press, 1965).

Bates, R. H, *Essays on the Political Economy of Rural Africa* (London: Cambridge University Press, 1983).

Beckman, Bjorn, *Organising the Farmers: Cocoa, politics and national development in Ghana* (Uppsala: The Scandinavian Institute of African Studies, 1976).

Beecham, J., *Ashantee and the Gold Coast* (London, 1968 [1841]).

Beinart, W & C. Bundy, *Hidden Struggle in Rural South Africa: Politics and popular movement in the Transkei and Eastern Cape* (London: James Currey, 1987).

Bentsi-Enchill, Kwamena, *Ghana Land Law: An exposition, analysis and critique* (London: Sweet & Maxwell, 1964).

Boahen, A., *Topics in African History* (London: Longmans, 1966).

———, *Ghana: Evolution and change in the nineteenth and twentieth centuries* (London: Longmans, 1975).

Bonne III, Nii Kwabena, *Milestones in the History of the Gold Coast: autobiography of Nii Kwabena Bonne III Osu Alata Mantse* (Diplomatic, 1953).

Bosman, W., *A New and Accurate Description of the Coast of Guinea* (London: Frank Cass, 1967[1705]).

Bourret, M, *Ghana: the Road to independence* (Stanford: Stanford University Press, 1960).

Bowdich, T. E., *Mission from Cape Coast Castle to Ashantee* (London: Frank Cass, 1966 [1819]).

Braudel, F., *The Mediterranean and the Mediterranean World in the Age of Philip II* (New York: Harp & Row, 1972). Translated by S. Reynolds.

Brokensha, D. W., *Social Change at Larteh* (London: Oxford University Press, 1966).

———, ed., *AkwapimHandbook* (Accra-Tema, Ghana Publishing Co., 1972).

Brown, E. J. P., *Gold Coast and Asianti Reader*, Book I (London: Crown Agents for the Colonies, 1929).

Buell, R. L., *The Native Problem in Africa* (New York: Macmillan, 1928).

Busia, K. A., *The Position of the Chief in the Modern Political System of Ashanti* (London: Oxford University Press, 1951).

Cardinall, A. W., *The Gold Coast 1931* (Accra: Government Printer, 1932).

Casely Hayford, J. E., *Gold Coast Native Institutions* (London: Frank Cass, 1970 [1903]).

———, *The Truth about the West African Land Question* (London: Frank Cass, 1970 [1913]).

Christaller, J. G., *A, Dictionary of the Asante and Fante Language Called Tshi [Twi]* (Basel: Basel Evangelical Missionary Society, 1933 [1881]).

Christensen, J. B., *Double Descent Among the Fanti* (New Haven: Human Relations Area Files, 1954).

Crowder, M., *West Africa under Colonial Rule* (Evanston: Northwestern University Press, 1968).

Crowder, M and O. Ikime, *West African Chiefs: Their changing status under colonial rule and independence* (Ibadan: University of Ife Press, 1970).

Cruickshank, B., *Eighteen Years on the Gold Coast of Africa* (London: Frank Cass, 1966[1853]).

Climo, V. C., *Precis of Information Concerning the Colony of the Gold Coast and Ashanti* (London: War Office, 1904).

Crisp, Jeff, *The Story of an African Working Class: Ghanaian miners' struggle 1870-1980* (London: Zed, 1984).

Danquah, J. B., *The Akim Abuakwa Handbook* (London: Forster Groom, 1928).

———, *Gold Coast Akan Laws and Customs and the Akim Abuakwa Constitution* (London: George Routledge, 1928).

———, *An Epistle to the Educated Youngman in Akim Abuakwa* (Accra, 1929).

———, *Liberty of the Subject A Monograph on the Gold Coast Hold-up and Boycott of Foreign Goods (1937-38)* (Kibbi, 1938).

———, *The Akan Doctrine of God* (London, Frank Cass, 1968[1944]).

———, *Journey to Independence and After (Danquah's Letters)* (Accra: Waterville Publishing House, 1970).

Debrunner, H., *Witchcraft in Ghana* (Accra: Presbyterian Book Depot, 1961).

Dickson, K. B., *A Historical Geography of Ghana* (London: Cambridge University Press, 1969).

Dupuis, J., *Journal of a Residence in Ashantee* (London: Frank Cass, 1966 [1824]).

Edsman, B. M., *Lawyers in Gold Coast Politics c.1900-1945* (Stockholm: Almqvist & Wiksell, 1979).

Ellis, A. B., *The Land of Fetish* (London: Chapman and Hall, 1883).

———, *The Tshi-Speaking Peoples of the Gold Coast of West Africa* (Chicago: Benin Press, 1964[1887]).

———, *Yoruba-speaking Peoples of the Slave Coast of West Africa* (London: Chapman & Hall, 1894).

Ephson, I. S., *Gallery of Gold Coast Celebrities* (Accra: Ilen Publications, 1969).

Field, M. J., *Religion and Medicine of the Ga People* (London: Oxford University Press, 1937).

———, *Akim-Kotoku An Oman of the Gold Coast*(London:The Crown Agents, 1948).

———, *The Social Organization of the Ga People* (London, 1940).

———, *Search for Security* (Evanston: Northwestern University Press, 1960).

Fieldhouse, D. K., *Economics and Empire 1830-1914* (London: Weidenfeld & Nicolson, 1973).

Fields, Karen E., *Revival and Rebellion in Colonial Central Africa* (Princeton: Princeton

University Press, 1985).

Fink, H., *Religion, Disease and Healing in Ghana* (Trickster Wissenschaft, 1990). Translated by Volker Englich.

Foster, Philip, *Education and Social Change in Ghana* (Chicago: The University of Chicago Press, 1965).

Fuller, Sir Francis, *A Vanished Dynasty Ashanti* (London: John Murray, 1921).

Fynn, J. K., *Asante and Its Neighbours, 1700-1807* (London: Longmans, 1971).

Gann, L. H. & P. Duignan, ed., *Colonialism in Africa 1870-1960* (London: Cambridge University Press, 1969).

Gardiner, Robert K. A., *The Role of Educated Persons in Ghana Society* (Accra, 1970).

Gaunt, Mary, *Alone in West Africa* (London: T. W. Laurie, 1912).

Gluckman, M., *Custom and Conflict in Africa* (Oxford: Blackwell, 1970).

Goody, J. ed., *Changing Social Structure in Ghana* (London: International African Institute, 1975).

Greenberg, J. H., *The Languages of Africa* (Bloomington:Indiana University, 1966).

Grove, David & L. Huszar, *The Town of Ghana: The role of service centres in regional planning* (Accra: Ghana Universities Press, 1964).

Guggisberg, Sir Gorden, *Gold Coast A review of the events of 1920-1926 and Prospects of 1927-28* (Accra: Government Printer, 1927).

Gunnarsson, Christer, *The Gold Coast Cocoa Industry 1900-1939, Production, prices and structural change* (Lund, 1978).

Gwendolyn, Mikell, *Cocoa and Chaos in Ghana* (New York: Paragon House, 1989).

Hailey, Lord, *African Survey* (London: Oxford University Press, 1938).

Hancock, W., *Survey of British Commonwealth Affairs* (London: Oxford University Press, 1964), Vol II.

Hargreaves, John D., *Prelude to the Partition of West Africa* (London: Macmillan, 1963).

Hill, Polly, *The Migrant Cocoa-farmers of Southern Ghana A study on rural capitalism* (London: Cambridge University Press, 1963).

Hill, Polly, *Studies in Rural Capitalism in West Africa* (London: Cambridge University Press, 1970).

Hindness, B. & Paul Q. Hirst, *Pre-Capitalist Modes of Production* (London: Routledge & Kegan Paul, 1975).

Hodgkin, Thomas, *Nationalism in Colonial Africa* (New York: New York university, 1956).

Hopkins, A., *An Economic History of West Africa* (New York: Columbia University Press, 1973).

Horton, J. A. B., *West African Countries and Peoples* (London: Kraus, 1970[1868]).

Howard, Rhoda, *Colonialism and Underdevelopment in Ghana* (London: Croom Helm, 1978).

Huber, Hugo, *The Krobo, Traditional social and religious life of a West African people* (St. Augustin: The Anthropos Institute, 1963).

Hutchinson, T. J., *Impressions of Western Africa* (London, Longmans, 1858).

Hutton, W., *A Voyage to Africa* (London: Frank Cass, 1971[1821]).

Hyden, Goran, *Beyond Ujamma: Underdevelopment and an uncaptured peasantry* (London: Heinmann, 1980).

Iliffe, John, *Tanganyika under German Rule 19005-1912* (London: Cambridge University Press, 1969).

Isaacman, Allen, *The Tradition of Resistance in Mozambique: Anti-colonial activity in the Zambesi Valley 1850-1921* (Berkeley: University of California Press, 1976).

Jones-Quartey, K. A. B., *History, Politics and Early Press in Ghana: The fictions and the facts* (Accra: University of Ghana, 1975).

Kea, R., *Settlements, Trade, and Politics in Seventeenth-Century Gold Coast* (Baltimore: The John Hopkins University Press, 1982).

Kemp, D., *Nine Years at the Gold Coast* (London: Macmillan, 1898).

Keta Study, University of Science and Technology, Faculty of Architecture, occasional paper No.15 (Kumasi, no date).

Kimble, D., *A Political History of Ghana The rise of the Gold Coast nationalism 1850-1928* (Oxford: Clarendon Press, 1963).

Klein, Martin A., *Peasants in Africa: Historical and contemporary perspectives* (London: Sage, 1980).

Konings, P., *The State and Rural Class Formation in Ghana: A comparative analysis* (London: KPI Ltd., 1986).

Kwamena-Poh, M. A., *Government and Politics in the Akuapem State 1730-1850* (London: Longman, 1973).

Latham, A., *Old Calabar The impact of the international economy upon a traditional society* (Oxford: Clarendon, 1973).

Lenin, V., *Selected Works* (Moscow: Foreign Languages Publishing House, 1961), Vol. III.

Lewin, T. J., *Asante before the British: The Prempean years, 1875-1900* (Lawrence: The Regents Press of Kansas, 1978).

Maier, D. J. E., *Priests and Power The case of the Dente Shrine in nineteenth-century Ghana* (Bloomington: Indiana University Press, 1983).

Mandala, Ellias C., *Works and Control in a Peasant Economy: A history of the lower Tchiri valley in Malawi, 1959-1960* (Wisconsin: Wisconsin University Press, 1990).

Manoukian, M., *Akan and Ga-Adangme Peoples of the Gold Coast* (London: Oxford

University Press, 1950).

Mao Tse-tung, *Selected Works of Mao Tse-tung* (Peking: Foreign Languages Press, 1965).

Marees, Pieter de, *Description and Historical Account of the Gold Kingdom of Guinea (1602)* (London: Oxford University Press, 1987). Translated by Albert van Dantzig & Adam Jones.

Markovitz, I. L., *Power and Class in Africa: An introduction to change and conflict in African politics* (New Jersey: Englewood Cliffs, 1977).

McPhee, Alan, *The Economic Revolution in British West Africa* (London: George Routledge, 1926).

Meek, C. K., *Land Law and Custom in the Colonies* (London: Oxford University Press, 1949).

Meillassoux, C., *Maidens, Meal and Money: Capitalism and domestic community* (London: Cambridge University Press, 1981).

Metcalfe, G. E., ed., *Great Britain and Ghana Documents of Ghana history, 1807-1957* (Accra: University of Ghana, 1964).

Meyerowitz, Eva, *The Sacred State of the Akan* (London: Faber & Faber, 1949).

———, *Akan Traditions of Origins* (London: Faber & Faber, 1952).

———, *Early History of the Akan State of Ghana* (London: Red Candle press, 1974).

Mikell, Gwendolyn, *Cocoa and Chaos in Ghana* (New York: Paragon House, 1989).

Newbury, C. W., *British Policy towards West Africa: Selected Documents, 1875-1914* (Oxford: Clarendon Press, 1971).

Nkrumah, Kwame, *Ghana The Autobiography of Kwame Nkrumah* (London: Thomas Nelson and Sons, 1957).

Nukunya, C. K., *Kinship and Marriage among the Anlo Ewe* (London: the Anlone Press, 1969).

Odonkor, T. H., *The Rise of the Krobos* (Tema: Ghana Publishing Co., 1971).

Ollennu, Nii Amaa, *Principles of Customary Land Law in Ghana* (Birmingham,   CAL Press, 1985).

Oppong, Christina, *Female and Male in West Africa* (London: George Allen & Unwin, 1983).

Owusu, M., *Uses and Abuses of Political Power* (Chicago, University of Chicago Press, 1970).

Phillips, Anne, *The Enigma of Colonialism: British policy in West Africa* (London: James Currey, 1989).

Proceedings of the West African International Cocoa Research Conference, 1953 (London: Crown Agents, 1953).

Pogucki, R. J. H., *Gold Coast Land Tenure* (Accra, 1955).

Ranger, T. O., ed., *Emerging Themes of African History* (Nairobi: East African Publishing House, 1968).
———, *Revolt in Southern Rhodesia 1896-7: A study in African resistance* (London: Heinmann, 1967).
Rattray, R. S., *Ashanti* (London: Oxford University Press, 1923).
———, *Ashanti Law and Constitution* (London: Oxford University Press, 1929).
Redwar, H. W. Hayes, *Comments on Some Ordinances of the Gold Coast Colony* (London: Sweet and Maxwell, 1909).
Reindorf, C. C., *The History of the Gold Coast and Asante* (Accra, Ghana Universities Press, 1966[1895]).
Report of a Conference on Cocoa (London, 1950).
Robertson, C., *Sharing the Same Bowl A socioeconomic history of women and class in Accra, Ghana* (Bloomington: Indiana University Press, 1984).
Robinson, R., J. Gallagher & A. Denny, *Africa and the Victorians, The official mind of imperialism* (London: Macmillan, 1970).
Rodney, Walter, *How Europe Underdeveloped Africa* (Dar es Salaam: Tanzania Publishing House, 1972).
Sarbah, J. M., *Fanti Customary Law* (London: Frank Cass, 1968[1897]).
Sarbah, J. M., *Fanti National Constitution* (London: Frank Cass, 1968 [1906]).
Sarpong, P., *Ghana in Retrospect* (Tema: Ghana Publishing Co., 1974).
Scott, James, *Weapons of the Weak Everyday forms of peasant resistance* (New Haven: Yale University Press, 1985).
———, *Domination and the Arts of Resistance* (New Haven: Yale University Press, 1990).
Smith, Anthony D., *State and Nation in the Third World* (Sussex: Wheatsheaf, 1983).
Sundkler, B. G. M., *Bantu Prophets in South Africa* (London: Oxford University Press, 1961).
Szereszewski, R., *Structural Changes in the Economy of Ghana, 1891-1911* (London: Wiedenfeld and Nicholson, 1965).
Taylor, Kobina, *Our Political Destiny: In commemoration of the 43rd year of the Gold Coast Aborigines' Rights Protection Society* (Winneba: Dapa Printing Press, 1941).
Thomas, W., *Adventures and Observations on the West Coast of Africa* (New York: Negro Universities Press, 1860).
Tilly, C., *From Mobilization to Revolution* (Reading: Addison-Wesley, 1978).
Urquhart, D. H., *Cocoa* (London: Longman, 1956).
Vogt, John, *Portuguese Rule on the Gold Coast 1469-1682* (Athens: University of Gorgia Press, 1979).

Wallerstein, I., *The Modern World-System* (New York: Academic Press, 1974), Vol.I.

Ward, W. E. F., *A History of Ghana* (London: George Allen & Unwin, 1967).

Warren, D. M. *The Akan of Ghana: An overview of the ethnographic literature* (Accra: Pointer, 1973).

Weber, Max, *From Max Weber: Essays in Sociology* (New York: Oxford University Press, 1958). Translated & ed. by H. Gerth & C. W. Mills.

Welman, C.W., *The Native States of the Gold Coast History and Constitutions Part I Peki* (London: Dawsons, 1969 [1925]).

Wight, Martin, *The Gold Coast Legislative Council* (London: Faber and Faber, 1946).

Wilks, Ivor, *Asante in the Nineteenth Century* (London: Cambridge University Press, 1975).

Williamson, C. J., *Akan Religion and the Christian Faith* (Accra: Ghana University Press, 1965).

Wilson, Louis E., *Krobo People of Ghana to 1892 A political and social history* (Athens: Ohio University International Studies, 1992).

Wipper, Audrey, *Rural Rebels: A study of two protest movements in Kenya* (Nairobi: Oxford University Press, 1977).

Young, C. M., *Politics in Congo* (Princeton: Princeton University Press, 1965).

Articles

Addo-Fening, R., "The background to the deportation of King Asafo Agyei and the foundation of New Dwaben," *Transactions of the Historical Society of Ghana*, 12:2(1973), pp.213-28.

————,"Asante refugees in Akyem Abuakwa 1875-1912," *Transactions of the Historical Society of Ghana*, 14:1(1973), pp.39-64.

————,"The Native Jurisdiction Ordinance, indirect rule and the subject's well-being: the Abuakwa experience c1899-1912," *Research Review*, 6:2(1990), pp.29-44.

Agyeman-Duah, J., "The ceremony of enstoolment of the Asantehene," *Ghana Notes and Queries*, 7(1965), pp.8-11.

Ajayi, J. F. A., "Colonialism: An episode in African History," in L. H. Gann & P. Duignan, *Colonialism in Africa 1870-1960*, Vol.I, pp.497-509.

————,"The continuity of African institutions under colonialism," in T. O. Ranger, *Emerging Themes of African History*, pp.189-200.

————,"Expectations of the independence," *Daedalous*, Vol. 111:2(1982), pp.1-9.

Arhin, Kwame, "Diffuse authority among the Coastal Fanti," *Ghana Notes and Queries*, 9(1966), pp.66-70.

————,"Rank and class among the Asante and Fante in the nineteenth century,"

Africa, 53:1(1983), pp.2-22.

Arhin, Kwame, "The political and military roles of Akan women," in Christina Oppong, ed., *Female and Male in West Africa* (London: George Allen & Unwin, 1983), pp.91-98.

Asamoa, A., "Classes in Ghana," *Ghana Journal of Sociology*, 13:1 (1979/80), pp.130-162.

Austin, Gareth, "Capitalists and chiefs in the cocoa hold-ups in South Asante, 1927-1938," *The International Journal of African Historical Studies*, 21:1(1988), pp.63-95.

Bagyire VI, Otutu, Abiriwhene, "The Guans: A preliminary note," *Ghana Notes and Queries*, 7(1965), pp.21-24.

Balandier, Georges, "Messianism and nationalism in Black Africa," in Pierre Van den Berghe, ed., *Africa, Social Problems of Change and Conflict* (San Francisco, 1965), pp.443-460.

Bening, R. B., "Administrative areas of the Gold Coast Colony, 1874-1899," *Universitas*, 3:3(1974), pp.59-78.

Boahen, Adu, "The origins of the Akan," *Ghana Notes and Queries*, 9(1966), pp.3-10.

————, "Ghana before the coming of Europeans," *Ghana Social Science Journal*, 4:2(1977), pp.93-106.

————, "Africa and the colonial challenge," in A. Adu. Boahen ed., *General History of Africa* (Unesco, 1985), Vol.VII, pp.1-18.

————, "Colonialism in Africa: its impact and significance," in A. Adu. Boahen ed., *General History of Africa*, Vol.VII, 782-809.

Boaten, Kwasi, "Trade routes in Asante before the colonial period," *Ghana Social Science Journal*, 2:2(1972), pp.109-16.

Brown, David, "Anglo-German rivalry and Krepi politics 1886-1894," *Transactions of the Historical Society of Ghana*, 15:2(1974), pp. 201-216.

Chukwukere, I., "Perspective on the *Asafo* institution in Southern Ghana," *Journal of African Studies*, 7:1(1980), pp.39-47.

Coleman, J. S., "Nationalism in Tropical Africa," *American Political Science Review*, 18(1954), pp.404-426.

Cooper, Frederick, "Peasants, capitalists and historians: A review article," *Journal of Southern African Studies*, 7:2(1981), pp.284-314.

Danquah, J. B., "The historical significance of the Bond of 1844," *Transaction of the Historical Societies of Ghana*, 3:1(1957), pp.3-29.

Datta, A., "The Fante *Asafo*: a re-examination," *Africa*, 42(1972), pp.305-314.

Datta, A. and R. Porter, "The *Asafo* system in historical perspective," *Journal of African History*,12:2(1971), pp.279-297.

Davidson, A. B., "African resistance and rebellion against the imposition of colonial rule," in T. O. Ranger, ed., *Emerging Themes of African History*, pp.177-188.

Dickson, K. B., "Origin of Ghana's cocoa industry," *Ghana Notes and Queries*, 5(1963), pp.4-9.

Fallers, Lloyd, "The predicament of the modern African chief: an instance from Uganda," in William John Hanna, ed., *Independent Black Africa: The politics of freedom* (Chicago: Rand McNally, 1964), pp.278-296.

Ffoulkes, A., "The Company system in the Cape Coast Castle," *Journal of the African Society*, 7(1907-8), pp.261-277.

———, "*Borgya* and *Abirwa*; or, the latest fetish on the Gold Coast," *Journal of the African Society*, 8(1908-1909), pp.387-397.

Fortescue, D., "The Accra crowd, the *Asafo* and the opposition to the Municipal Corporations Ordinance, 1924-25," *Canadian Journal of African Studies*, 24:3 (1990), pp.348-375.

Fynn, J. K., "The *Nananom Pow* of the Fante: myth and reality," *Sankofa The Legon Journal of Archaeological and Historical Studies*, 2(1976), pp.54-59.

Gallagher, J and R. Robinson, "The imperialism of free trade," *Economic History Review*, 2nd series, 6(1953), pp.1-15.

Goody, J., "Anomie in Ashanti?" *Africa*, 27(1957), pp.356-363.

———, "Ethno-history and the Akan of Ghana," *Africa*, 29(1959), pp.67-80.

Hill, Polly, "The history of the migration of Ghana cocoa farmers," *Transactions of the Historical Society of Ghana*, 4:1(1959), pp.14-28.

Howard, R., "Formation and stratification of the peasantry in colonial Ghana," *Journal of Peasant Studies*, 8:4(1981), pp.61-80.

Hyam, R., "The colonial office mind, 1900-1914," *The Journal of Imperial and Commonwealth*, 8:1(1979), pp.30-55.

Iliffe, John, "Organization of the Maji-Maji rebellion," *Journal of African History*, 8(1967), pp.495-512.

Ikime, O., "The anti-tax riots in Warri Province, 1927-1928," *Journal of Historical Society of Nigeria*, 3:1(1966), pp.559-573.

Irwin, G., "The origins of the Akan," *Universita*, 4:5(1961), pp.138-141.

Isaacman, Allen, "Peasants and rural social protest in Africa," *African Studies Review*, 33:2(1990), pp.1-120.

Isaacman, Allen & Barbara Isaacman, "Resistance and collaboration in Southern and Central Africa, c.1850-1920," *The International Journal of African Historical Studies*, 10:1(1977), pp. 31-62.

Johnson, J. C. De Graft, "The significance of some Akan titles," *The Gold Coast Review*, 2:2(1927), pp.217-219.

————, "The Fante *Asafu*," *Africa*, 5(1932), pp.307-322.

Johnson, J. W. deGraft, "Akan land tenure," *Transactions of the Gold Coast & Togoland Historical Society*, 1:4(1955), pp.99-103.

Johnson, T., "Protest tradition and change: An analysis of southern Gold Coast riots 1890-1920," *Economy and Society*, 1:2 (1972), pp.164-193.

Kea, R., "'I am here to plunder on the general road': Bandits and banditry in the pre-nineteenth-century Gold Coast," in D. Crummey, *Banditry, Rebellion and Social Protest in Africa* (London: James Curry, 1986), pp.109-132.

Law, Robin, "In search of a Marxist perspective on pre-colonial tropical Africa," *Journal of African History*, 19:3(1978), pp.441-442.

Li Anshan, "*Asafo* and destoolment in colonial southern Ghana, 1900-1953," *The International Journal of African Historical Studies*, 28:2 (1995), pp.327-357.

————,"*Abirewa*: A religious movement in the Gold Coast, 1906-8," *The Journal of Religious History*, 20:1(1996), pp.32-52.

————,"Rural protest and historical study," *Hong Kong Journal of Social Sciences*, 12 (Autumn, 1998), pp.155-174.

Macmillan, W. M., "Political and social reconstruction, the peculiar case of the Gold Coast," in C. K. Meek, ed., *Europe and Africa* (London: Oxford University Press, 1940), pp.94-115.

Mauny, R. A., "The question of Ghana," *Africa*, 24(1954), pp.200-212.

McCaskie, T. C., "Anti-witchcraft cults in Asante: An essay in the social history of an African people," *History in Africa*, 8(1981), pp.125-154.

McLeod, M., "On the spread of anti-witchcraft cults in modern Asante," in Goody, ed., *Changing Social Structure in Ghana*, pp.107-117.

Milburn, Josephine, "The 1938 Gold Coast cocoa crisis: British business and the Colonial Office," *African Historical Studies*, 3(1970), pp.57-74.

Miles, John, "Rural protests in the Gold Coast: the cocoa hold-ups, 1908-1938," in C. Dewey and A. Hopkins, *Imperial Impact Economic development in Africa and India under colonial rule* (London: Athlone, 1978), pp.152-170.

Omosini, Olufemi, "The Gold Coast land question, 1894-1900: some issues raised on West Africa's economic development," *The International Journal of African Historical Studies*, 5:3(1972), pp.453-469.

Owusu, M., "Custom and coups: a juridical interpretation of civil order and disorder in Ghana," *The Journal of Modern African Studies*, 24:1(1986), pp.69-99.

————, "Rebellion, revolution, and tradition: Reinterpreting coups in Ghana," *Comparative Studies in Society and History*, 31:2(1989), pp.372-397.

Platt, D. C. M., "The imperialism of free trade: some reservations," *Economic History Review*, 2nd series, 21(1968), pp.296-306.

———, "Further objections to an 'imperialism of free trade' 1830-60," *Economic History Review*, 2nd series, 26(1973), pp.77-91.

Ranger, T. O., "Connection between 'primary resistance' movements and modern mass nationalism in East and Central Africa," *Journal of African History*, 9(1968), pp.437-454 and 631-642.

———, "Resistance in Africa: From nationalist revolt to agrarian protest," in Gary Okihiro, ed., *In Resistance: Studies on African, Caribbean, and Afro-American History* (Amherst: University of Massachusetts Press, 1986), pp.32-52.

Rattray, R. S., "Tendencies in the British colonial administration," *Journal of African Society*, 33(1934), pp.29-33.

Rey, P. P., "Class contradiction in lineage societies," *Critique of Anthropology*, 13&14:4(1979), pp.41-60.

Rhodie, Sam, "The Gold Coast hold-up of 1930-31," *Transactions of Historical Society of Ghana*, 9(1968), pp.105-118.

Rodney, Walter, "African slavery and other forms of social oppression on the upper Guinea coast in the context of the Atlantic slave-trade," *Journal of African History*, 7:3(1966), pp.431-443.

Shepperson, G., "Nyasaland and the Millennium," in Sylvia L. Thrupp, ed., *Millennial Dreams in Action* (The Hague: Mouton, 1962).

Simensen, J., "Rural mass action in the context of anti-colonial protest: the *Asafo* movement of Akim Abuakwa, Ghana," *Canadian Journal of African Studies*, 8:1(1974), pp.25-41.

———, "The *Asafo* of Kwahu, Ghana: a mass movement for local reform under colonial rule," *The International Journal of African Historical Studies*, 8:3(1975), pp.383-406.

Sklar, Richard L., "The nature of class domination in Africa," *The Journal of Modern African Studies*, 17:4(1979), pp.531-552.

Stone, R., "Protest: tradition and change: a critique" and T. Johnson's reply, *Economy and Society*, 3:1(1974), pp.84-105.

Tait, D., "Akan Traditions of Origins," *Man*, 53(January 1953), No.10, pp.11-12.

Twumasi, Yaw, "Prelude to the rise of mass nationalism in Ghana, 1920-49: nationalists and voluntary associations," *Ghana Social Science Journal*, 3:1(1976), pp.35-46.

Ward, B., "Some observations on religious cults in Ashanti," *Africa*, 26(1956), pp.47-61.

Wilks, Ivor, "The rise of the Akwamu empire 1650-1710," *Transactions of the*

Historical Society of Ghana, 3:2(1957), pp.99-136.

———, "The growth of the Akwapim State: A study in the control of evidence," in J. Vansina, R. Mauny & L. V. Thomas, ed., *The Historian in Tropical Africa* (London: Oxford University Press, 1964), pp.390-411.

———, "The Mossi and Akan states 1500-1800," in J. F. A. Ajayi & M. Crowder, *History of West Africa* (London: Longman, 1971), pp.344-386.

Wyllie, R. W., "The *Aboakyer* of the Effutu: A critique of Meyerowitz's account," *Africa*, 37:(1967), pp.81-85.

IV. Unpublished Theses and Articles

Addo-Fening, R., "Akyem Abuakwa C.1874-1943: A study of the impact of missionary activities and colonial rule on a traditional society" (PhD. Thesis, University of Ghana, 1980).

Dickson, K. B., "Cocoa in Ghana" (PhD. Thesis, University of London, 1960).

Holmes, A. B., "Economic and political organizations in the Gold Coast, 1920-1945" (PhD. Dissertation, University of Chicago, 1972).

Jenkins, P., "Towards a definition of social tension in rural Akan communities of the high colonial period: The *asafo* movement in the Eastern Province and Eastern Asante" (Seminar Paper, Department of History, University of Ghana, 9 Feb, 1971).

Okoro, Ako, "A short history of Awukugua-Akwapim" (B.A. Paper, Institute of African Studies, University of Ghana, 1984).

Quarcoopome, Samuel S., "Political activities in Accra 1924-45" (M.A. Thesis. University of Ghana, 1980).

Quaye, I., "The Ga and their neighbours 1600-1742" (PhD. Thesis, University of Ghana, 1972).

Rathbone, R. J. A. R., "The transfer of power in Ghana 1945-57" (PhD. Thesis, University of London, 1968).

Simensen, J., "Commoners, chiefs and colonial Government: British policy and local politics in Akim Abuakwa, Ghana, under colonial rule" (PhD. Thesis, University of Trondheim, 1975).

Twumasi, E. Y., "Aspects of politics in Ghana, 1923-39: A study of the relationship between discontent and development of nationalism" (D.Phil. Dissertation, Oxford University, 1971).

Yegbe, J. B., "Research material at the Ghana National Archives on the history of Anlo 1850-90" (Institute of African Studies, University of Ghana, 1966).

SOCIETY AND POLITICS IN AFRICA

Yakubu Saaka, General Editor

This multidisciplinary series publishes monographs and edited volumes that provide innovative approaches to the study and appreciation of contemporary African society. Although we focus mainly on subjects in the social sciences, we will consider manuscripts in the humanities that treat context as a significant aspect of discourse. Within the social sciences, we are looking for not only analytically outstanding studies but, what is more important, ones that may also have significant implications for the formulation and implementation of public policy in Africa. We are especially interested in works that challenge pre-existing hierarchies and paradigms.

For additional information about this series or for the submission of manuscripts, please contact:

> Peter Lang Publishing
> Acquisitions Department
> 275 7th Avenue, 28th floor
> New York, New York 10001

To order other books in this series, please contact our Customer Service Department:

> 800-770-LANG (within the U.S.)
> (212) 647-7706 (outside the U.S.)
> (212) 647-7707 FAX

Or browse online by series at:

> www.peterlangusa.com